Beyond the Walls of Separation

Beyond the Walls of Separation

Christian Faith and Ministry in Prison

TOBIAS BRANDNER

CASCADE *Books* • Eugene, Oregon

BEYOND THE WALLS OF SEPARATION
Christian Faith and Ministry in Prison

Copyright © 2014 Tobias Brandner. All rights reserved. Except for brief quotations in critical publications or reviews, no part of this book may be reproduced in any manner without prior written permission from the publisher. Write: Permissions. Wipf and Stock Publishers, 199 W. 8th Ave., Suite 3, Eugene, OR 97401.

Cascade Books
An Imprint of Wipf and Stock Publishers
199 W. 8th Ave., Suite 3
Eugene, OR 97401

www.wipfandstock.com

ISBN 13: 978-1-62032-463-9

Cataloguing-in-Publication data:

Brandner, Tobias.

    Beyond the walls of separation : Christian faith and ministry in prison / Tobias Brandner ; forewords by Howard Stone and Ron Nikkel.

    xxii + 212 p. ; 23 cm.—Includes bibliographical references.

    ISBN 13: 978-1-62032-463-9

    1. Church work with prisoners. 2. Prisoners—Religious life. I. Stone, Howard. II. Nikkel, Ron. III. Title.

BV4465 B73 2013

Scriptures marked (NRSV) come from the New Revised Standard Version Bible, copyright 1989, Division of Christian Education of the National Council of the Churches of Christ in the United States of America. Used by permission. All rights reserved.

Manufactured in the U.S.A.

For Joel, Elia, and Jill Pina

Contents

Foreword by Howard Stone • ix
Foreword by Ron Nikkel • xi
Acknowledgments • xv
Introduction • xvii

1 Life in Prison • 1

2 Prisons and Offender Rehabilitation—Then and Now • 32

3 Religion and Spirituality in the Context of Imprisonment • 51

4 Christian Faith and Spiritual Transformation in Prison • 68

5 Christian Care for Prisoners: Chaplains and Lay Visitors • 92

6 A Communication Guide to the Visiting Ministry • 111

7 Roles and Relationships: Visiting in an Unequal Context • 139

8 Prison Ministry as a Social Ministry • 159

9 Towards a Theology of Prison Ministry • 175

Appendix: Questions for Reflection and Group Discussion • 201
Bibliography • 205

Foreword

by Howard Stone

THE APOSTLE PAUL WROTE several of his epistles from prison. Jesus was imprisoned before he was put on the cross. Paul portrayed his imprisonment as an opportunity to grow spiritually, to understand better Christ and his sufferings. He believed that suffering through imprisonment advanced the gospel. Prison is certainly not unknown in the history of the church or in the Scriptures.

Beyond the Walls of Separation, by Tobias Brandner, is a handbook for prison ministry covering all elements of prisoners' faith life and pastoral visitors' ministry. Brandner writes this very helpful guide to prison ministry with the hope that the book "can lead to a deeper understanding of those in prison and uncover the relevance of religious life in such a place" (see xviii below). I met Reverend Brandner while lecturing at the Divinity School at the Chinese University in Hong Kong. I was impressed by the wisdom he had about pastoral ministry and especially prison ministry but also by his personal warmth, compassion, and grace.

My personal interest in prison ministry came from my work and writings on crisis intervention and ministry to those experiencing a crisis. Certainly most individuals who enter prison for the first time experience a crisis. Brandner believes it is "one of the most serious crisis experiences one can imagine, causing high levels of stress and disruption to life" (see 69 below). *Beyond the Walls of Separation* draws from the work of the social sciences, theology, the tradition of pastoral care in the church, and Brandner's own twenty years of experience doing prison ministry.

I think readers will find fascinating the opening of the book, for Brandner allows readers to imagine themselves as a new ward entering a prison and getting to know the context of prisons. He looks at the daily life of inmates, their feelings, their thoughts, and the ways they begin to discover how they will survive and hopefully thrive in such an environment where all areas of life are no longer under their control. Readers get a look at what life in prison is like—its effect on the individual physically and emotionally. *Beyond the Walls of Separation* goes on to describe interest in religion for those who are incarcerated; Brandner states that inmates are not uninterested in religion, but many have a strong desire for it.

As a teacher of pastoral care ministry, I was especially interested in chapters six and seven which cover how we can actually offer ministry to those in prison; this is the how-to section of the book. First Brandner looks at the attitudes and communicative acts of those offering pastoral care ministries. Then he turns to the issue of how inmates are affected by the context of inequality and the roles that pastoral visitors take on. He sees that the primary stance of the caregivers is one of presence; it is a ministry of presence.

The section of the book that meant the most to me was Brandner's examination of the suffering of Christ, or what Luther referred to as the theology of the cross. We do not meet God in the strength of the world or the power of the church but in the sufferings of others. In *Beyond the Walls of Separation* Brandner helps us see how when we visit those who are suffering, when we visit the imprisoned, we have the opportunity to see the Christ, to experience his grace. As he puts it, "prisoners thus become . . . a lens through which to see God. *In them, we see Christ; in Christ, we see God*" (see 180 below).

I think you will truly appreciate this book.

Foreword

by Ron Nikkel

OVER THE PAST THIRTY or more years I've had the opportunity of visiting prisons in more than one hundred countries in every region of the world. To enter a prison is to enter an alien world, a world that is very different and often unrecognizable from the world of our normal everyday existence. It is not only the walls, the razor wire, and the security that separate the prison world from the outside. Rather it is a separation painfully experienced in the relationship of the husband who can no longer embrace his wife, the child who cannot understand her father cannot provide for them any longer, the imprisoned son who can only picture the face of his mother, and families who can no longer celebrate their birthdays and anniversaries together or share the joys and sorrows of life together.

A fundamental longing in all people is the longing for freedom. While there are those who abuse or take advantage of their personal freedom at the expense of other persons, punishing those offenders by depriving them of freedom inevitably does more harm than good. Life in enforced captivity does not prepare a person to live more responsibly in the free world. Taking away an individual's responsibility to make even the basic decisions of life (when to eat, what to eat, where to go, what to do, when to get up, and when to sleep, and the like) does not prepare a prisoner to make responsible decisions upon release.

The fact is that imprisonment constitutes an unnatural environment—a distorted and contorted reality. It has often been observed that the tragic impact of imprisonment is not that it keeps offenders out of the community but that prison walls keep the community out of prison. Prison's wall of separation may be necessary to protect the community from crime and violence, but that wall of separation should never become a barrier that prevents the responsible community from caring, reaching out, and encouraging offenders through humanizing activities and personal interaction.

Vivien Stern, a British criminologist, observes that prisons are simply magnifying mirrors of what is wrong in society. In other words, prisons are us: prisons are part of our community. Prisons reflect what is wrong in our community, and the ills of our community cannot be cured apart from our involvement as a community. Crime is a problem of our community and our community, not just our designated criminal-justice agencies, must become part of the solution.

There is probably no more strategic a place in any community for followers of Jesus Christ to be involved in ministry than in the prison. Prisons represent the core human issues that the gospel addresses—issues of violence and peacemaking, guilt and forgiveness, alienation and reconciliation, brokenness and restoration, anger and love, rejection and embrace,. The gospel is the antidote to the fallen human condition, the answer to what is wrong in our community. We know that prisons and justice systems and law enforcement agencies and even education and rehabilitation programs cannot change the heart of a human being; we cannot make bad men good.

The heart of what imprisonment represents is the heart of the offender. What place in society is more significant for Christian witness than prison—where the walls of separation between prisoners and the community, between offenders and victims, between human beings and God, can only be removed through the love and grace of God? I have seen firsthand the transforming and reconciling impact of the Christian community—caring churches and caring believers—in countries all over the world.

Some years ago I met a man named Peter, who after a very successful professional career, decided to forego retirement and devote himself to caring for inmates in the miserable little prison outside his community. Prison rules and walls, however, prevented him from spending much time in prison, so he appealed to the authorities for permission to spend more time inside. He was strongly advised that prison is for prisoners, and that if he wanted to spend more time inside, he would have to be a prisoner. Peter took the challenge literally and took up residence as a prisoner in that prison in order to become closer to the inmates he felt God wanted him to care for.

During my meeting with Peter, I commented that it must have been a very difficult adjustment to give up his lifestyle and freedom. "Oh no, not at

Foreword by Ron Nikkel

all," he immediately replied. "I thought it would be, but surprisingly I found myself much closer to Jesus in that little cell than I had ever been in my own big home." His answer astonished me until I realized that Peter was doing exactly what Jesus did in bridging the separation between humanity and God—the incarnation. There was a time when I thought that I was bringing Jesus into the prisons I was visiting, until I realized that Jesus was already in the prison, and that I was merely joining him in expressing his love among the prisoners. Prison walls do not keep Jesus out of prison.

Like Peter, Mother Antonia has lived for many years inside La Mesa State Penitentiary in Tijuana, Mexico. Previously known as Mary Clark and living in Los Angeles, she dreamed of being a wife and a mother. By the age of fifty, she had raised seven children. Feeling deeply unfulfilled and lost after her husband left her, Mary turned to charitable work where, during a mission trip to the drug-trafficking and violence-ridden city of Tijuana, she visited La Mesa State Penitentury. It was during that first prison visit she experienced an intense feeling of finally finding her true lifework. "I felt like I had come home," she said.

At the age of fifty, Mary Clark gave up her comfortable life in Los Angeles and moved across the wall of separation into a tiny prison cell to let them know that prison bars cannot keep out the love of God. Today, more than thirty years later, she is known as Mother Antonia, "the prison angel," living in a prison cell surrounded by prisoners.

Not everyone who wishes to reach beyond the walls of separation can or should take up residence in prison. For many others it involves a challenging commute between the community and prison, and serving as an ambassador of God's love behind the wall. This book, *Beyond the Walls of Separation* is born in the experience of Tobias Brandner of Hong Kong, who like Peter and Mary recognized that God's love and grace does not stop at the prison gate. Through his writings he takes readers behind the wall of separation into the very different and unfamiliar world of imprisonment. The wisdom, insights, and experiences he offers in the pages that follow compose a guidebook to that world, offering not only a wealth of information and very practical advice but also a vibrant and challenging theological reflection on prison ministry.

    Ronald W. Nikkel
    President & CEO emeritus
    Prison Fellowship International

Acknowledgments

I AM INDEBTED TO many people who have made possible my ministry and the experiences and reflections shared in this book. All of them have had a special impact on me during my twenty years of learning: the coworkers of the Swiss mission agency Basel Mission (now Mission 21), who supported me during all my years in Hong Kong, particularly director Madeleine Strub-Jaccoud, Reverend Albrecht Hieber, and Doris Grohs; all the staff of the Hong Kong Christian Kun Sun Association (Prison Fellowship Hong Kong), particularly the director of the Board, Reverend Thomas Chow; the general secretary, Reverend John Poon; and Susan Chan: they have shown tremendous patience and respect despite our different backgrounds. Professor Dr. Lo Lung-kwong, principal of Chung Chi Divinity School of Theology continuously supported the prison ministry through his interest, passion, and flexibility around my teaching obligations. The staff of the Hong Kong Correctional Services Department opened many doors and gates to me; the welfare officers patiently explained many rules of prison and often enough struggled with my stubbornness; the commissioner and the senior leaders of the department showed me respect and friendship despite our different visions on penal questions; the late Father Sean Burke, previously head chaplain in Hong Kong has always given critical advice and inspiration.

I am also grateful to leaders on my spiritual journey, among them Hans Lutz, my senior coworker in Hong Kong; Walter Hoffmann, the first one to mentor me in prison ministry; and Patrice De Mestral, who discussed with me many issues of prison ministry.

I enjoyed camaraderie with a great number of fellow pilgrims, volunteer visitors, inmates, and ex-inmates who were a source of constant

Acknowledgments

encouragement to me. To name anyone individually would not do justice to the many others.

My gratitude goes to Luke DeKoster and Tim Summers, who served as proofreaders of this manuscript. Besides giving me linguistic advice, they encouraged me with critical and thorough feedback, and inspired many changes.

Finally, the past years of ministry and the writing of this book would not have gone as they did without my wife, Gabi Baumgartner, who has accompanied me on the way. Her equanimity, her confidence, and her faith have given me crucial support. Raising our three children with her is a source of much joy, inspiration, and strength.

Introduction

THIS BOOK IS DEDICATED to all the inmates who have had an impact on my life, who transformed me during the past years of fellowship, who shared something with me and allowed me to accompany them in their experience of brokenness. It is further dedicated to all those Christians, foremost among them my students, who joined the fellowship in prison, and who greatly enriched my time as prison chaplain, turning the work of the lonely prison chaplain into a community ministry.

The first day I entered a prison was a cold and gray winter day more than twenty years ago. It was a high-security prison in Switzerland, and I remember well the heavy air, the dry central heating, the lack of ventilation, and the stale odor of food and bodies, an altogether unique and alien smell. Since that very first day, prison has remained part of my life. I treasure a certain roughness of the people I met, often disguising an underlying softness; the directness in their communication, concealing a deep vulnerability; and their honesty, obviously aware of how their lives have been shattered. Underneath the hustle and bustle of prison society and the tough bodies of male inmates, I meet people who are genuinely and earnestly searching for meaning in life.

After some years of pastoral ministry in that high-security Swiss prison, I had the chance to serve in a radically different cultural environment—in Hong Kong. Prisons in Hong Kong, although mainly populated and staffed by ethnic Chinese, follow the British prison model and maintain a standard comparable with other prisons in the West, in some ways better than in Europe or North America, in other ways worse. The independent common-law judiciary and, likewise, the independent civil service administering the prisons make Hong Kong prisons comparable particularly to those in other parts of the Commonwealth.

Introduction

After thorough language training (in Cantonese, a language of Southern China and Hong Kong, with some Mandarin, the official language of China), I have since 1998 continuously served as a prison chaplain in Hong Kong, mainly visiting adult male prisoners. The ministry of a prison chaplain offers a unique insight into prison and into the spiritual experience of incarceration. Within the highly controlled environment of prisons, the chaplain is possibly the only one who is completely independent of the correctional administration but still has unlimited access to all parts of a prison. He effectively shares the everyday life of inmates without being subjected to the strict administrative and disciplinary order of the correctional service. At the same time, he or she has special access to outside volunteers and church groups who participate in prison ministry. This position, bridging the gap between the world inside and the Christian community outside, is part of what accounts for the distinctiveness of prison chaplaincy.

While I was serving as prison chaplain, my church invited me to teach at a local seminary, the Divinity School of Chung Chi College, Chinese University of Hong Kong. This school values the link between critical, academic theology and practical ministerial practice. It was my privilege again to build a bridge: this time between the theological training of the seminary and the prison environment, by regularly inviting students to join the prison visits.

This book is a result of my dual role as prison chaplain and teacher. It is a handbook for prison ministry covering all aspects of prisoners' faith life and visitors' ministry. I hope the information it contains, including insights from the social sciences, can lead to a deeper understanding of those in prison and uncover the relevance of religious life in such a place. Paradigmatic stories of change and spiritual transformation allow readers to understand how the crisis of imprisonment breaks open basic issues of human existence. The accounts of inmates' spiritual change allow us to witness the life-changing power of faith. The book hopes to foster the mutuality of chaplain-based and lay-based ministry that together build the ministry of the whole people of God.

The visiting ministry to those in prison is a journey to a focal point of society. Prisons reveal in a nutshell the values and rules of a society and harbor many of our society's burning problems. Possibly more than in other ministries, visitors are confronted with issues of power, justice, and

Introduction

equality—and the lack thereof. A book on ministry in prison thus needs to be aware of these issues and respond to them sensitively, without neglecting the individual dimension in the experience of wrongdoing, suffering, and alienation. This book integrates insights from liberation theology into a pastoral theology for those in prison. Although I have never been an inmate myself, I try as much as possible to develop a prison theology, which takes as its starting point the experiences and life realities of those in prison.

The book starts by following a virtual visitor entering prison and getting to know the context of prison and the daily life of inmates, their feelings, their thoughts, and their survival strategies in an environment where all aspects of life are subject to control. In light of the difficult prison environment discussed in chapter 1, the second chapter asks how prisons came into being and how rehabilitation became a central motive in modern punishment. Chapter 3 uses an outside, sociological perspective to assess the role, importance, and effect of *religion in prison*. Why do inmates participate in religious life, what do they expect, and how do they benefit from it? Chapter 4 describes how faith transforms inmates. It offers a *psychology of spiritual transformation*, which shows how change starts from the radical, upside-down crisis experience of being in prison, and how this critical point in a person's life triggers a process of healing. With Chapter 5, we turn to the different *agents of prison ministry* and describe how the ministry developed along two different lines—the more priestly tradition of chaplains and the more revivalist tradition of lay ministry. The next two chapters offer a kind of how-to-do-it. Chapter 6 introduces basic attitudes and communicative skills essential for a *healing prison ministry*, and chapter 7 analyzes *visitors' role behavior* and asks how, in a context of radical inequality, they avoid the pitfalls of a condescending attitude. Chapter 8 reverses the usual direction of ministry and describes *how the ministry of visitation affects visitors* and, through them, society outside. The final chapter is a *theological conclusion* that links faith experiences with the Christian theological tradition. It develops a theology from the perspective of the suffering of a specific people group—those in prison—and responds to their experience.

This book should appeal to different kinds of readers. To make the reading of the book easier I suggest several *reading options*. A reader may of course choose to follow the book's whole argument. Alternatively, readers may choose a more selective approach. Those who are less interested in faith and spiritual questions but rather want to learn about the secular reality of prison—prison life, the history of prisons, and the role of religion

Introduction

in prison—will find chapters 1 to 3 most inspiring. Readers interested in spiritual aspects of prison ministry and stories of change should read chapters 1, 4, 5, 6, and 7. Issues of justice linked to prison ministry are featured in chapter 8. Those interested in theology, and in the link between pastoral care and a politically aware theology, should read chapters 1, 4, and 6 to 9.

To improve the overall readability, I have kept the *footnotes* to a minimum, trying to avoid hiding important ideas there. Where given, notes simply indicate the source of a quote or a thought; occasionally they provide additional information that would have interrupted the main thrust of the account. However, I compensate this academic deficit with bibliographical notes that offer plenty of advice on finding more information. Some paragraphs appear in smaller print. This usually indicates a story of an inmate, or of an encounter with an inmate, to illustrate an argument. Sometimes such paragraphs introduce further material—quotes or short methodological or academic reflections—to deepen the main thought. Questions for group discussion can be found in the appendix.

∼

Every book has its natural *limitations*. First, this book focuses on prison ministry in the narrow sense and says little about ministry to ex-offenders or to inmates' families, who are both part of prison ministry in the wider sense. The emphasis is on contextualizing Christian faith in one very specific area, namely, the prison. Still, the narrow context of prison may interest people who have experienced other forms of deprivation, or who feel spiritually imprisoned. Next, the book is written from the perspective of a man working with male inmates, so the perspectives of female inmates are not sufficiently reflected. Third, this is not a Christian perspective on justice or punishment in general. Others have done this—on biblical, theological, philosophical, or psychological grounds—better than I could. Finally, Christians are obviously not the only ones caring for inmates; other faith groups are equally committed to this ministry. However, as I am rooted in the Christian tradition and find meaning in the message of Christ, it is meaningless to attempt a neutral position. This book thus reflects a Christian perspective on spiritual transformation in prison.

A particular limitation is due to the *cultural perspective and background* of both the writer's experience and the academic literature. Most experiences of the book reflect an Asian or, more specifically, a Hong Kong/Chinese context, which could be described as *authority centered*. Prisons in Hong Kong are in many ways different from prisons in other parts of the world—more submission, less violence and probably less rebellion. The inmates, despite being rebellious and unadjusted, still maintain deep-rooted respect for authority and submission to existing rules. The contextual limitations of my observations are, to some degree, balanced by the partiality of academic literature that I take into account: most academic research responds to North American or British situations. The comparison of pastoral experiences in East Asia with scholarly descriptions of prisons in the West reveals substantial similarities between the two. The different cultural contexts cause only gradual, not categorical, differences in prison life and pastoral ministry. Readers should be able to distinguish where experiences are related more to a specific context and where they have broader relevance.

Finally, I hope to show the symbolic weight that prisons—both their reputation and their reality—have in our society. Prisons are charged places that fascinate many of us. Hidden from the public and avoided by most people, they arouse curiosity. Removed from genuine experience, prisons carry connotations of a counterworld of darkness and lawlessness. The concept of prison is a powerful symbol of our basic existential situation, our human limitation and finitude; our common experience is that people can be imprisoned spiritually or mentally as much as physically. When entering the reality of prison, visitors are confronted not only with a deeply unsettling experience, but also with the accompanying spiritual and cultural connotations. On their way to visit those in prison, they pass through spiritual walls, just as they pass through physical ones. Once they meet the inmates, they find ordinary people in an extraordinary situation. Often enough, such visits turn into a revelatory encounter, unearthing one's own questions of imprisonment and liberation.

This book is intended as more than just a random account of a prison chaplain. I hope to offer spiritual inspiration, theological insight, and counseling tools to all those involved in faith-based prison ministry: chaplains, Christian volunteers, and church groups, correctional staff and, last but clearly not least, inmates themselves. The following pages reflect only a glimpse of the tremendous joy and love I have experienced in fellowship with inmates, and of the respect I have for inmates who struggle to survive in an environment that gives little hope.

1

Life in Prison

WHENEVER VOLUNTEERS JOIN A prison visit for the first time, I routinely ask about their impressions and feelings. The most common answer is complete surprise about the kind of people they have encountered—that the inmates are not brutes, but well-behaved and friendly people who express themselves reasonably well and usually show abundant gratefulness toward the volunteer. The encounter with the real people in prison stands in stark contrast to the gruesome and stereotypical media-driven images that shape public perceptions.

Of course, this first impression is not the whole reality, but it is an important starting point. Inmates are ordinary people who have, among many other things in life, committed a crime, and who have been unsuccessful—or perhaps simply unlucky—enough to be caught. They may be good husbands or not, they may be good fathers or not, they may be good citizens or not. At some point in their life, whether early or late, they transgressed the boundaries of what society considered acceptable and were caught in crime.

This chapter introduces the *social environment* that shapes inmates' faith and life, the environment that provides the context in which Christian faith is received and responded to. The main thrust of this chapter reflects inmates' viewpoints and perspectives. The observations are based mainly on the ethnically Chinese and specifically Hong Kong administrative context,[1]

1. *Hong Kong* refers to the geographical entity, the small region that has belonged to

complemented by experiences and descriptions from other contexts. Readers will easily recognize, which parts refer more to the Hong Kong context and which parts apply to other contexts as well. The feelings of inmates, their suffering, and the important issues in their life are, in many ways, similar and comparable despite the cultural differences.

The chapter discusses the following questions:

- Who are the people in prison?
- How do they live?
- What do they feel, think, and hope?

WHAT KIND OF PEOPLE?

Going through a fraction of the vast criminological literature (see the bibliographic notes at the end of the chapter), one finds a broad range of views and typologies. Some see prisoners as self-centred and egoist criminals who commit criminal acts for their own excitement and for their greedy selfishness; prisoners are thus fundamentally different from normal people.[2] Some see them as driven by rebelliousness and a deep-rooted anger[3] or as sick or mentally disturbed individuals who are incapable of free human action and need help.[4] Again others see them as socially and educationally deprived people on the fringes of society, who need to be educated to change

---

China since 1997, but is under special administration widely independent from the central government in Beijing. When speaking about *Chinese* I refer to ethnically Chinese people who share in the same cultural, linguistic, and religious traditions independent of whether they come from Hong Kong or China. Often there are some educational and social differences between the two groups, but overall they interact well and understand each other. *Chinese* refers also to those ethnically Chinese people from Chinese communities elsewhere in Southeast Asia or in the wider world. Speaking about *inmates*, I usually refer to male inmates. My primary ministry experience is with men, and many observations are specific and gender related.

For more about the Hong Kong context and the development of prisons in Hong Kong, see the next chapter.

2. An example from a Christian perspective is Cowart, *Prison Minister's Handbook*, 61ff.

3. Spitale, *Prison Ministry*, 22–59.

4. Such a view underlies the treatment model under the leadership of medical doctors, psychiatrists, and clinical psychologists; more about this model appears in chapter 2.

and adjust. They are weak people, corrupted by an evil society.[5] Others see in them a kind of antibourgeois hero who rejects conformity to the rules of an unjust society,[6] or who exploits the ruling system to its extremes by beating a materialistic system with its own logic. For systematic purposes, the whole range of theories about crime can be divided into (a) theories that seek the origin of crime *in a person's environment*, and (b) theories that seek the origin of crime *in the person committing the crime*. The former sees the roots of crime in extrinsic factors like unemployment, poverty, poor schooling, abusive parents, peer pressure, or drug and substance abuse. It is an approach that shows understanding for important causal factors in criminal careers. However, it can result in exculpating an inmate and in failing to take him and his potential seriously. The latter theory emphasizes personal responsibility and sees the criminal as making an active choice. This approach can result in a negative view of inmates as persons who have made wrong choices out of purely selfish motives. Such a view can be useful in specific situations—for example, when confronting an inmate who is trying to avoid accountability for his own actions. It may, however, equally undermine good communication because it shows little empathy (see also chapter 7).

Yet there is no such thing as a typical prisoner. Milton Burglass, founder of a humanistic counseling program for prisoners and formerly an inmate himself reminds us: "Despite nearly 200 years of organized research into the question of crime, no one can today claim validated knowledge of the specific causes of criminal behavior or of a consistently effective means for its prevention. Every major 19th- and 20th-century theory of man, his psychology, his sociology, or his biology seems to have had its day in one form or another."[7] Chuck Colson, famous for his role in the Watergate conflict and his subsequent conviction and his founding of Prison Fellowship International, correctly said, "the simple truth is that offenders cannot so easily be stereotyped . . . Prisoners are fellow sinners and we shall share with them a common heritage of sin."[8] This statement is still valid today. People in prison do represent a cross-section of society—the majority

---

5. An example of such a view is Elmira Reformatory in the United States or the Borstal concept (see again chapter 2).

6. The theories of Foucault, discussed in the next chapter, helped to inspire the antipsychiatry and the prison-abolition movements. Both see institutional inmates partly as creative nonconformists.

7. Burglass, *Thresholds Program*, 20.

8. Colson, "Understanding of Imprisonment," 165–66.

rather young, often rather poor, with insufficient education, and often with a limited sense of social responsibility or seeking immediate satisfaction. A disproportionately high number were neglected or abused as children and have some kind of mental-health problem.[9] But such a description does not help much because it indicates only general trends. To be sure, prisoners are not better than people outside of prison, but on the average they are also not much worse. They share the same petit-bourgeois life goals: a nice wife or husband, well-educated children, a decent salary, occasional family get-togethers. In short, they seek a peaceful, stable, and harmonious life.

Given an awareness of the dangers of generalizations, the following remarks build an attempt to gain a deeper and nondiscriminatory understanding of inmates. First, the terms *prisoners* and *criminals* are *not to be equated*. The vast majority of criminals (that is, people who have committed a crime) never go to prison. Only a small minority of people who commit criminal acts are ever caught, and of those, only a few are convicted.[10] Further, *crime* is more than its narrow legal definition, which *in*cludes and sanctions only those acts that have been declared illegal and *ex*cludes *legal* destructive acts like killing during warfare; some acts of environmental destruction; the consumption, possession, and trading of *legal* drugs; and certain destructive economic practices. Besides, not all inmates are criminals, as it can never be excluded that some inmates are innocent and have been wrongly convicted. The identification of *prisoners* with *criminals* automatically reaffirms the injustice to those wrongly convicted, even if this applies only to a small minority. We can thus say that *prisoners are just the visible top of an iceberg*. They represent a small part of the problem of destructive behavior, which extends also to those committing a criminal act without being sentenced, without being caught, or doing it legally.

Second, for a majority of inmates the *crisis experience* of being in *prison* is not a singular mistake in an otherwise smooth life. It is rather the *latest in a series of difficulties*, possibly in family relationships, in school, or at

---

9. According to Nacro, a British charity working to prevent crime and resettle offenders, 40 percent of young prisoners in the UK had been neglected or abused as children, and 72 percent of prisoners had some kind of mental health problem, see Cavadino, *Current Issues in Penal Policy*, Nacro, March 2004, quoted in The Catholic Bishops' Conference of England and Wales, *Place of Redemption*, 21.

10. Referring to the US context, some studies estimate that only around 1.5 percent of all committed felonies result in the imprisonment of the perpetrator, see McHugh, *Christian Faith and Criminal Justice*, 61–62. The British charity Victim Support estimates that 97 percent of crimes never reach court: see *A Place of Redemption*, 17.

work. This can be said even while acknowledging that no theory about the origins of criminal behavior can sufficiently explain the problem of crime. The prevalence of family problems does not necessarily mean that inmates always come from broken families, although a good number do. Some inmates come from caring families but were unable to adjust to society and stood in conflict with them. In the same way, school problems are common in inmates' biographies, but they should not be taken as indicators of inmates' lower intelligence. Inmates are not significantly less intelligent than the average population.[11] Past experience of job problems, another typical inmate trait, often relates to unstable performance and difficulties adjusting to regular requirements. However, this does not mean that inmates have no professional skills; as a matter of fact, they can show great creativity and skill.

Third, *prisoners* are usually *not heartless* individuals. Of course, some inmates have committed terrible crimes and have done so cold-bloodedly. Some have disturbed personalities or are in one way or another emotionally detached. But often it is the intensity of their feelings that overwhelms them and causes them to lose control. Mostly they are impulsive, not cold-blooded. One of the deepest impressions of ministry in prison is how passionate inmates are, and how strongly and directly they express their affection. What makes working with prisoners so fascinating is exactly this: they have an originality and directness that is less spoiled by traditional behavior patterns, education, or social status. They have a frankness in their expressions that allows refreshingly open interaction.

Finally, *inmates* are *not totally immoral*. Many inmates have received little moral teaching and grew up in war zones and in an atmosphere of contempt for the law. This obviously impairs their moral strength. Still, they usually know the moral codes of a society quite well and largely stick to them. The problem is that they *selectively suspend* what is morally required, or rather that they do so to a higher degree than others. Many prisoners, though having lived at the fringes of society and having thus developed a critical distance to its values, still accept most social norms. Their distance from the normal society does not make them indifferent to society's rejection.

---

11. Pierson and Kelley, "HSPQ norms on a Statewide Prison Population," 185–92; quoted in McHugh, *Christian Faith and Criminal Justice*, 73.

PRISONERS AND THE PRISON: LIVING IN A TOTAL INSTITUTION

How do people live inside prison? Life in prison is *life in deprivation*. What a person feels most directly and immediately when entering the prison system is manifold deprivation: the loss of liberty, the loss of most common goods and services, the isolation from family and friends, and the frustration of sexual desire.[12] The prisoner understands his or her confinement and deprivation as a deliberate, moral rejection by the free community. The loss of liberty is a double loss: first, a confinement *to* the institution and second, a confinement *within* the institution. In most high-security prisons—with the exception of facilities in many African countries and in Latin America—prisoners' movements are highly restricted. The loss of heterosexual contact in those prisons that have not introduced conjugal visits undermines an essential component of a person's, and particularly a man's, self-image. Men are used to receiving much of their meaning and motivation from women; deprived of contact with people of the other gender, they lack an important part of their identity—how women perceive them. The constraints of a monogender environment profoundly shape the atmosphere in prison.

The sociologist Erving Goffman in his classic study on institutional life described the *prison as an example of a total institution*.[13] What Goffman says about prisons is still generally valid: all aspects of life are carried out under one roof; all activities happen in groups and within a strict schedule; and all activities are planned with a rational goal, whether to keep different inmate groups separated, to make the administration of inmates easier, or simply to enhance the authority of the institution. In a total institution, power is unevenly distributed, as the coercive force and the sanctioning power are completely with the institution.[14] However, reliance on pure coercive force is insufficient to secure obedience. Weapons, for example, are generally forbidden in prison as they can easily be turned against the guards. Instead prisons follow a system of *punishments and rewards* to exert control. Punishments include isolation, withdrawal of privileges, loss of earnings, or loss of a part of the typical remission of one-third of the sentence. This last one is the most severe—a direct extension of the time to be

---

12. Sykes, *Society of Captives*, 63ff.
13. Goffman, *Asylums*.
14. On the mechanisms of power, see Sykes, *Society of Captives*, 40–62.

served. On the other hand, control is delivered through granting rewards. This can be an early parole, furloughs, conjugal visits, access to special activities, or any goods or services not commonly granted in prison. In the case of Hong Kong, rewards are granted sparingly. There is no ordinary furlough system, there are no conjugal visits, and hardly any special activities could be used as incentives. The parole system is very conservative and allows only a small number of inmates to be released before the two-thirds point in their sentences (a release after two-thirds of the sentence is well-established practice in most places across the world).

The reality of prison is, however, not one of the management commanding unlimited power over the inmates and randomly establishing its own order, but one of the management *sharing power with inmates*.

Sykes (1958) develops the thesis that despite formal power being totally in the hands of official bureaucracy, the prison authority necessarily and for the benefit of a reasonable and pragmatic prison management, transfers some of its controlling power to the inmates. Sykes's findings that the reciprocal dependence of staff and inmates mitigates the totalitarian character of the institution are still valid and also apply to the context of East Asia. In order to be effective, prison officers have to learn how to get things done without using force. This does not happen by yielding to inmates but by using authority without using force and by showing consistency and fairness. The best way to establish such authority might be by earning the respect of the inmates.[15] Sykes's study analyzes the patterns of compromise between the rulers and the ruled and how they affect the prisoners' lives. His thesis that such an arrangement is inherently unstable and contains the seeds of its own destruction[16] can be explained by the historical context of his research: the 1950s, when many riots occurred in US prisons. It is not confirmed by observations in Hong Kong, where the situation has been rather stable.

Some countries, especially in Latin America but also in Asia, rely for a major part of internal prison life on inmates who function as a kind of co-opted staff. These inmates take over many supervisory duties and receive rewards for the services they provide. Such an administrative policy usually goes together with a strong prison subculture that effectively manages the prison. The inherent inequality and injustice that results when inmates manage much of internal prison life is the reason why more affluent prison

---

15. Liebling et al., "Appreciative Inquiry and Relationships in Prison," 83.
16. Sykes, *Society of Captives*, 109ff.

systems avoid such management methods. Power sharing is also possible in a different form. Many prisons (especially, but not only, in Europe) allow areas of self-determined life even under the restrictions of confinement. Some provide facilities where inmates can prepare their food themselves; others allow inmates ample freedom in decorating their private rooms and having mutual visits of fellow inmates. However, many prison administrators still seem to regard it as integral part of punishment not only to deprive inmates of their freedom but also to prevent them from positively experiencing achievement and self-determination inside the walls.

The *system in Hong Kong* tends to a *strict monopolization of power* in the custodial staff. Such an administrative policy relies on a high number of officials, among whom the most pivotal figure is the official in the lowest ranks. He (she, in women's prisons) is the person who supervises and controls the inmates in concrete and detailed terms.[17] The lowest-ranking guards are in many ways in a similar position to the inmates in their charge. They share life with the inmates and find themselves partly in a community of solidarity with them. Both inmates and staff suffer from unreasonable custodial policies and regulations. Long-serving officers may know some inmates from earlier custody in juvenile centers or from previous incarcerations. Guards can hardly maintain a constant social distance, so they naturally befriend inmates. It is not rare to see affectionate relations between the two. This communality has a humanizing effect and undermines the system of power, and it exposes the limits of the total institution. Besides, even in a strict power monopoly, it is unavoidable that some duties are handed over to inmates, who receive rewards for their cooperation (see the section below—Prison Culture: Strategies of Survival pp. 12–15).

PRISON RULES AND ROUTINE: DEPERSONALIZATION

The daily routine in prison is extremely monotonous; it undermines all personal initiative and saps an independent mind. In Hong Kong, inmates are obliged to work six days a week, but the work they do is mostly menial, meaningless to the inmate, and without educational or vocational value. The time in prison thus appears as a total waste towards a prisoner's future reintegration into society, which increases the possibility of relapse into crime. Rather than qualifying a prisoner for productive living outside the institution, prison work has a *disqualifying* effect. Rehabilitation, one of

---

17. For a comparison with the United States context, ibid., 53ff.

the pillars of a modern correctional system, occurs in the work of a small minority of workshops, and then only implicitly. The daily workload can be done in a fraction of the time allotted, and the inmates end up idle. Some use their unused working time for study, but this requires a lot of self-discipline within a noisy and highly distracting environment and, in summer, in scorching heat.

The rules allow minimal room for personal creativity. The cell, or an inmate's part of a dormitory, has to be kept strictly tidy, with no personal decorations like photos of loved ones or posters. Only a small range of personal items for hygiene is permitted, and books or any other special items need approval. The same applies to the inmate's body, which has to be kept in strict order. Sloppy haircuts, beards, and accessories like necklaces, bracelets, or watches are prohibited. The uniformity strips the prisoner of all individuality. The continuous subjection to endless routine and senseless coercion gradually destroys the inmate's spirit and drains the energy that keeps a person alive.

Many rules are hard to understand, make little sense to the inmate, or seem randomly implemented. For example, many inmates in Hong Kong's prisons have altered their prison uniform to include trouser pockets, which are not usually provided. This common practice contradicts the rule but is usually tolerated. Still there are occasions when prisoners receive punishment for it. Also, there have been exceptions to the cell rules—for example, an inmate being allowed to keep some special belongings in a cardboard box, until during a routine cell search the items are declared illegal. Certain activities like playing Chinese chess are prohibited but commonly tolerated until senior officers decide the contrary. The encroachment of prison authority in private life and other areas seemingly irrelevant to the maintenance of good order causes irritation. Being kept in the dark about matters that concern the daily life of the prisoner community or its individuals is a powerful manifestation of the supreme authority of the penal and judicial system.

The *lack of clarity and the permanent need to seek approval* for minor needs keeps inmates in a status of constant *dependence* and *insecurity*. In a system run by people, even if they work with good intentions, decisions are obviously always dependent on a person's mood or his relationship to a supplicant, making it impossible to maintain complete coherence and justice. However, in the small world of prison, these differences in implementation can become a source of frustration and confrontation. The complete dependence on decisions by prison authorities has in the long term a dehumanizing impact. An inmate has to live with the bitter daily experience that it is *not his* or *her* decision, *his* or *her* intention *that counts*, but that of some dark and inaccessible authority: a classic kafkaesque situation, menacing, disorienting, and distorting one's life. Such constant vagueness of rules, the mix of clear prohibition and a certain pragmatic laxness, makes life uncertain and fosters an attitude of passivity. In the long term, inmates become dependent on the strict routine that defines every moment of life in prison; they lose initiative and feel paralyzed by the daily experience of powerlessness—or, in other words, they *learn helplessness*.[18]

Furthermore, prison guards in Hong Kong change on a regular rotational basis. Staff changes at the top echelons of a prison can cause a sudden disruption of familiar rules and established regulations, and habits suddenly seem to lose their validity. Inmates are often rotated in similar fashion and are always conscious that they can, at any time, be transferred to another correctional institution. Such transfers happen without any prior notice and take immediate effect. The inmate usually has no time to bid farewell to his peers and, even worse, needs to start anew with the difficult process of readjusting to a new environment. This adds to a general sense of *constant uncertainty*, of having no say, and of being in danger of losing the pillars of one's life.

A number replacing an inmate's name amplifies the depersonalizing effect of imprisonment. One inmate said, "The worst of all is the loss of human dignity when one's individuality is gone and each prisoner is identified by a number. No longer are we regarded as human beings, but as non- or subpeople."

Wearing standardized clothing, keeping a uniform hairstyle, and having most personal accessories confiscated, the inmate loses any sense of uniqueness. Furthermore, being a number within a total institution and within a narrow daily schedule makes an inmate lose all sense of individuality and self-esteem. It is indeed painful for inmates to experience how the whole system, deliberately or not, strips a person of his or her personhood, pride, personal value, and (worst of all), human dignity. A depersonalizing impact may to some extent be inherent in the management of a complex institution, as it appears to be the most cost-effective way to supervise and control a big group of rebellious and maladjusted people. Also, a strict regime appears necessary to maintain order and safety. However, an

---

18. Haney, *Reforming Punishment*, 14.

additional intention goes with it: if a person is rebellious, bad or generally unadjusted and in need of correction, the logic goes, his or her specific needs, wishes, or orientations, should be broken and given new direction, and a destructive character should be suppressed.

THE PRISON AS PHYSICAL REALITY: SHAPING INMATES' MINDS

The architecture and overall design of prisons creates a depressing feeling. Rare is the occasion that inmates see colors beyond the brown of their own uniforms and the green of the officers.' Seeing colorful clothes worn by prison visitors can in itself become a pleasure to which inmates respond strongly. The ubiquity of barbed wire, the monotonous forms, the lack of wall colors or paintings, and the insufficient light all add to a pervading mood of hopelessness. In most cells the light bulb only spreads a sparse, sickly light, which is hardly enough for study during lockup time. A former inmate describes the physical reality of prison in following words: "Nearly everything one sees, hears, and touches can be described as hard. The senses are confronted with hardness at every turn."[19]

The *interior design* increases the feeling of *humiliation*. In a newly built complex for prisoners with long sentences within Stanley Prison, Hong Kong's biggest and oldest prison, the openings in the massive cell doors are so low that inmates who need to communicate with staff during lockup time need to kneel down: Deliberate design or architectural mistake? Cell doors in the older parts of the prison and in other prisons consist of iron bars, which allow constant supervision and deny privacy.

All over the world many prisons are *overcrowded*. This is particularly an issue in the United States, where since the early 1970s a series of policies and decisions has led to the imprisonment of whole groups of the population, namely, young black males in large urban centers.[20] By the beginning of 2008 the incarceration number for the first time crossed the critical threshold of one in 100 adult US Americans.[21] Overcrowding has a direct

---

19. Spitale, *Prison Ministry*, 88.

20. See Garland, *Mass Imprisonment*, 2. On the criminal justice policy changes that triggered such mass imprisonment, see Mauer, "Causes and Consequences of Prison Growth," 4–14; on the link between mass imprisonment and racial inequality, see Wacquant "Deadly Symbiosis," 82–120.

21. See the report published by the Pew Center on the States, *One in 100*. See more on

impact on the daily life of inmates: no places for withdrawal, overused facilities, a sports ground large enough only for a minority of inmates during break times, small cells (designed for one person) shared with another prisoner who is allocated randomly. In Hong Kong, the inmates have to use the toilet right in front of their cellmate, without a partition. Living together in cramped conditions with inmates, many of them with severe emotional problems and difficult personalities, can create serious tensions.[22]

A prison is full of *noise*: noise from workshops, noise from inmates or from officers shouting, and noise from the television. During breakfast, lunch, or dinner in the common room, the set is switched on at a volume, which drowns all creative thinking and peace of mind. Being exposed to constant noise increases tension, causes irritability, and can lead to sleeplessness.[23]

The hardware of the prison, the impact of its architecture and design, and the software (its habits and rules) all emphasize the overriding purpose and spirit of strict *obedience* and *submission*. This spirit is further reinforced by a behavioral assessment system that officially sanctions and rewards obedience. In Hong Kong, inmates with life sentences can be released only if they exhibit clear obedience and submission to judicial and correctional authority, including open expressions of remorse.[24] A deviant inmate is urged to go through a process of mortification of the old self and strict submission under the authority of the given order.

PRISON CULTURE: STRATEGIES OF SURVIVAL

Goffman describes four typical strategies of how inmates respond to total institutions. This typology also fits Hong Kong's prison population. Some inmates react with *withdrawal*. This happens physically, through deliberate isolation confinement; it happens socially, through withdrawal from interaction with other inmates; and it happens psychologically, through escape

---

this in chapter 8, "Prison Ministry and Penal Reform."

22. On the psychological effects of overcrowding see Haney, *Reforming Punishment*, 199–240 (chapter 7).

23. Collins, *Christian Counseling*, 467–68.

24. In Hong Kong, a so-called Long Prison Sentence Review Board reviews life sentences every two years and considers commuting them into a determinate sentence. This is a necessary precondition for a release of inmates with life sentences. Often such commutation happens after twenty-two to twenty-six years; depending on the severity of the case, it can also happen later.

into a world of fantasy. Spiritual techniques or studies can support an inmate in his withdrawal. Such an attitude is often accompanied by a negative view of other inmates and an elitist view of oneself: those who withdraw from community life see themselves in a different light, as not belonging to the same kind of people as the fellow inmates.

Others react with *rebellion*. Rebels cause the staff many problems but can be institutionally useful, as they provide an opportunity to demonstrate authority. Rebels are to some degree popular among inmates, particularly if their protests are reasonable. They show character, raise morale, and demonstrate that some room for self-determination still remains. They remind inmates that the authority of the institution has its limits. On the other hand, rebels constantly threaten the order of the institution and may cause increased repression with negative consequences for all inmates, particularly if the management, through collective punishment, cancels benefits, which all prisoners enjoy. The goal of such punishment is to induce the majority of adjusted inmates to pressure rebellious individuals to conform to the rules.

A third and very common reaction is *colonization*. Inmates become indifferent to the institution, and the prison turns into their home. They integrate the rules into their personal routine and live well with them. Colonized inmates are those whom staff like most, who are most easily governed, and who respond to the rules with a sense of duty. The administration often mistakes colonization for change in an inmate's mind and may reward it with positive assessments and support for parole. Fourth, the colonization can turn into *conversion* when inmates completely adopt the staff's or outsiders' stereotypical views of themselves. They internalize a low and negative image of inmates and identify with it.

This typology emphasizes interactions between inmates and the system but says little about interactions between inmates. The prison system is indeed a closed society with its own economic and political system. Inmates are constrained to live with their neighbors more intimately than anyone lives with his own family. Every day they sleep in the same room or in adjacent rooms with little separation. They work in the same narrow workshop, eat together, shower together, and spend their leisure time together. An inmate seems to have only three ways to survive in such an environment: by withdrawing from mingling with other inmates; by mitigating the hardship through establishing a system of solidarity, which provides mutual aid, loyalty, affection, and respect; or, by seeking one's own advantage and exploiting the other prisoners as far as possible.

Hong Kong inmates have established a system to which the majority adapts and that combines mutual solidarity with exploitation. In this prison subculture, the *Triads* play a crucial role. Triads are criminal groups mainly in Hong Kong and Macao, but also in Taiwan, across the Chinese diaspora of Southeast Asia, and elsewhere; their number is increasing again in mainland China. Similar to the Yakuza in Japan or the Mafia in the West, they make their living from smuggling, money laundering, contract and black–market crimes, extortion, prostitution, gambling, and counterfeiting. Historically they go back to the eighteenth century when they were established as secret patriotic societies to overthrow the foreign Manchu emperor of the Qing dynasty in China. They are still a dominant force within the criminal world of Greater China, although only a minority of crimes in Hong Kong is Triad related. Nowadays, they seem to be less strictly and ritually structured, and Triad affiliation is complemented by clan loyalty, political links, or bonds through growing up in the same place. Many youth gangs loosely belong to one of the known Triad groups, but gang leaders act largely independently from any senior command. Triad-related violence is directed mostly against members of other Triad groups, who settle their differences by violence when deals cannot be reached peacefully.

What is relevant for visitors from outside is less the reality of the Triads and more its spirit, a special Triad culture where it is common that so-called little horses (*mazai*), junior group members follow a big brother (*dalao*), who has ample command and authority. Reflecting the Confucian spirit of the Chinese context, these groups or gangs exert strong influence on their members. The criminal society has, like the outside world, a top–down structure, and it is the responsibility of the big brother to protect and support his little horses, who owe him unconditional loyalty. In such a context, Christian or other visitors may be tempted to behave similarly. The question about how to relate to the Triads remains a continuous challenge for the Christian community: Should the church accept them as part of the fabric of prison society, as part of the context of prison ministry, like the creation order of the broken prison world? Or are they a fundamentally evil reality that needs to be rejected? What about members of the Christian community who are at the same time leaders of Triad groups inside the prison? We will discuss this point later.

Within prisons in Hong Kong, Triads coexist relatively peacefully. The many different Triads that exist outside prison fall into four local Triad groups, plus an additional fifth group of those from mainland China. These groups do not usually compete for members and have an important regulatory function within the prison. We can regard them as a specific form of civil society—that is, the social middle structure between (on the one hand) the individual and (on the other hand) the macrostructure: the given rules. Probably around 95 percent of ethnic Chinese inmates belong to one of these groups. Only foreign inmates or inmates with special authority or status can live a dignified life without becoming a member of such a group, and only inmates whose criminal conduct disqualifies them (for example, sexual offenders) are unwelcome. All areas of everyday prison life are arranged through negotiations between the four local groups: who sits where in the dining hall, who can play football during leisure time on the crowded pitch, who gets what position in the workshop, or who takes a shower in what place. As the prison functions like any other community, the inmates need to set the prices of commodities, services, and privileges. Everything has its price. If someone opts not to join the Triad groups, he is not only less safe, but he is often also excluded from certain services and privileges.

Each of the subgroups in prison, usually also in each section of prison, democratically elects its own leader. If there are conflicts between members of different groups, it is the responsibility of the leaders to negotiate an agreement that can settle the conflict. Besides performing this internally pacifying function, the leaders also act as spokespeople, communication channels between the prison administration and the prison population. If the food rations are too small, if the food is too salty, if there are conflicts with specific junior members of staff, or if there are new rules that are unpopular, it is these leaders' duty to voice complaints. The advantage of this system for the prison management is that it makes administration easier. Complaints are channelled through the common-sense assessment of the experienced leaders and are not expressed randomly. The regular inspection tours of senior prison officials and of members of independent supervisory boards are less likely to be interrupted by freak and minority complaints; instead, the Triad leaders discuss necessary improvements with less-senior officials. Nonconformist inmates who disturb the stable coexistence of prison can be disciplined by joint sanctions.

PRISON ECONOMY AND GAMBLING

In Hong Kong every inmate who works receives a small salary for his work. Depending on the kind of work, there are different salary levels, from US$10 to US$70 a week. With this salary, inmates can officially purchase food, cigarettes, hygiene items, and stationery. Obviously, this sum is hardly enough to purchase the many amenities that the prison does not provide, and this imposed poverty can be regarded as fringe punishment.[25] Part of the salary is deducted and put in a reserve fund, which is accessible only after release. An inmate may also at any time pay some of his salary to family or friends outside prison.

However, this official economy has little significance compared to the more important (illegal) underground economy, which is one of the most central areas of Triad regulation and control. In Hong Kong prisons, the common tender is the cigarette, as official currency is not accessible. The black market price of cigarettes is fluctuating, but may stand at three to four times the price at which they are officially purchased. Any commodity or service among inmates can be paid for with this unofficial currency.

An important element of the underground economy is *food* taken illegally from the daily food allocation of the kitchen. Through illegal food preparation, creative and skilled inmates can even in the absence of common private kitchen facilities improve the monotonous diet. Converting a sink into a cooker, a flatiron into a toaster or a laundry machine into a stove are just some of the ways through which inmates show extraordinary ingenuity in mitigating their deprivation. Accordingly, work in the kitchen can be financially very lucrative.

Important within this economy is *gambling*, an important leisure activity for many inmates. It is communitarian and relaxing, and it gives some spice to a time dominated by overwhelming monotony. In Chinese culture, playing a game rarely happens without some pecuniary incentive, though an exception may be Chinese chess, which is also popular among inmates. In all other games, there is at least a small amount of money at stake. When gambling, the time of meaningless idling turns into a thrilling and possibly profitable activity. Gambling can be an important source of income for many inmates.

In the absence of any limiting factor, it is easy for an inmate to become *addicted* to gambling. For some inmates, the potentially huge gambling

---

25. See Williams and Fish, "Formal and Informal Economic Systems," 162.

revenue provides one of the few opportunities to support their families and regain a valuable purpose in life. For others, it is the pure thrill of a possible win. Tragically, a significant number of inmates' crimes were related to gambling debts and to subsequent illegal attempts to recouping them—through robbery, kidnapping, or other means. Gambling can prove equally destructive and can bring tremendous misery when continued in prison, with the Triads controlling the debt economy and receiving their share. As the financial power of inmates is very limited, it is usually the inmate's family who has to repay the debt through out-of-prison payments to the family of the winner. If the loser does not want to burden his family, the only way is to withdraw into solitary confinement, where an inmate is safe from forced debt collection. The harm caused by gambling is one of the reasons why, in the past years, the Hong Kong prison administration has relatively successfully repressed such illegal activities.

Not only gambling, but the whole underground economy is periodically jeopardized by stricter implementation of the prison rules, particularly when some incident has brought the whole system into public awareness, or when there is a change in senior management. However, despite all measures to suppress the underground economy, both are related to inmates' needs, and the prison economy is no different from any other economy in its response to needs. Administrative pressure, on the whole, often simply causes prices to rise. The strict implementation of rules has its natural limits in the readiness of frontline staff to cooperate. They work daily with the inmates and need to maintain steady relationships with them, balancing pressure from senior officers with pressure from the people of whom they are in charge.

VIOLENCE

Hong Kong's Triad-dominated prison culture described above creates a relatively stable, safe, and predictable environment with much less violence than in most other contexts. Random violence rarely happens. There may be a cultural factor at work: Chinese people seem to have more concern for the social order and are more used to suppressing negative feelings such as anger and aggression, and to giving priority to the needs of the community. People do not express negative feelings as much as in the Western context, as this would disturb social and interpersonal cohesion. The person who fails to control his or her emotions and erupts in anger attacks not simply another individual but the harmony of the community at large. In a Western context, there is a greater concern for the individual, for whom suppression of negative feelings is believed to have a counterproductive effect, which results in other destructive expressions. It is thus thought to be healthier for the individual to express his or her anger in controlled ways. A senior prison official describes this impact as follows: 'The emphasis in Chinese culture on harmony and on the Confucian hierarchical structure of respect for authority has helped to maintain peace in Hong Kong's jails. Put simply, most inmates want to live orderly lives. Most do, most of the time.'[26]

We can thus say that this cultural factor, the management style of Hong Kong prisons, and the stabilizing influence of the Triads add up to an environment that compared to other countries shows little violence. Nevertheless, for many inmates, violence is a reality of prison life much more than in the outside world. In a place where a high number of unadjusted people live together involuntarily, this is no surprise. Violence is obviously an issue for particular groups of inmates, but it can also affect ordinary, nonviolent inmates who happen to live close to people with violent tendencies.

The most common form of violence is a *spontaneous attack*, when a conflict between two individuals turns violent. Often a previous history of animosity between the two exists. External factors like negative news from one's family may affect the mood of the attacker and undermine his morale. Such attacks easily turn into collective fights because inmates are linked to each other through bonds of loyalty owed to other members of their group. A second form of violence springs from *ongoing latent animosity* between different groups of inmates, sometimes between Hong Kong Chinese and inmates from Mainland China, or between Vietnamese[27] and local inmates. This animosity can occasionally turn into bigger, collective fights. A third form is *violence against outsiders*—against, for example, unadjusted or unpopular inmates and, most commonly, sexual offenders. These inmates, like former police officers, or prosecution witnesses, usually opt to withdraw into solitary confinement or, if available, into a special workshop for inmates who are threatened in normal association. This form of violence is often not carried out but remains a threat. An inmate convicted of a

---

26. Prison Commissioner Chan Wa-shek in the 1980s, quoted from Sinclair, *Society's Guardians*, 113.

27. Vietnamese inmates constitute a significant group in Hong Kong prisons. Most of them grew up in the narrow context of refugee camps where they were kept upon their arrival in Hong Kong as boat people. Often it was also there that they committed their crime.

sex-related crime may choose to stay in normal confinement while paying a regular ransom tax of as much as one month's salary to the leaders of the Triad groups to avoid the threat's being realized. A fourth form is *violence by staff against inmates*. Of course, Hong Kong has an intact and independent judicial and penal system. Prisoners are granted standard rights and may raise their complaints through independent channels; human-rights violations are certainly not the rule. Nonetheless, just as in other countries, so in Hong Kong there are cases of staff exerting violence against inmates. This violence can happen through other inmates who are hired as proxy attackers against an inmate regarded as a troublemaker. Or the staff may conduct the attack themselves, well out of sight of the closed-circuit cameras. It is practically impossible for an inmate to lodge a successful complaint in such a case, as the staff will support each other and claim that the inmate initiated the attack. The fifth form, *violence of inmates against staff*, is extremely rare. Not only is violence generally less expressed, but a person of authority also receives much more respect in the Chinese context than in the West. Strict supervision and a very high staff-inmate ratio (around one member of staff per two inmates[28]) further contribute to the virtual absence of inmates attacking staff.[29]

Violence (or possibly more pertinently, living under the threat of violence) can create a deep sense of anxiety, depression, and fearful withdrawal from the community; it can cause an inmate to lose all feeling of being valued. An atmosphere of violence affects all parts of an inmate's life: he will find it very hard to mobilize constructive energy for stability and for transforming progress.

> Ah-Lung[30] was sentenced for a sexual offence, which involved a relative of a senior staff member. He requested isolation for fear of reprisals by prison staff. Even there in the relative safety of solitary confinement, he was for several months dominated by the fear of

---

28. Annual report of the Correctional Services Department of Hong Kong. The staff-to-inmate ratio is reached by dividing the overall number of departmental staff (around 6,800) by the number of inmates (around 12,000). This number also includes staff working in the administration.

29. Different from this is the assessment of Lahm, "Inmates Assaults on Prison Staff," 145, with reference to the U.S. context: Lahm observed that with an increase in the staff-to-inmate ratio there is an increasing probability for an inmate to assault a prison employee.

30 ˙ All names are changed if not otherwise noted. Names in colloquial Cantonese are often preceded by a prefix *Ah-*.

revenge. It was only after a long period of counseling, and through the emotional stability resulting from such counseling, that he gradually lost his fear. He eventually agreed to be transferred to normal confinement and became an active member of the prison's Christian community.

Until now, we have focused on the social and structural side of prison life. We turn next to the more individual side of how inmates commonly experience life in prison and what they feel.

SELF-PERCEPTION: FAILURE, SHAME, GUILT

It is a common misperception that prisoners feel no remorse for their crimes. In fact usually the opposite is true. That does not mean that all inmates freely show feelings of guilt; the prison environment is not conducive to such expression. But failure, shame, and guilt are usually not far from the surface. Inmates' most immediate feeling is one of *failure*: They have failed to fulfil their families' or friends' expectations, no matter whether these expectations were real or imagined. This feeling of failure is, in a Chinese context, particularly directed towards the parents because inmates are unable to take up the responsibility of filial obedience. They have been brought up with the expectation that they will return the parental support they received during their childhood and youth by later caring financially and emotionally for their parents. The lack of a sufficient welfare system in Hong Kong makes support from one's children an economic necessity for a large part of the population. Inmates often have to watch helplessly while their parents struggle.

The inmates also understand their situation as *individual* failure. This is partly the product of a social discourse, which emphasizes individual responsibility and preaches the theory of equal opportunity. On the other side, it is the result of a context that stresses submission of the individual under a communitarian order. Accordingly, most of the inmates I have met direct the blame for their failure at themselves. Parents—or those in charge of the inmates' education, often a sister of the father, a grandmother or another close relative—are rarely blamed but are usually described with gratefulness.

> One inmate, Ah-Ban, who had been convicted for an outburst of violence and causing heavy bodily harm to somebody who bullied him over a long period of time, felt so deeply ashamed about his

behavior that he wanted to divorce his wife. He hoped that at least by doing so he could avoid the harm that he had inflicted on his family. Through a slow process of counseling he regained identity, self-respect, and the strength to face his own family.

This tendency to blame oneself stands in contrast to groups of other cultural backgrounds, which I met in Hong Kong prisons or in other prisons around the world, who more easily blame society, a racist judiciary, or their upbringing in poverty and deprivation.

Failure is experienced as a deep *shame*, often described as a *loss of face*. *Face*—a famous word in Chinese and other Asian contexts—refers to all public expression of one's person, and how that expression is publicly perceived. Face is one of the main driving forces in a person's public behavior and should enhance harmonious relations with others. This means, as seen above, to hide one's feelings and not to show weakness and anger, as they should not interfere with interpersonal relationships. Human relations are structured less along subjective and random lines of personal feelings and more along objective lines of social positioning or hierarchy. Having been convicted of a crime brings shame not only on an individual but also on a whole family, and destroys the harmony of its relationships and the social order in which its members live.

A good number of inmates in Hong Kong prisons hide their imprisonment from their own *children*. They still try to maintain a relationship with them through letters sent indirectly or through the occasionally allowed phone calls. They usually explain that they are working in a faraway place or on a boat, in very primitive conditions—and in this latter point, at least, they are right. Inmates hide the truth for fear that children (a) may not be able to cope with seeing their father under prison conditions, (b) may not keep this secret and end up being bullied by peers, or (c) may be otherwise affected, emotionally or academically, by the incarceration. Indeed, declining academic performance frequently follows a parent's imprisonment.[31] For some, a deeper reason might be the worry that a disclosure could destroy a father's credibility with his children. Many inmates are painfully aware that their crime could deprive them of the respect of the next generation and could endanger future support and communal togetherness. The loss of face in relation to their children, they fear, could permanently undermine the family's coherence and structure. Hiding the

---

31. Friedman and Esselstyn, "Adjustment of Children of Jail Inmates"; quoted in Van Ness, *Crime and Its Victims*, 50.

fact of imprisonment can, however, increase shame, as there is no chance for reversal. A long period without direct interaction can be more harmful than a disclosure, and it is difficult to maintain the story of permanent absence for a long period of time. Children may find out somehow about the real whereabouts of their father or mother and feel betrayed.

Guilt is an attitude that stands rather at the end than at the beginning of a process and, in this sense, signifies a deeper understanding of the roots, the effects, and the related factors of a person's harmful actions. Guilt has thus a spiritual dimension and is shaped by the experience of forgiveness and a forgiving community (more on this in chapter 4).

EMOTIONAL PAIN: USELESSNESS, LONELINESS, DEPENDENCY

Most inmates, although admitting it in various degrees, share a deep emotional pain. This pain is a feeling of *overwhelming sadness*, like an endlessly painful sting in the heart, continuously present in the background even if an inmate has adjusted well to life in prison. Of course, some inmates find it difficult to adjust to the outside world after their release and thus regularly return: drug addicts, caught in an endless cycle of addiction and petty crimes to sustain their living; a few foreign inmates from poor backgrounds, who relish the opportunity to earn a bit of extra money while imprisoned in a more affluent context; some older fellows, who feel better taken care of in prison than in the rough outside world. They all somehow take their captivity more easily. But the pain of being unable to contribute to society, to set up a family and a meaningful life results in an overwhelming feeling of *uselessness*: Nearly all inmates regard prison as a complete waste of time. They wait until it is over, and nearly all inmates find it difficult to gain purpose and meaning. This feeling of uselessness is exacerbated by the outside world's perception of prisoners. Many inmates reduce their activity and change their sleeping patterns; they withdraw and gradually *unlearn their skills*, not only their vocational skills, but maybe more important their communicative and relational skills.

The separation from the family and the inability to sustain family members are particularly strong in relation to the *mother*. Instead of gratefully returning the dedication that she gave through education and upbringing, the inmate remains dependent on her support and care. Often the relationship to the mother lasts when others have decayed. This inability to return what one has received during childhood further aggravates the feeling of uselessness. Inmates seem not to experience the same feeling of pain in relation to their *fathers*. Rather, they feel a more objective sentiment of failure—of not living up to his standard.

Equally, the pain caused by separation from *children* is experienced as a painful inability to educate them in a good direction, a loss of relation and influence, or powerlessness at witnessing how they too slowly slide into criminal activities. In contrast to my impression from the European context, my sense of Hong Kong is that many inmates accept separation from the *wife* more easily and rationally. They understand that the wife needs to give them up and find a new partner in order to sustain a family.

> Ah-Wa is a young man who committed a murder and was subsequently sentenced to life in prison. He had a young wife and a newborn baby. During the first five years in prison he witnessed how his wife increasingly distanced herself from him. However, the deepest pain was when his daughter started to address the new man in his wife's life as Daddy. He realistically feared that he would slowly fade out of his daughter's memory. When discussing the divorce agreement, his only point was to make sure his daughter's regular visits would continue.

Another dominant feeling while in prison is *loneliness*. Separation from the family strips an inmate from his most basic network, even if many inmates had been neglecting their family relations while outside. Loneliness in prison has an additional dimension: prisons are extremely loud places where one is never alone. An inmate finds himself constantly in the midst of intensive social interaction, and the inability to escape the crowds can make the feeling of loneliness even worse. An inmate will continuously try to maintain a facade of normality and avoid showing weakness in order to protect himself from other inmates' bullying. He can hardly share his true feelings and is, *in the midst of people, alone*. Solitary confinement can be an exacerbation of loneliness, as physical and psychological isolation drive people into deep desperation. However, it can also be an opportunity to avoid the enforced and overwhelming social interaction and an opportunity to deal with one's own loneliness.

An effect of the separation from the regular network of support is that inmates *face the issues of their lives alone*. When communication with the family or with friends has to go through a slow process of written and censored mail, communicating about their well-being becomes a complicated exercise, and minor events can become big issues: a letter that is not answered within the common time span; a birthday card to the parents that never arrives and gets lost in the jungle of the internal mail system, censorship, or the public mail; a family member's sickness; a verbal allusion to some financial problem; an air of fatigue during a visit —all these and similar issues could under normal circumstances easily be clarified through a phone call or through a reassuring visit. However, when nothing happens, these minor issues take on their own existence and continue to occupy the inmate's mind while, in reality, the fatigue, the sickness, or the financial problem may long ago have been resolved. The detachment from the outside world means that realism in assessing problems of the outside world is gradually lost.

Another aspect of this loneliness is the *feeling of being abandoned*. Some inmates drew news headlines at the time of the crime and during the trial, but once they are locked up, they gradually fade out of public interest and are forgotten. Some particularly infamous inmates have to face the fact that their cases are mentioned in the media on special occasions, with the corresponding experience of being more and more reduced to just a case rather than a person. The loneliness and the feeling of abandonment can instil fear: of the future, obviously most strongly towards the end of imprisonment; of meeting the family after release; of being ill prepared and poorly educated for a future work life. If the inmate has no opportunity to verify his aptitude, such fears can grow unabated.

The isolation of prison causes many inmates to live as though *frozen in time and space*. While the outside world continues to develop, inmates keep an understanding of their outside relationships and of the outside world that remains the same as at the time of their arrest, even as time passes. They live in the past and orient themselves based on the past. The growing gap between the inmates and an ever-changing outside world can be a constant source of *misunderstanding*, and may jeopardize successful communication between inmates and relatives or friends. Put simply, inmates have difficulties realizing how life outside of prison moves on. It can thus be painful when they witness how their family has learned to cope without them.

> There are inmates who are well aware of this difficulty. Ah-Hon had been in prison for over twenty years. He has four daughters, the youngest not even born at the time of his arrest. After his arrest, the daughters were raised by his own family, as is common in

the patrilineal Chinese context, and he was thus able to maintain a stable relationship with all four of them. Once, when sharing about his relationships with his daughters he conceded that, when talking to them, he couldn't comment on their lives. He needed to completely restrain himself from any interference. They had grown up without him and wouldn't accept any fatherly imposition.

It is this endless feeling of pain, due to the experiences described above, that lasts far beyond the actual time in prison and makes continuous postrelease care so crucial. Many inmates reminiscing about their time in prison end up bitter even many years after release. They experience anew what has been called the "deferred pains of imprisonment."[32]

A context that deprives people so fundamentally of all common elements of good life makes it very difficult to build up self-esteem. Placing someone in a dependent position where he or she cannot reciprocate will undermine self-respect. It is difficult for inmates to contribute to and build up their personal life and to experience a sense of achievement. It is accordingly difficult to grow into a balanced person with a sense of value and self-awareness. The most important *motor in personal growth* and in transformation is the chance to receive positive feedback, to feel that personal efforts do have an impact, and an environment that facilitates and encourages even small-scale improvement. The overall failure of the prison system to support inmates' sense of value undermines all rehabilitative efforts.

POSITIVE VALUES: PRIVATE LIFE, GOALS, AND HOPES

As in any other community that lives in hardship and deprivation, plenty of positive values are to be found also in the prison community. There is friendship, there is joy, there is laughter, and there is rich interaction between many young, interesting, and energetic people. The causes of what is *positively* experienced are not much different from life outside prison. Anything that interrupts the monotony of incarceration is essentially welcome.

Surely of highest value to inmates is a *visit*. A visit from a family member reminds inmates that they are not forgotten and gives them the experience of being loved. During the visit, inmates can catch up with the latest news and receive support in material or emotional form. Visits have an additional social effect. Being called to a visit elevates inmates within the prison community: they are regarded as being taken care of and thus

32. Haney, *Reforming Punishment*, 13.

receive additional status. Some request visits from prison ministry volunteers explicitly to get such a feeling.

Letters have a similar effect, though not quite the same warmth. But they have the additional effect of lasting beyond the short thirty minutes of an ordinary visit. And they may inspire the inmate to respond, which has an activating effect. Whether visit or letter, the most important is to receive good news from loved ones. What happens to one's family becomes extremely important when one's own world shrinks to the narrow confinement of prison. In the absence of anything happening in their own lives, inmates focus on the lives of others. The same interest in the lives of others appears regarding the lives of volunteers or the chaplain. Anything known about their lives is treasured and continuously remembered.

Friendships with people outside prison can play a similar role to family relationships. However, at least in the Asian context, people usually prefer to burden the family rather than friends in case of having special needs. Friendships *with other inmates* provide important emotional support. Many relations between inmates show tremendous care and mutual affection; some of these go back to previous incarcerations or to juvenile prison. On the other hand, many inmates confess that, despite apparently close links between inmates, truly strong friendships are not possible in prison. To really confide in another inmate is too risky and means giving away too much. Much distrust remains.

Within the narrow confinement of prison, a physical workout and a *well-formed body* become important values. Many male inmates do weight lifting and other physical exercises. Such exercises are not only a way to use up energy but also have an emotionally comforting and rejuvenating effect. Physical activity is also a popular and legitimate way of caring for one's body and involves tenderness directed at oneself. On the other hand, physical strength establishes male identity and enhances masculinity in a context where male assertiveness is strongly valued, and in a society that is highly conscious of each member's abilities and strengths.[33]

Sexual desires can hardly be satisfied in prison. Masturbation is of course possible, but where inmates share a narrow cell with other inmates, they lack the necessary privacy. Sexual intimacy between inmates may occur, but is equally hard to imagine when there is so little privacy.[34] There

---

33. See further Sabo, "Doing Time, Doing Masculinity," 61ff.

34. In contrast to this impression stands the estimation of Sykes, *Society of Captives*, 72, regarding the US context. Sykes estimates that around 35 percent of inmates in that

are no indications that violent and enforced forms of sexuality, as known from prisons in the United States, occur in Hong Kong. A popular form of intimacy that can at least partly substitute for direct sexual contact is the massage. It is common that inmates, some with experience and technique, massage another's backs and necks. Physical contact is also common in other casual forms, which partly compensate for the lack of sexual contact. Inmates may hold hands while walking in the courtyard, or they may closely lean on each other while watching television.

Goals in life are similar to those of people outside prison: progress in academic studies, maintaining positive family relations or positive developments therein, or anything that causes oneself or one's family to be proud.

Finally, what inmates most basically *hope* and yearn for is *to be respected*. Every inmate hopes that there is a way out of the daily rejection, which they experience through the dehumanizing elements of imprisonment while confined behind prison walls. Inmates wish to live and be treated with dignity. This is the bottom line for any prison worker, be it a member of the staff, a chaplain, or a volunteer visitor. Inmates are highly sensitive about how they are perceived. No matter how good the counseling techniques, how profound the psychological understanding, or how deep the spiritual commitment of a visitor, if there is anything in the visitor's attitude that makes the inmate feel looked down upon, he will react with mistrust and will not be ready to establish a good relationship. To respect inmates implies trust—that they are able to change even if such change does not happen in the way that the visitor expects. To change, to be able to change, and to experience true transformation is what many inmates ultimately hope for. This is what the remainder of this book is about.

Bibliographical Notes

> One of the *most basic reference book* for all aspects of prison, particularly the penal context of the United States is Mary Bosworth, ed., *Encyclopedia of Prisons and Correctional Facilities*, 2 vols. (Thousand Oaks, CA: Sage, 2005). Its nearly 400 entries provide a comprehensive view of all aspects of prison life, prison history, punishment theories, penal policies, and issues of the prison population.

---

context engage in homosexual acts. For a more recent discussion of sexuality in prison, see Kunzel, *Criminal Intimacy*.

Beyond the Walls of Separation

To my knowledge no study exists on prison life in the *context of Hong Kong* besides one, which will be noted in the next chapter, a historical study commissioned by the Correctional Services Department. However, it does not give much insight into the details of prison life.

A good number of studies exist describing and analyzing other contexts. They offer useful background and comparative information and inspire beyond their own context. Several *sociological theories about the mechanisms of prisons* have become standard and are commonly referred to. Graham Sykes, *The Society of Captives: A Study of a Maximum Security Prison* (Princeton: Princeton University Press, 1958) gives a classic and very readable description of prison life and prison subculture in the US. His thesis is that the specific features of prison life emerge as a mitigating reaction to five fundamental areas of deprivation: of liberty, of goods and services, of autonomy, of security, and of heterosexual relationships. This *deprivation theory* is not the only one to explain how a distinctive society forms in prison. An alternative approach is the *importation model*, suggested by John Irwin and Donald Cressey that asserts that inmates bring with them or import their values and norms from their outside world. The 'prison code' of loyalty to one's peers, of being strong, of not informing on other inmates, and so forth, not only has relevance in prison, but is the same code that criminal groups outside prison share. An example that tries to combine deprivation and importation theory is John A. Slosar, *Prisonization, Friendship, and Leadership* (Lexington, MA: Lexington Books, 1978). His findings distinguish between inmates who were less involved in a life of crime and to whom the deprivation theory applies more, and those with a longer criminal career, who are less affected by the deprivation experiences in the penal institution. The discussion between deprivation theory and importation theory is not a purely academic debate but is the simple and old question of whether prisoners are made in prison or whether they bring their attitudes and values into prison from outside. This has important repercussions on how to manage prisons. Another classical study that describes the dynamics of an institution is Erving Goffman, *Asylums: Essays on the Condition of the Social Situation of Mental Patients and Other Inmates* (Garden City, NY: Anchor, 1961). The study describes life in a closed mental-health clinic, but it serves as example for any closed institution. The famous book of Michel Foucault, *Discipline and Punish: The Birth of the Prison* (New York: Pantheon, 1977) offers, not only a historical account about how prison as main form of punishment emerged, but also a fascinating analysis of the microphysics of power. He describes how the prisoner is trained, normalized, and disciplined. The interesting book edited by Don Sabo, Terry A. Kupers, and Willie London, *Prison Masculinities* (Philadelphia: Temple University Press, 2001) describes (male) prison life from the perspective of gender studies. The thesis of the book to which persons from inside and outside prison contributed is that the existing prison system serves to reproduce destructive and hegemonic forms of masculinity. Regina Kunzel, *Criminal Intimacy: Prison and the Uneven History of Modern American Sexuality* (Chicago: University of Chicago Press, 2008) examines the sexual world and the multiple sexual cultures through the course of nineteenth- and twentieth-century America. Although sex in prison has not been as much a taboo as is often claimed, Kunzel's historical study fills an important link between the history of prisons and the history of sexuality.

On the *politics of imprisonment*, see several of the essays in David Garland, editor. *Mass Imprisonment: Social Causes and Consequences* (London: Sage, 2001). The essay by M. Mauer, "Causes and Consequences of Prison Growth," 4–14, describes the criminal-justice policy changes and shifts in sentencing policy that triggered such mass imprisonment, most important, the so-called war on drugs and the shift toward the use of determinate sentencing. The essay by L. Wacquant, "Deadly Symbiosis: When Ghetto and Prison Meet and Mesh," 82–120, shows how the prison has replaced the ghetto as a device for caste control and to keep (unskilled) African Americans in a subordinate and confined position (83). More bibliographic information on the politics of imprisonment can be found at the end of chapter 8.

On the *psychology of imprisonment*, see Craig Haney, *Reforming Punishment. Psychological Limits to the Pains of Imprisonment* (The Law and Public Policy, Washington DC: American Psychological Association, 2006). Haney studied the psychology of imprisonment in the United States for more than thirty years, and his research has been widely discussed. He shows how mass incarceration has brought the American criminal-justice system to the brink of collapse, how pain has become a primary purpose of imprisonment, and how prisons themselves generate new crime. The book offers valuable information about the psychological effects of imprisonment. Haney applies the insights of psychology to offer an alternative to the excess and harm caused by penal policies. His study contains valuable and recent information about the punitive state of the prisons in the United

States. Haney was also one of the scholars in charge of the Stanford Prison Experiment, conducted in 1971. This famous study showed in a very concentrated form how inmates' and guards' behavior patterns derive not from their personalities but from inmates' and guards' roles in imprisonment and from their power or powerlessness. See C. Haney, et al., "Interpersonal Dynamics in a Simulated Prison," *International Journal of Criminology and Penology* 69 / 1 (1973); Craig Haney and Philip Zimbardo, "The Socialization into Criminality: On Becoming a Prisoner and a Guard," in *Law, Justice, and the Individual in Society: Psychological and Legal Issues*, edited by June Tapp and Felice Levine (New York: Holt, Rinehart & Winston, 1977), 198–223; information can also be found on a special website that presents the whole study through accounts and images, see http://www.prisonexp.org/.

On formal and informal *prison economies* see Vergil L. Williams and Mary Fish, "Formal and Informal Economic Systems," and Sandra E. Gleason, "Hustling: The 'Inside' Economy of the Prison." In *Correctional Institutions*, edited by Robert M. Carter et al. 161–73 and 174–87 3rd ed. (New York: Harper & Row, 1985); Michael Welch, *Ironies of Imprisonment* (Thousand Oaks, CA: Sage, 2005), 139–62, looks at the topic from a different perspective. He focuses on the role of prison in the wider economic context and discusses the role of prison industry and privatization of prisons.

For *prison management*, penal policies, and rehabilitation concepts *in international comparison* see the study by Michael K. Carlie and Kevin I. Minor, editors. *Prisons around the World: Studies in International Penology* (Dubuque, IA: Brown, 1992). The volume contains also contributions that cover penal issues close to the context of Hong Kong. So one article discusses prisons in Taiwan, and another treats prisons in the People's Republic of China.

Several publications on Christian ministry in prison offer some descriptions of *what kind of people* inmates are, *how they feel*, and what the important issues in their life are. Good descriptions from a Christian perspective can be found in Lennie Spitale, *Prison Ministry: Understanding Prison Culture Inside and Out* (Nashville: Broadman & Holman, 2002); Henry G. Covert, *Ministry to the Incarcerated* (Chicago: Loyola University Press, 1995), 13–63; or Gerald Austin McHugh, *Christian Faith and Criminal Justice: Toward a Christian Response to Crime and Punishment* (New York: Paulist, 1978), 68–85. All these books reflect experiences from an

American prison background; however, despite clear cultural differences, they overall compare well with the Asian context.

2

Prisons and Offender Rehabilitation—Then and Now

IN THE LAST CHAPTER, we got a glimpse of life in prison and its effect on the individual—physically and emotionally. Passing through, at times, more than half a dozen locked gates until actually meeting an inmate, visitors realize that prisons are as hard to break *into* as they are to break *out of*. They enter a social institution that is radically different from what they are used to in normal life. They do not simply step into a randomly built, randomly managed place but into an institution that is the crystallization of a past history of penal ideologies. They may therefore want to know why prisons are what they are.

In this chapter, we step back and look at prisons from a distance. We ask how the modern prison, as known and used throughout the world today, has developed. Past attempts to cope with crime continue to shape prison life to the present, even though penologists—those who manage prisons and those who analyze their functioning in theory—increasingly doubt the effectiveness of current prison-based penal practices. Or, in the words of David Garland, who wrote an account of punishment and penal philosophies, "A growing sense of doubt, dissatisfaction, and sheer puzzlement has now begun to emerge around our modern penal practices. The contemporary period is one in which penological optimism has given way to a persistent skepticism about the rationality and efficacy of modern penal institutions."[1]

Ever since ancient times, imprisonment has been a societal response to violations of the law. From ancient Mesopotamia, Assyria, Egypt, and Israel through Athens to Rome we find references to prisons.[2] Ancient China also detained offenders in prisons, as did India. However, the ways prisons were managed and the roles they played in the punishment and rehabilitation of offenders have changed through the centuries. Looking into how imprisonment became what it is today broadens our understanding, and prepares us to respond appropriately to those living in such confinement. A look into the history of imprisonment enables us to avoid regarding imprisonment as necessary, God-given, and the only possible response to crime, and instead sees it as historically developed and changeable. Our account will focus on penal developments in the West because Occidental penal philosophies shaped the modern prison most strongly.

Questions that this chapter addresses follow:

- Why has corporal punishment been largely abolished and replaced by punishment through imprisonment?
- What is the penitentiary? How is the penal philosophy behind the penitentiary still alive and influencing modern prisons?
- How did the idea of rehabilitation emerge? What have been its modes through history?
- How have Christian ideas affected penal reforms?

A SHIFT IN PUNISHMENT TECHNIQUES: FROM CORPORAL PUNISHMENT TO IMPRISONMENT

Before modernity, the main purpose of imprisonment was the *detention* of inmates awaiting trial, of debtors until they paid, or of vagrants before they were sent away. Imprisonment *as punishment*, though known throughout medieval times, was never the principal method. Different justice systems used it in varying degrees: It was more commonly applied in England and Italy, less so in Germany and Scandinavia; more often through ecclesial

---

1. Garland, *Punishment and Modern Society*, 4.
2. See on the whole Peters, "Prison before the Prison," 4–21.

courts, also called canon-law courts, less so through secular courts.³ Other forms of punishment were more important, the most common being *corporal punishment*, administered in different degrees of severity: whipping, branding, mutilation, instant execution, or, most severely, slow execution. Branding was also a common form of identifying recidivists. *Exile or deportation* to some colonies was a punishment that was increasingly used from the sixteenth century on, as attitudes toward idleness and poverty changed. Similarly, *bondage* and *forced labour*, service in the army or in the navy, or punishment to perform public work, became popular in early modernity for lesser crimes, as for vagrants or for beggars. *Financial punishment* and restitution was required in the case of offenses against property and was a penalty normally reserved for the rich.

Corporal punishment was based on several ideas. First, based on the concept of the king's peace, introduced by the English King Henry I (1068–1135), crime was regarded as violation of the king. The king thus took the place of the victims before the law.⁴ Second, crime was regarded as a violation of the sovereign's—the monarch's—body, and corporal punishment was a way to restore justice and regain proper power relations.⁵ Punishment happened visibly, the justice system's public celebration imprinting itself on the body of the punished person. The suffering of the delinquent and the physical presentation of justice served as powerful and public demonstration that justice prevailed and as a means of social control.⁶ However, from the eighteenth to the nineteenth century, a radical change in punishment occurred. Corporal punishment widely disappeared, and imprisonment became the major form of punishment:

> The French philosopher *Michel Foucault* (*Discipline and Punish: The Birth of the Prison,* 1977) offers a thorough description of the shift from a punishment that focused on the body of the delinquent to a prison-based punishment that exerts its power through internalization and discipline. The study has become a seminal work in the understanding of the modern penal system. Foucault rejects the common understanding that the disappearance of torture in Western justice systems happened simply as a step in the growing humanization of society. Instead, the development of

---

3. Ibid., 22–23.
4. Colson and Van Ness, *Convicted*, 46.
5. Foucault, *Discipline and Punish*, 47: "the crime attacks the sovereign; it attacks him physically, since the force of the law is the force of the prince."
6. Ibid., 32–69 (Part 1, chapter 2: "The Spectacle of the Scaffold").

the prison signified an attempt to discipline and dominate, and to shift punishment from the body to the soul of the offender.[7] Or, in Foucault's terminology, the shift to the prison was the surface expression of a deeper shift in the "microphysics" of power that exerts its control through an internalization of its commands. Punishment in the penitentiary responds to deviation from what society prescribes as normative and what it describes as normality. The dominant nineteenth-century society merely imposed a new mechanism of power and control, a discipline of time and of work, over the body of the delinquent. Modern imprisonment is not a milder form of punishment but simply a more ascetic way of imposing suffering, a form that aims more at the *soul* of the delinquent than at the bodily surface. Foucault describes (tongue in cheek) a loop that allows him to turn the roots of Occidental thinking upside down: whereas traditionally the body was the prison of the soul (following a Greek word game, *soma* ["body"] = *sœma* ["prison"]), the soul now becomes the prison of the body.

Of course, the shift to imprisonment did not completely abolish corporal punishment. The continuing existence of the death penalty as many countries' ultimate corporal punishment and the ongoing use of torture, even in disguised or hidden forms, both reflect how deeply rooted this form of punishment is in many societies. In some American states, whipping took place until the middle of the twentieth century,[8] and England formally abolished flogging as a punishment only in 1967.[9] Singapore maintains this form of punishment to our time. It is also obvious that many elements of imprisonment and prison labor are very much directed against the body. Still, generally speaking, we observe how within two centuries a shift in the surrounding culture, usually called the spirit of Enlightenment, radically changed corporal forms of punishment.

There were at least five reasons for this shift. First, executions and corporal punishments turned more and more into *problems of public order*. When spectators sympathized with the convict or expressed admiration for his or her boldness, the authorities' public demonstration of power turned into a mockery of the law. The justice system thus started to move punishment out of sight to avoid public demonstrations of excessive violence or torture.

---

7. See about Foucault's use of *soul*, Garland, *Punishment and Modern Society*, 137.
8. Rotman, "Failure of Reform," 164.
9. McConville, "The Victorian Prison," 145.

A growing *industrial economy* that badly needed an able work force made mutilation and the death penalty appear uneconomic. From early modernity, forced labor grew increasingly popular in many European countries, and prison workhouses were built to accommodate those convicted of less serious offenses.

A *shift in values* supported the shift from corporal punishment to imprisonment and to an emphasis on the integrity of the human body. People felt increasingly appalled by the crudeness of corporal punishment. Mutilation disappeared around the seventeenth century or was maintained only in connection with the death penalty; branding was applied more discreetly. The value of personal liberty increased dramatically through the process of modernization, and new technological possibilities and a growing emancipation from the bonds of tradition encouraged people to value the feeling of freedom. The threat of its loss consequently appeared as a serious deterrent.

Justice in the new spirit of the Enlightenment opted for more *rational and egalitarian forms of punishment*. In cases where the death penalty was implemented, a criminal's socioeconomic status did not come into play. Both rich and poor alike underwent simple execution on the gallows or under the guillotine. When the death penalty was not called for, prison sentences varied in length depending on the severity of the crime. Both reforms made punishment appear less random, more humanitarian, more egalitarian, and more rational.

Finally, and most important, Enlightenment thinking emphasized an orientation towards goal and purpose. This purpose-driven philosophy influenced penal thinking. The essential element of punishment was not punishment as such but its *teleological function*, pointing beyond punishment and bringing about *improvement, education, and healing*. Underlying the changes in penal policies is a faith in human perfectibility that was paralleled by Christian revival movements.

Indeed, Christians played an important role in the changing penal philosophies. Churches supported the shift from corporal punishment to imprisonment because they regarded imprisonment a more spiritual form of punishment than the inflicted corporal pain. Important inspiration for penal reforms came from Christian evangelicals like John (1703-91) and Charles Wesley (1707-88) and entrepreneurs like Jonas Hanway, who were convinced that faith would have a positive impact on the rehabilitation of prisoners. They advocated solitude as an effective tool to reform offenders and thus prepared the way for a radical shift in the conception of imprisonment.

THE PRISON REFORM MOVEMENT IN THE EIGHTEENTH AND NINETEENTH CENTURIES

Until the eighteenth century, many jails and prisons in England were under the private control of lords, bishops, or noblemen, or under local authority. Prisons were self-financing operations, and since the running of a prison or jail involved pecuniary interests, many of the prisoners were charged various fees: for bed and blankets, for shackles or chains to be removed, for all kinds of services like food or alcohol, and even for turning the key at the time of discharge. Prisons were places where people were simply locked up. Little penal authority was exerted in the daily life behind bars. As long as inmates could afford it, they could eat and wear what they liked, they could interact with whom they liked, and they could engage in the activities they liked. On the other hand, those who could not afford the fees or were away from supporting families survived only through charity. Those who could not afford the imposed release fees ended up in prison for extended periods of time.

By the end of the eighteenth century, there was a trend towards *central administration and central control*, with several factors at hand. Most important was the crisis that the British judiciary faced when increased criminality, a growing number of convicted offenders, and the interruption of banishment to the American colonies after their independence led to heavily overcrowded prisons. The prison-reform movement that began in the late eighteenth century is often associated with John Howard and the publication in 1777 of his book *The State of the Prison in England and Wales*. Howard was driven by a Christian zeal to transform the world, and he was shocked to find prisons in such a stark contrast to Christian love. He visited prisons across England and Europe and successfully urged the British Parliament to abandon the fee structure and to appoint salaried officials for the administration of prisons. The reform movement that he initiated strengthened control by the central administration and allowed a more equal treatment of prisoners across England; it established the prison as the central form of punishment, shifting all other forms of punishment aside; and it contributed to an orderly prison management that segregated different kinds of prisoners. The reforms gradually transformed prisons from physically and morally filthy places of confinement into clean and rationally functioning reform machines. The reformers rejected the public spectacle of punishment and removed punishment from the public sight. One effect was that punishment disappeared from most people's experience. As the prisoner disappeared, the prison turned into an object of public imagination. The prisoner, removed from experiential reality, produced more, rather than less, anxiety.[10]

Christian reformers, most prominently the *Quakers*, continued to play an important role in the prison reform movement. The most famous of these Christian prison reformers was Elizabeth Fry (1780–1845), who started a prison-visitation program that brought Christian education to female inmates. She and other Christian reformers believed that spiritual conversion was a more powerful way to change prisoners than whips. The task of punishment should be only the *reformation* of prisoners and could be achieved through personal influence. The Quaker reformers were concerned not only about the prisoner as individual but also about the prison system as a whole. Elizabeth Fry proposed, though without immediate success, reforms of prison labor that would allow prisoners to see the fruits of their efforts, but she would not live to see this happen. The treadmill, symbol of dire meaninglessness, remained a common feature in prisons well into the second half of the nineteenth century (and was given new life in modern-day gyms). Even as late as 1860, a medical committee reaffirmed its use and decided that the amount of labor that a prisoner could be expected to fulfill was to take 8,640 steps per day on the treadmill.[11] It was a particularly cruel device, exhausting prisoners not only physically but also mentally, as it produced absolutely nothing. Elizabeth Fry was also consistently opposed to the death penalty, and she forcefully advocated the segregation of male and female inmates in prison. It was partly due to her efforts that female prisoners were finally separated from male prisoners and their constant sexual exploitation came to an end.[12]

---

10. McGowen, "The Well-Ordered Prison," 98.
11. McConville, "The Victorian Prison," 132.
12. Zedner, "Wayward Sisters," 298ff.

THE EMERGENCE OF THE MODERN PRISON: THE PENITENTIARY

The prison-reform movement fell into a time of fear about the disintegration of society and family. In Europe, it was the time of Restoration and Romanticism, with conservative movements responding to the chaos of the French Revolution. In North America, it was the early years after the foundation of the United States, when enthusiasm about the new nation slowly gave way to fear that the stable social order was threatened by the mobility, unlimited freedom, and lawlessness of a frontier society. It was in this context that prison reformers and their Christian supporters discovered the prison as a place to teach order and discipline to offenders, who were otherwise perceived as a fundamental threat to the societal stability.[13]

It is in this context, and reflecting such penal philosophies, that *new models of prison* emerged, most famously the *penitentiary system*. The penitentiary developed in the United States in two different forms: the *Pennsylvania* or *separate system* and the *Auburn* or *silent system*. In England these were known as the Millbank Prison, designed after the ideas of Jeremy Bentham and completed in 1821, and the Pentonville Prison, which opened in 1842 and followed the separate system. The basic idea of the penitentiary was to hold prisoners in solitude in order to shield them from the supposed contaminating influence of other convicts. Being left in complete silence with only the company of one's conscience and the Bible was to bring about the spiritual renewal of the offender.

The completion of the Eastern State Penitentiary in Philadelphia in 1836 introduced advanced technology unmatched in other public buildings: central heating, flush toilets, and shower baths. It used a system of isolation and lonely labor in individual prison cells to lead the inmates to reflection, repentance, and the eventual change of the criminal person. In Pentonville Prison, even the guards wore padded shoes so that they would not disturb the silence. In the Auburn system, developed in New York as an alternative to the Pennsylvania system (and gradually replacing it) individuals were isolated in separate cells by night but worked under complete silence in congregate workshops during the day. The Auburn system had the same goal as the Pennsylvania system, reforming inmates through redemptive discipline and penitence, but it wanted to do so through more effective means and through strict domination of the inmate's body and

---

13. Rothman, "Perfecting the Prison," 105.

spirit. The idea of the Auburn system was that isolation alone would not lead the prisoner to change; instead, the criminal's spirit needed first to be broken through hard labor and through specific forms of degradation, including by having their heads shaved, by having to wear striped uniforms, and by having to be referred to by numbers rather than by names.

The penitentiary—particularly the separate system—was strongly influenced by Quaker reform ideals. Here the idea of reforming or rehabilitating a criminal was forcefully expressed and the previously dominant, purely vindictive punishment abandoned. In isolation and silence the criminal individual was alone with his or her own conscience and was supposed to be illuminated by it. Or, as two noblemen from France on a fact-finding tour to the new penitentiaries noted, "Thrown into solitude, the convict reflects. Placed alone in the presence of his crime, he learns to hate it, and, if his soul is not yet blunted by evil, it is in isolation that remorse will come to assail him."[14] Others stated, "Alone in his cell, the convict is handed over to himself; in the silence of his passions and of the world that surrounds him, he descends into his conscience, he questions it and feels awakening within him the moral feeling that never entirely perishes in the heart of man."[15] It is through relating to his or her own conscience that change and transformation of a criminal happens.

The penitentiary concept of isolating prisoners clearly reflects the Quakers' mystical belief in the inner light and in an innate sacredness of each individual. The Quakers understood the criminal not as innately evil, as was the traditional view of Puritans, but at least partially as a victim of conditions created by society. It was therefore the moral obligation of this society to help the offender toward reform.[16] Deviancy was the result of corruption pervading the whole of society, with the family and even the church failing to provide counterbalance. Through isolation, religious instruction, practice, and reflection, and by avoiding interaction with other convicts, the criminal would be reeducated and rehabilitated in prison. The penitentiary relied on moral instructors to assist the inmates in their reformation through conversion. How powerfully, it was thought, would the threat of eternal damnation or the promise of eternal salvation through

---

14. De Beaumont and Tocqueville, Note sur le système pénitentiaire (1831), quoted from Foucault *Discipline and Punish*, 237.

15. *Journal des économistes*, II (1842), quoted from ibid., 238.

16. McHugh, *Christian Faith and Criminal Justice*, 35.

faith in Christ, spoken through a prison chaplain, a religious visitor, or even a warden, reach the soul of the inmate in such isolation!

The penitentiary model of imprisonment is described here so thoroughly because it had, in both its systems (the Pennsylvania and Auburn), a strong impact on penal thought and practice, in America and beyond. Both models, though in different ways, expressed a belief in the *reformability of criminal offenders*. The idea of the offender as *a person to be reformed* is the important heritage of the penitentiary even though its importance in actual history soon waned: by the second half of the nineteenth century, it was widely abandoned, and only the mere prison was left. Reasons for the decline of the penitentiary were manifold. It couldn't cope with the overcrowding, brutality, and disorder that characterized prisons after the American Civil War;[17] separation was no longer possible and prisoner unrest increased; and, responding to social change and a growing number of immigrants, politicians criticized what they called pampering of prisoners and called for more punitive penal discipline. However, one internal factor must be considered as well. An inherent flaw of the penitentiary system was that, when offenders were restricted to their cells, conversion did not happen voluntarily, and it turned into coercion. Punishment, in the penitentiary system, *preceded* the expected repentance instead of *flowing out* of it as a voluntary act of penance. This flaw has, ever since, been a challenge for all penal models that emphasize rehabilitation.

Eventually, when success in rehabilitation failed to appear, when prisoners instead of repenting became ever more hardened and desperate, when penal bureaucrats who lacked religious or ethical concern for the rehabilitation of the inmates replaced the early reformers, and when the belief in the reformability of criminal offenders waned, only the physical shell of the penitentiary remained: solitude in the isolation of individual cells and hard labor. Many present-day prisons remain as silent witnesses of this early belief in transformation through coerced repentance.

PRISONER REHABILITATION IN THE TWENTIETH CENTURY

Although the ideal of the prison penitentiary failed, the *idea* of reformation or rehabilitation survived. Ever since the nineteenth century, prison

17. From 1850 to 1890, the US prison population grew twelvefold, see Haney, *Reforming Punishment*, 32.

punishment, while maintaining a deterrent and a punitive element, was also designed to *reform or reeducate* the criminal offender. This principle has been widely adopted and has entered judicial and penal contexts beyond the Western and Anglo-American context, even though sometimes in tragically perverted forms such as reeducation through labor, applied by totalitarian governments both in East and West. In practice, the fragile idea of rehabilitation was always threatened by popularly more appealing penal ideologies that emphasize deterrence and retribution, and was always undermined by the reality of overcrowded prisons. Still, at least in etiquette and official rhetoric, it was hardly abandoned.

In a growingly secular environment, penitentiaries turned into reformatories and later into correctional institutions, relying on a mix of punishment and treatment programs. What different times regarded as the most scientific methods replaced the original religious motives of rehabilitative ideals. Instead of in religious and moral terms, criminality was described as the consequence of specific physical and psychological dispositions. The *treatment model* was developed with the leadership of various professional groups in the social and medical sciences: educators, medical doctors and psychiatrists, clinical psychologists, and social workers. They were supported by the belief that the medical profession, social sciences, and education could resolve many of the problems of crime. The treatment model does not see the prisoner as morally evil or inferior but as psychologically deficient or ill. It is not punishment he needs, but healing. Medicine, psychiatry, and clinical psychology were used to explain why certain people acted in criminal ways and as prognostic tools to determine who was cured and who still needed further treatment. The treatment model fostered a more individualized approach to offenders. It became common in Anglo-American and European prisons to classify and segregate inmates in different categories according to security needs, reformability, criminal disposition, number of convictions (first-time offender or recidivist), and age (juvenile or adult). Following the logic of the treatment model, the judiciary started to set *indeterminate sentences*, thus making the release of an inmate dependent on the assessment of his or her psychological and behavioral changes. The prison authorities gained tremendous additional power, as a positive assessment depended heavily on reports issued by the authorities themselves. One famous example combining an indeterminate sentence with reforming efforts was the Borstal system of juvenile reformatories, implemented in England during the first half of the twentieth century. The Borstal system worked from the assumption that the inmate first of all needs to be reformed. This system influenced treatment of juvenile offenders around the world. The prison reforms during this era, known in the United States as the Progressive Era, had deep impacts on prison life. As the perception of the offender changed, prison life became less depersonalized and allowed more space for the individual. The radical separation of inmates from fellow inmates and from the inmates' families was abolished; instead, interaction between prisoners was allowed. New prison structures encouraged communal life and even introduced recreational activities.

Not surprising is that the treatment model faced similar *problems* to those of the earlier model of religious conversion. In the Anglo-American context, in marked contrast to continental Europe, the emphasis on treatment could not supersede the security, prevention, and deterrence rhetoric of imprisonment. Tensions between (a) professionals in charge of rehabilitation and (b) guards in charge of maintaining order undermined efforts to carry out individualized treatment. Equally, increases in prison population undermined such treatment. While in the early twentieth century many countries of continental Europe introduced a wide variety of noncustodial punishments in addition to imprisonment[18] and subsequently succeeded in reducing the prison population (and thus were able to focus their rehabilitative efforts on a relatively small number of prisoners), there was little such development in England and the United States. Finally, as during the period of penitentiaries, coercion as the basis of therapeutic or behavioral treatment was destined to fail. Creating a therapeutic environment in what is ultimately and overwhelmingly a punitive institution is futile. Inmates do *not* prefer being seen as psychologically deficient instead of being labeled morally unworthy. What modern correctional institutions achieve is the production of inmates who know how to play the system and how to show effective adjustment. Social sciences substitute the previously dominant religious ideology. Treatment appears successful where inmates accept the rules and the dominating values of society at large. This is the point where the treatment model of prisons reveals its hidden premises, being exactly what Foucault calls a disciplinary apparatus that corrects and constrains individuals, forces them to abide by the rule of societal norms, and produces productive, hard-working, and loyal conformists: people who are normal according to society's dominant values.

---

18. For more information about these developments, see O'Brien, "The Prison on the Continent," 187ff.

Beyond the Walls of Separation

By the end of the twentieth century, one can observe a *renewed appreciation of religious programs* in the rehabilitation of prisoners. This revival of religious participation in rehabilitation was partly the result of a growing disillusionment with earlier penal approaches. The repeated failure of all kinds of prisoner-reform programs has led many people to think that nothing works in offender rehabilitation. It may indeed appear so, but as a matter of fact, it is very difficult to measure the reformative effects of any prison program. Social scientists have become skeptical about monistic explanations of the roots of crime and monistic ways of responding to it. Further contributing to this renewed appreciation of religious involvement in the care for prisoners are cultural shifts in our societies. Many people are disillusioned with the ideological battles of modernity and accept that neither so-called rational or scientific principles alone (as in a typical modern society) nor religious principles alone (as in a premodern society) can govern social life. Instead they are looking for a more pluralistic, integrated, holistic view, which sees religious programs *in combination* with educational, psychological, and social formation. There is an increased readiness for coexistence and cooperation of different actors who contribute to prisoners' rehabilitation. Religious counselors have for some time realized that the insights of psychology and other human sciences do not threaten but rather broaden and quite often sharpen their understanding of the human soul and human behavior. Many secular counselors now also realize that despite all secularization, the spiritual dimension is an essential element of a person's healing. The awareness of multiculturalism, particularly visible in prison environments, has further helped secular counselors to appreciate the role of religion.[19]

Today we face a dilemma: On one hand we call for caution about too much rehabilitative optimism. We are skeptical about a belief—ultimately based on the optimism of the Enlightenment—according to which deviant people could be dealt with through punishment techniques and be perfected. Even penal systems that give priority to rehabilitative ideas and seriously implement them realize that their success is limited. On the other side we argue that the old ideas of treatment, of rehabilitation, or of a more individualized response to the problem of crime have in many places not been implemented seriously enough. What frustrates the success of rehabilitation in these penal systems is the unwholesome mix of rehabilitation and punishment. It is a halfhearted implementation of rehabilitative

---

19. Sundt et al., "The Role of the Prison Chaplain," 60.

Prisons and Offender Rehabilitation—Then and Now

ideas that is too narrowly concerned with results and not with the process that leads to them, and it is the constant subordination of rehabilitation to custodial and security concerns. What undermines rehabilitation, in addition, is the lack of *simultaneously introduced penal reforms* that reduce the widespread problem of overcrowding. The history of rehabilitative efforts has amply shown how constant overcrowding thwarts good efforts and subverts more individualized treatment.

Rehabilitation builds the context for religious programs, and Christians naturally support a wider and more serious implementation of rehabilitation. However, Christian care for those in prison, although rightfully claiming a positive impact on the rehabilitation of offenders (as our next chapter will show), needs to affirm an identity *beyond and independent of rehabilitation*. Christian participation in rehabilitation will always stress that it happens not for the sake of results but as a response to God's call.

EXCURSUS: A SHORT PENAL HISTORY OF HONG KONG[20]

From 1841, when first occupied by the British army, until 1997, Hong Kong was a British colony. Its judiciary and prison system essentially *followed the British legal system and British penal policies* with local characteristics in the actual implementation. Historically, the prison was run in a highly disciplined and military style. Many British penal reforms were slow to reach Hong Kong, if they did so at all. Since World War II, changes in penal policies have been introduced more swiftly. More recently, the Correctional Services Department (CSD), as the department in charge of prisons has been called since 1982, has developed more independently and has set up dialogue with partners worldwide, particularly with penal experts from Canada, Australia, and Singapore, since 1997 increasingly also with experts from mainland China. However, British common law and the British penal system still provide the general framework for justice and penal administration.

Soon after British occupation of Hong Kong, the first prison, Victoria Prison, was provisionally set up to accommodate unruly sailors, local bandits, and pirates. It was finally completed in 1867. In the nineteenth century imprisonment was purely designed to *deter crime*. Reflecting the deterrence-based penal policies of

---

20. The following account is, for the period before 1990, based on Sinclair, *Society's Guardians*, a historical account that was officially commissioned by the Hong Kong Correctional Services Department.

45

late nineteenth-century England, feeling surrounded by a hostile environment, and failing to understand the Chinese culture and language, the colonial government was unable to devise ways of education or rehabilitation. Prisoners were assigned to hard and maddening labor: breaking stones, carrying stones back and forth, plodding on the treadmill, or toiling at specially designed punishment machines, such as one that required turning a wheel thousands of times each day. Some inmates were also deployed to serve in much-needed public work.

To further deter the growing number of offenders, the government reintroduced public flogging and branding to stigmatize criminals, practices that had long been abolished in England. Only in 1885 were they finally also abolished in Hong Kong. The government cited the special context of Hong Kong to legitimate its practice of harsh treatment and radical deterrence. Facing grim poverty in China and a culture of much stricter punishment and more severe prisons, only the harshest treatment would provide sufficient deterrence for the influx of offenders from across the border.

In rapidly growing Hong Kong, Victoria Prison was soon desperately *overcrowded*, and despite all attempts to further increase deterrence through even tougher prison conditions, the problems remained unresolved. The enlargement of Victoria Prison, finished by 1898, and a new prison in Lai Chi Kok, constructed in 1924, brought only temporary relief. Stanley Prison, designed to hold 1,500 prisoners, opened in 1937 to great acclaim. Many saw it as a masterpiece of penal architecture, an example of the enlightened treatment of offenders, and proudly called it the finest prison of the British Empire. Ironically, soon after its opening, it was used by the Japanese occupation army to detain local and British prisoners of war.

After the Second World War, Hong Kong experienced an unprecedented population surge as refugees from China sought shelter there. This growth was paralleled by a steady growth in the prison population that overwhelmed the capacity of prison management: lack of room, faltering prison industries, untrained staff—these were just some of the problems the prison service faced. The 1950s and '60s were a time of rapid development. In one year alone, 1960, construction was underway on no less than seven prisons. This was also the time of the first and very tentative steps towards rehabilitation. Prisoners were segregated and classified into different categories, and the government established juvenile training centers in the tradition of the Borstal system, a concept for treating young offenders that developed in Britain in the early twentieth century. The original idea of training prisoners through personal relationships, trust, and responsibility, was adapted locally to include discipline, good manners, order, and hard work.

A serious riot at Stanley Prison in spring 1973 led to important changes in Hong Kong's prison system. The causes of the riot were not only serious overcrowding and a lack of well-trained staff, but also the widespread availability of drugs that were trafficked through a network of Triads and staff, and the recent measures to curb the drug trade. The '70s and '80s were a time of *uprooting the deep-rooted corruption and Triad power* that had controlled much of Hong Kong's prison system. It was also a time when new penal policies were established—with cautious steps toward the rehabilitation of drug addicts; the introduction of vocational training for some inmates; and improvements to prison infrastructure, sanitary installations, and health services. At the same time the prison services faced an unprecedented challenge when put in charge of accommodating and supervising tens of thousands of Vietnamese refugees in closed camps. The number of refugees surpassed thirty thousand at one point. Another important penal event during this period was the abolition of the death penalty.

Since the late 1990s there has been a stronger *emphasis on rehabilitation*, but the *priority is still on deterrence, retribution, security, and strict rules*. Rehabilitation resources have been mostly allocated to juvenile detention centers. The increased rhetoric of rehabilitation has not yet been matched by genuine penal or (even more important) judicial reforms that would thoroughly introduce noncustodial forms of punishment, as are widely and successfully applied in continental Europe, Canada, and elsewhere. Many well-tested prison reforms that allow a higher degree of prisoner autonomy within the confinement of prison and that help inmates maintain family links are still only under consideration. The prison management is still reluctant to share responsibility with other social agencies in order to allow for more individualized treatment of offenders.

There are several reasons for such reluctance to initiate thorough reforms. A first reason is the history of lawlessness and Triad domination. The prison management has successfully eradicated drugs, previously easily available, and is now anxious to maintain the strict orderliness it has achieved. Also, there is a deep-rooted spirit of deterrence that goes back to the early years of Hong Kong's prisons, then supported by a military-led prison service and now matched by an equally discipline-minded local prison service. Another important reason is a civil-service culture that is overly conservative when considering change. An equally conservative and, overall, still mostly punitive attitude toward offenders (and a paternalist authoritarianism rooted in Confucianism) has also prevented courageous reforms. Finally, and surely quite important, the wider geographic context of relative poverty and stricter punishment, both in China and in other Southeast Asian nations, has continued to serve as an argument for retribution, discipline, and deterrence rather than rehabilitation.

The return of Hong Kong to the People's Republic of China did not affect the penal policies. While overcrowding was an issue some years ago and was responded to by enlarging existing prisons and thus extending capacities of imprisonment, the penal population has, in the past years, remained stable or has even been declining. Presently, an important concern of penal management in Hong Kong is the improvement of aging facilities. Rehabilitative services have not significantly developed. Equally, judicial reforms that reduce the overall number of prisoners (and the number of those serving in high-security institutions more particularly) have not really happened.

Bibliographical Notes

The most *comprehensive information for the history of the prison system in general* can be found in Norval Morris and David J. Rothman, editors, *The Oxford History of the Prison: The Practice of Punishment in Western Society* (New York: Oxford University Press, 1995). Although focusing on the history of justice and punishment in the West and with little reference to Christian contributions to the judicial and penal developments, it includes important sections about prisons from ancient and medieval times to the present. Each of the different chapters points to plenty of additional literature on the history of prison. A recent and wide-ranging penal history of America is Thomas G. Blomberg and Karol Lucken, *American Penology: A History of Control*. 2nd ed. (New Brunswick, NJ: Aldine Transaction, 2010). It covers the whole history from the ancient and European roots of punishment in America to the most recent developments after 2000, when the number of people in prison or under any form of supervision is still increasing, although at a lower rate compared to the 1980s and '90s. Older, but reflecting the ambiguity of prison reforms that have repeatedly failed to achieve their aims is the book by Blake McKelvey, *American Prisons: A History of Good Intentions* (Montclair, NJ: Smith, 1977).

On *punishment in China and elsewhere* see Klaus Mühlhahn, *Criminal Justice in China: A History* (Cambridge: Harvard University Press, 2009). The book offers a comprehensive examination of the criminal justice system in modern China, from late imperial China to the Deng reform era. The study by Terance D. Miethe and Hong Lu, *Punishment: A Comparative Historical Perspective* (Cambridge: Cambridge University Press, 2005) compares different punishment philosophies, in particular those in American history, in Chinese history, and under Islamic law. On punishment in Republican China see some of the research by Frank Dikötter: *Crime, Punishment and the Prison in Modern China* (Hong Kong: Hong Kong University Press, 2002); "The Promise of Repentance. Prison Reform in Modern China" (*The British Journal of Criminology* 42 [2002] 240–49); and "Crime and Punishment in Early Republican China: Beijing's First Model Prison, 1912–1922" (*Late Imperial China* 21/2 [2000] 140–62). On the Chinese penal system of "reform through work," better known as *laogai*, see the research by James D. Seymour and Richard Anderson, *New Ghosts, Old Ghosts: Prisons and Labor Reform Camps in China* (Armonk, NY: Sharpe, 1998). The book rests on the study of three northwestern provinces (Xinjiang, Gansu, and Qinghai), but it gives important insights into the whole of the *laogai* system.

On the history of *prisons in Hong Kong* see Kevin Sinclair's *Society's Guardians: A History of Correctional Services in Hong Kong 1841–1999*, online: http://www.csd.gov.hk/misc/csd_history/main.pdf/. Commissioned by the Correctional Services Department and essentially a departmental self-portrait, particularly regarding the most recent years, it still offers important information and interesting details.

On *Christian contributions to the evolution of penology and criminal law*, see Gerald Austin McHugh, *Christian Faith and Criminal Justice. Toward a Christian Response to Crime and Punishment* (New York: Paulist, 1978). McHugh reaffirms Christians' responsibility to confront contemporary penal practices. Since the 1980s there has been increased research on the link between religion and law. A good overall image can be gained by a collection of essays on Christian perspectives on legal thought, edited by Michael McConnell et al., eds., *Christian Perspectives on Legal Thought* (New Haven: Yale University Press, 2001). Lee Griffith's *The Fall of the Prison: Biblical Perspectives on Prison Abolition*

Beyond the Walls of Separation

(Grand Rapids: Eerdmans, 1993) provides many insights about churches' participation in prison and justice. His history offers interesting information about the dissident and prophetic tradition of the church. His overall aims are, as the title suggests, to remind the church of Jesus's prophecy that the captives shall be set free, and to advocate the abolition of prison.

A study in the *shifts of penal philosophy* is Michel Foucault's *Discipline and Punish: The Birth of the Prison* (New York: Vintage, 1979). It has become a classic in the history of justice and punishment and still offers highly rewarding reading about the shift from punishment focused on the offender's body to a prison-based punishment system. His thesis has inspired a good amount of academic literature with summaries and critical analyses. A good summary and discussion of Foucault's thesis can be found in David Garland, *Punishment and Modern Society: A Study in Social Theory* (Studies in Crime and Justice, Chicago: University of Chicago Press, 1990), 131–75. Daniel W. Van Ness's *Crime and Its Victims* (Downers Grove, IL: InterVarsity, 1986), dealing mainly with the concept of restorative justice, has a relevant chapter about important shifts happening in the late medieval times, when crimes started to be understood as offenses against the king.

3

Religion and Spirituality in the Context of Imprisonment

A COMMON ASSUMPTION OF people in our society is that a prison must be a very difficult spiritual environment. People suppose that bad people are unlikely to be interested in something good. Obviously this assumption is wrong. Prisons all over the world are full of spirituality and of religious activities. They are spiritual powerhouses in the sense that spiritual questions are most vibrant and vigorous, as we will more clearly see in the next chapter. Obviously the circumstances of life behind bars shape inmates' religious expressions and give them a special flavor.

Prison employees often tell visitors that they shouldn't be naïve, and that the inmates are not as good as they present themselves. This is obviously true—in the same way it is true for every church where the ordinary churchgoer participates in singing, praying, or the Eucharist with devout fervor and then, upon leaving the church, may go back to a less than saintly life. Prison officers see inmates at their worst, whereas chaplains and prison visitors see them at their best. Neither view contains the full truth.

This chapter continues to describe prison life but focuses on how it affects and is affected by religion. The chapter introduces this rich spiritual life with an *analytical and outside perspective*. The questions addressed in this chapter follow:

- Why do inmates attend religious services more often than those outside prison—both more often than the average population and more often than they would outside prison?
- What is the role of religion in a total institution?
- What is the significance of conversions? Are they credible, and do genuine transformations happen, or are they just ways of conning prison visitors and officials?
- What are the elements of folk religion, popular religious beliefs, and practices in prison?
- How do the prison context and the criminal subculture affect specific expressions of faith?
- What impact does religious faith have on recidivism?

RELIGION AND DEPRIVATION: WHY DO INMATES PARTICIPATE IN RELIGIOUS ACTIVITIES?

There are various reasons why inmates participate in religious activities. Certainly religious activities mitigate the psychological and physical deprivations of being incarcerated. Many inmates, if not most, start to attend religious services for *reasons not directly related to faith*. These may be called *nonreligious reasons*.

> Social scientists distinguish between (a) *intrinsic* reasons (i.e., reasons of a spiritual nature, referring to inner motives as defined by religious beliefs, and (b) *extrinsic* reasons, where religious activity is chosen for its utilitarian benefits.[1] Others take up the inmates' own categories and distinguish, more judgmentally, between *sincere* and *insincere reasons*.[2]

Prisons are terribly boring, so worship is a welcome *break in the monotony* of a prison day. Worship services offer a rare chance to *meet people from outside* face-to-face, without a separating screen, in contrast to all personal visits in high-security institutions that commonly only allow an encounter through glass screen. In some prisons, worship is the only opportunity to *meet inmate friends from other units*. Services are a chance

---

1. See Clear, "Value of Religion," 56ff.
2. See cf. Dammer, "Reasons for Religious Involvement," 38.

to exchange information, settle debts, or transmit contraband. Religious gatherings are places to *enjoy social life*. The faith-based fellowship offers a chance to *set up friendships* beyond the typical and often problematic prison friendships. For inmates such as sexual offenders, who suffer pressure and bullying in normal association, the gatherings with people from outside provide an important space where they *feel safe* and don't experience exclusion.[3] An important initial reason for some male inmates is to *meet female visitors*. Some inmates even ask the chaplain directly how many female visitors will join, and they may make their participation dependent on female visitors. Meeting female visitors allows the inmate to reclaim at least part of an important aspect of outside life. Other important reasons for participation in religious activities are to *line up friends* who can be of help during imprisonment and to *find access to certain goods or services* that are crucial in the life of prisoners: religious visitors usually love to support inmates with spiritual material to help them grow in their faith. But many visitors will be willing to go beyond spiritual support and help inmates with their studies. In the case of inmates who are on life sentences, the enlarged network of prison visitors offers a chance to find *support for the parole board* or for the committee that decides about commuting life sentences into determinate sentences. Inmates commonly ask the chaplain, and sometimes also visitors, to write a letter in support of their application for a determinate sentence or an early release. Personally I doubt that the relevant boards care much about religion.[4] Nevertheless, even when expectation of their impact is low, written support letters provide an important service that gives psychological strength to the inmate. Finally, well-established contacts with visitors can be helpful when former convicts are looking for a *job* or are adjusting *after release*.

Some inmates describe their own or others' participation more in psychological terms, often simply as a *psychological crutch*. Indeed, inmates receive quite basic emotional and psychological strength from the fellowship and the religious activities, which help them to deal with a negative self-image widespread among inmates. Religious activities allow inmates to experience and receive trust and to experience relationships that can be relied upon. Visitors provide psychological support for the inmates to persevere

---

3. This is more important in other contexts where violence in prison is more virulent, as several studies show: see Dammer, "Reasons for Religious Involvement," 43; Clear, "Value of Religion," 64ff.

4. Both Dammer and the inmates he interviewed in the US (ibid., 55), and Clear and his interviewees (ibid., 63) share this impression.

when experiencing frustrations in daily life, or when going through moments of crisis. To join worship may, quite simply, make inmates feel better about themselves: at least they are doing something useful, and something that is usually regarded as positive by the prison administration or by their families. In fact, quite a number of inmates started to join worship after being encouraged by a relative. Participating in religious activities is also a public way of claiming to be a different person from the one who was sentenced to prison.[5]

A reason that stands between the nonreligious and the more spiritual reasons is the *music*. Singing is a powerful way of tapping into life's emotional dimensions; it is a channel for expressing joy or venting anger; it often has a direct, positive, immediately tangible impact on one's mood; and it doesn't distinguish between believer and nonbeliever. Music is a low-threshold entry point for people who are skeptical about or not ready for a clear religious commitment. It is a tremendously important form of receiving healing in prison: the joint singing is not only a deep experience of fellowship but also a touching moment of reconnecting with dimensions of life beyond the visible. The music in prison stands in radical contrast to the surrounding atmosphere. Some of my most precious experiences in prison have much to do with music: the sonority of powerful male voices audible throughout the prison; the soft, meditative worship and a tranquility hard to imagine in a place like prison; the concentrated participation of inmates momentarily forgetting where they are. Music provides a good first opportunity for inmates to take up leadership or to participate with guitars or other instruments and thus to have a chance to learn something meaningful.

If inmates join worship for an extended time, their reasons and motivation usually change. The original nonreligious reasons remain important, but they are supplemented by *more genuine, spiritual reasons*. On the one hand, there is pressure from other inmates to move beyond mere nonreligious reasons. Some inmates are openly critical of those who only join worship for what they regard as selfish benefits. These call the others pretenders and remind them that joining religious activities has deeper implications and should, on the long term, be reflected in one's behavior. On the other hand, and through continuing interaction with the chaplain or with visitors, inmates discover spiritual dimensions of life that can become important.

---

5. Similarly Clear, "Value of Religion," 72.

Spiritual reasons for joining religious activities can vary. Some inmates had been in touch with religion previous to their imprisonment, and the time in prison offers them the chance to *recover a neglected dimension* of their previous lives. Many inmates feel that they came to a dead end in their previous life and are now looking for *new direction*. They sincerely *hope to change their lifestyle*, and as long as they are in prison, where they are not exposed to many of the temptations of the outside world, they often succeed. The visitors from outside are much-needed role models in this process of change. Many inmates indeed discover *a different form of fellowship* that they did not know about, and that they find meaningful—at least in the context of deprivation. They discover that community and celebration are possible even with very few material goods. Participation in religious activities can further *teach basic spiritual techniques* that are helpful for coping with the loneliness of imprisonment. Such techniques help inmates maintain a peaceful and positive mindset and accept circumstances that, for the time being, cannot be changed. Faith then provides a type of freedom even within the walls of the prison. In the words of an inmate,

> It is not the prison that incarcerates us, it is a man's mind. I am able to live a normal life and uphold my character with dignity. The first objective of prisons is to strip you of your dignity. It takes your self-esteem, your dignity, and everything about you. Religion has helped me to regain this.[6]

Spirituality offers some inmates a *framework for understanding*. Quite a number of inmates understand their imprisonment in spiritual terms, as *God's way of punishing—or even saving—them*. They remember their previous existence as dangerous (Triads) or as unhealthy (drugs) and always close to death. Participation in religious activities is a response to the new understanding of their identity and an expression of gratitude for the new chance given.

I agree with other chaplains[7] that the distinction between genuine reasons and nonreligious reasons is useful only for an outside perspective; it is not helpful when one is actually interacting and working with inmates. Although inmates themselves apply it and sometimes talk critically about nonreligious participants in worship, I avoid such reasoning as judgmental. I don't mind *why* people join. If they join, they hear the gospel, they

---

6. Quoted in Clear, "Value of Religion," 62.
7. Shaw, *Chaplains to the Imprisoned*, 48; Rideau and Sinclair, "Religion in Prison," 49.

receive words of comfort and encouragement, they experience the warmth of Christian fellowship, and they may or may not be affected by what they receive. Nonreligious reasons are valid and good reasons to join; they are perfectly genuine and sincere—even though they miss the point of deeper spirituality. The different reasons are simply different stages in a process of spiritual growth.

CONVERSION AND CHANGE: HOW GENUINE ARE CONVERSIONS IN PRISON?

The same ambiguity discussed above also applies to conversions. Some people who work in prison for a long period become cynical about the genuineness of conversions. A good number of inmates respond to altar calls at evangelistic rallies more with the desire to satisfy the preachers' need for some sort of success than with a sudden spiritual breakthrough. And many devout and born-again inmates regularly turn up in disciplinary confinement.

> Daniel had grown up as a Christian and went through a renewal of his conversion after his admission to prison. He had impressed me with his genuine faith and his strong rhetorical skills. I consequently didn't hesitate much when one day he asked me if he could give a message in the worship. His message was theologically sound and inspired the group of visitors to have a good discussion about the content of the sermon after the service—something that does not always happen. So I was quite glad to have him preach again when he asked for a second time. My surprise was great when, upon arriving at prison on the morning when he was supposed to preach, I learned that Daniel was in the isolation ward because he had beaten up another inmate the day before. When I went to see him, he insisted that he was actually the victim, not the offender. Indeed, the prison administration often doesn't distinguish much between victim and offender in a fight. I still don't know if Daniel was more the victim or more the offender. However, the incident reminded me how our assessment of a person's faith often stands on shaky ground. Was he conning me? Was he just putting on a show?

There is surely more than a kernel of truth in the statement of a prison chaplain who said 150 years ago: "I find that the men generally are more anxious concerning their release from confinement than their delivery

Religion and Spirituality in the Context of Imprisonment

from the bondage of sin."[8] Without a doubt, some conversions are faked—to please Christian visitors (who often push for conversion), to gain higher attention from visitors or the chaplain, or to put up some playful act and see what happens. I believe, however, that most conversions are not *deliberate* fakes. Rather, they show another side of an inmate's personality, possibly a side they would like to extend and develop further. Some conversions do not result from a genuine spiritual process but are rather a spontaneous and emotional response to a good evangelistic sermon, to touching music, or to nice fellowship. Admittedly, conversions that truly result from a spiritual process and a genuine experience of deliverance and redemption often fade after the initial spiritual excitement. Some inmates have such distorted personalities or such deep wounds from their past that they fail to sustain and build on their conversions.[9]

Still, some conversions are more lasting and are part of more thorough transformation processes. The point of conversion, a clearly identifiable point in a person's biography where a person accepts Jesus Christ into his or her life, is actually just one element in a continuous process of transformation, preceded by a time of searching, and setting in motion a cycle of positive developments. It becomes an important landmark to be remembered when facing spiritual weakness or disintegration. The conversion is a celebration of a turning point that one experiences or of a new step that one has taken in life. Converted inmates, similar to converted drug addicts, can become important peer counselors (see more in chapter 5). They have a deeper understanding of inmates' and drug addicts' spiritual needs and pain, and they have immediate access to their world, which makes this kind of peer counseling highly effective. The road to such thorough transformation is a difficult one, though. Many genuinely converted Christians have relapses, as the brokenness from their past continues to affect their spiritual renewal.

POPULAR RELIGION AND INMATE PERSONALITIES: RADICAL FAITH IN PRISON

Three main factors shape prison spirituality and religiosity and give it a unique character. Religious faith in prison reflects (a) the popular faith of

---

8. Quoted from Shaw, *Chaplains to the Imprisoned*, 25.
9. Pace, *Christian's Guide*, 239–41, offers some useful reflection on the topic of converts who revert to crime.

the cultural context and the religious environment, (b) the reality of prison, and (c) the personality of many inmates.

The first factor shaping religious faith in prisons in the context discussed here is *Chinese popular religion* that has its roots in animism and ancestor worship.[10] In simple terms, Chinese popular faith expects people to venerate their ancestors: to express their gratitude to them and to bring offerings that provide a good life in the realm of death. The fate that people await after death and the judgment that they receive depend first on their behavior and deeds during their lifetime (i.e., the merits that they have accumulated), and second on offerings from their offspring.[11] If someone has died in tragic circumstances, possibly as result of a killing or an accident without subsequent redemption of the negative energies, he or she may return to the world and haunt the living offspring. In this worldview, spirits are all around us, and humans need to pacify them through religious rituals like prayers or offerings. It is common to hear inmates use the vocabulary of magic to interpret their crimes or their relapses. Equally, stories of encounters with spirits and demons during the night are widespread. Inmates, accordingly, find it easy to understand the biblical message because it depicts individuals in a continuous struggle within a world populated by demons and evil spirits.

Chinese popular faith is practical and believes that the spiritual realm can be influenced through our religious acts and moral lifestyle: we will receive as we have done, if not in this life, then in the life after death. Prayers are straightforward. People pray for wealth, for health, for success in examinations, or in the context of prison, for early release. Prayers, similar to other religious acts, are believed to directly influence people's fates and the spiritual realm. Such a belief can lead to a manipulative understanding of God—especially for someone accustomed to manipulative human relationships. Many inmates have grown up learning that feelings and relationships are for sale; they have behind them a history of manipulation and emotional abuse. They have learned to assess relationships in terms of *material benefits* and to emphasize the importance of money in human relationships. They easily extend this manipulative understanding of relationships to God: "If you bless me materially, I will believe in you."

10. Some of the following paragraphs are taken from Brandner, "Charismatic Faith and Prison Ministry," 26–30, where the link between Chinese popular religion and charismatic faith in prison is further discussed.

11. Liu, "Nameless but Active Religion," 388–89; Tam, "Local Religion in Contemporary China," 66.

Religion and Spirituality in the Context of Imprisonment

A deal with God can, however, be a starting point for serious spiritual growth. I remember Ah-Keung, who had been a regular gambler. At one point, he promised God that if, this last time, God would bless him with winning the game, he would give up gambling and turn to Christ. It happened—and Ah-Keung has become an honest and committed Christian.

The second factor is the reality of prisons. Where many inmates face day after day with little hope, where isolation from life outside prison keeps them in an emotional and spiritual limbo, *superstition and credulity* grow. Many prisoners cling to anything that can positively influence their present misery. Any *simplistic form of faith* that promises instant change and redemption seems particularly appealing. Inmates thus respond particularly positively to a religious faith that is based on a magic understanding of the effect of faith. They believe something like a magic potion is necessary to break through the vicious circle in which they find themselves caught. Only a radical break with the previous life, a change and complete discontinuity with all that has shaped the preceding life, is adequate to respond to the present misery. The isolation of prison life further shields inmates from a critical reality check. In such an environment, spiritual processes can gain momentum and turn into dominant forces of a person's identity.

A third factor that shapes religion and spirituality in prison is a specific kind of personality commonly found in prison. Many inmates have a strong body but a *weak personality*: they have a weak sense of personal identity and worth, they have little self-esteem, and they have no clear concept of who they are. They have a rather low ability to tolerate frustration, to control impulses, or to organize their life. Many inmates are unwilling to take up adult responsibilities or to handle everyday relationships in a mature way. They have a strong tendency to form dependent relationships, and many deep wounds from their childhood or adolescence have brought chaos to their emotional lives. Such persons are easily attracted by strict theological views, by a faith within narrow margins, and by the promise of instant success.

These three factors shape religious faith in prison, independent of religious adherence. However, *Christian* groups are most active and particularly successful in their adjustment to prisons. They benefit from a special *convergence between interests of Christians from the outside and the needs of inmates on the inside*. Radical Christian faith groups are attracted to prisons for outreach programs, because prisons symbolize deep darkness and the realm of the antichrist that needs to be won over to Christ. This battle, to them, has an important strategic impact in the extension of God's kingdom. Inmates respond positively to such black-and-white spirituality: it strengthens and encourages them to play such a crucial role in God's plan of salvation.

Radical religious groups have, all over the world, been successful in prisons. They offer a radical break with the past and a new beginning that puts the failed old self completely to rest. Many inmates crave (as other people do) for certainties in their life, which they eventually find in the narrowly understood teaching of religion. Additionally, the strict religious framework offers a way to better understand one's crime, namely, as a result of a failed spiritual life and rejection of God, or, in the words of an inmate, "I was bound by desires for drugs, for sex, and for money. Now I am free. I have laid down my bondage at the foot of the cross." Some may go a step further and blame the devil for their crime: "It was not me, but somebody else was at work within me. Now, Christ is at work within me and he has helped me to drive out Satan."

> I remember a group of inmates convicted of sex offenses who, during our prayer fellowship, regularly shared how the demons (*mo gui* or *xin mo*) were still at work in their bodies. They expressed how much they felt obsessed by sexual fantasies and how they had failed to put them to rest. This way of explaining their obsessions within a religious framework is psychologically questionable, because it separates desire from self and puts the blame on an outside power, Satan. However, it does reflect their genuine and obviously true feeling of lacking control and of being subject to something beyond their own power.

Blaming an external agent, any spiritual and demonic power, for a particularly detestable crime helps mitigate the terrible burden of guilt at a point where a person is not yet ready to fully face responsibility for a crime. It also gives support where a person is at his or her weakest, surrounding the person's failure with a stable framework. Inmates who have turned to faith then look back on their previous moral failures with a sense of moral achievement and even superiority. A radical spiritual life offers a meaningful way of coping with the daily emptiness of prison life. This radical spirituality offers a strong surface identity and an idealized self-image that is reinforced by applause from religious volunteers, who are impressed by the spiritual fervor of many inmates. The daily experience of powerlessness stops causing constant pain, as true power is found elsewhere. The daily frustrations and unpleasant events are merely the small challenges of a benign God who thus raises the faithful inmate's ability for self-control.

CHURCH BEHIND BARS: INMATES' INDEPENDENT FAITH LIFE

The spirituality described above also shapes the church behind bars, which is not the same as faith-based prisons.[12] The latter are prisons run by Christian organizations that try to bring about change among the inmates through religious programs (see more in chapter 5). The church behind bars, in contrast, is more independent from the outside church. Prison ministry specifically encourages inmates to conduct *their own* religious activities in addition to the occasional programs by outside visitors. A church led by inmates is a truly local and indigenous church, and only such a church can grow to become a solid spiritual home for inmates. A church that depends on occasional visits from outside volunteers—or even on the more regular visits of the prison chaplain—does not provide the inmates with a feeling of ownership. Thus, aiming at a church behind bars is a simple missiological necessity. And in many prisons around the world vibrant independent prison faith groups have emerged; two of the most famous are the work of the Nation of Islam in US prisons and the Christian revival at the Los Olmos High Security Prison in Argentina.

One of the preconditions for a strong church behind bars is freedom from internal restriction. Only then can inmates gather freely and enjoy a self-determined religious life. In a context like Hong Kong, where there is a very high level of internal segregation and restriction, only small prayer groups, restricted to the rather small number of interested inmates from one workshop, may gather for joint prayer, Bible reading, and occasional singing. They depend on at least one charismatic leader who draws the small group together and encourages them.

A good number of such groups go on steadily and keep attracting new inmates. If they survive the transfer of the founding leader, they have obviously reached an important stage of maturity. Groups are usually more stable among prisoners with long sentences who do not face frequent transfers, but they may also become monotonous without fresh input from

---

12. Some of the following is from Brandner, "Charismatic Faith and Prison Ministry," 24–26.

new members. Some of these groups consist of only two or three inmates regularly reading the Bible during lunch break and discussing it. Others have full worship services with music, prayer, joint Bible study, and possibly a message from one of the leaders. Despite the narrow theological perspective of many of these groups, they show openness towards other inmates and the staff, and they can have a positive impact on the whole atmosphere of a unit. Many prison officers have revised their negative image of prisoners after witnessing the steadiness and reliability of such faith groups over an extended period. Prison management does not mind these groups meeting, as long as their overall authority is not jeopardized. These groups are particularly powerful tools of evangelism: many inmates start to believe because the spirit, the gentleness and the genuine interaction of such a group has touched them.

One of the biggest *dangers of the church behind bars* is that it absorbs and reflects the dominant Triad culture. Such is the case when evangelism turns into Triad-driven recruitment and when this recruitment happens along the lines of Triad kinship, or when the main recruitment agents are "big brothers" who push their "little brothers" into the church fellowship. This danger applies, however, not only to independent gatherings of inmates but also to those with visitors involved. It is indeed a temptation for Christian visitors or a chaplain—often unintentionally—to take the position of the senior brother and to dominate a group in the spirit of an authoritarian head who expects unquestioned loyalty in response to his service and support. (Indeed, this is mostly a male behavior.) Loyalty means dependence, an exclusive relationship, and a feeling of ownership by the authoritarian head of the group. This process can be exacerbated through the radical spiritual tendencies described above: the church then turns into both a rigid club that lacks the openness necessary to welcome God's diverse children, and an association of individuals who use their faith as a mechanism to repress chaos—the chaos of prison life in general or the chaos of each person's personal life in particular.

RELIGION AND REHABILITATION: DO RELIGIOUS PROGRAMS AFFECT REHABILITATION?

The question as to whether religious programs have a positive impact on the rehabilitation of offenders is an old one. Despite the natural inclination of most Christians to answer yes, the reality is not that simple.[13] A fully conclusive answer also depends on how *rehabilitation* is defined. Still, overall, there is some evidence to suggest that involvement in religious programs positively affects rehabilitation.

> Factors that social science uses to assess rehabilitation may include (a) the number of *in-prison infractions*—a relatively objective behavioral measure of adjustment, (b) the *adjustment to prison*—a subjective, psychological measure indicating how well an inmate is able to cope with the deprivations and difficulties of prison life, (c) *recidivism*—the likelihood of renewed crime after release and the time span of nondeviant behavior, and (d) the *adjustment to life after release*, which again can be measured psychologically, economically, and other ways. Rehabilitation has, in a spiritual context, another dimension that goes beyond the mere ability to adjust to given rules of society. The term then refers to deeper transformations and to the ability to cope with life in a constructive way.
>
> All studies on religion and rehabilitation face one or more methodological difficulties, such as how to measure religiosity; how to distinguish between religious involvement and personal, privately practiced religiosity; how to avoid bias in the selection of participants; and how to identify a control group that clearly lacks religiosity. Recent empirical research and a comprehensive review of previous empirical reviews by O'Connor and Perreyclear conditionally confirm that religious involvement reduces in-prison infractions: the more inmates participate in religious activities, the fewer infractions occur.[14] The studies show no evident difference between programs of different faith groups or different Christian denominations,[15] although factors like training, style, content, frequency, and quality of leaders undoubtedly influence the rehabilitation process.

---

13. See Hoyles, *Church and the Criminal*, 98. Pace, *Christian's Guide*, 39–40, summarizes the history of the failure to establish an evident link between the religious activities and successful rehabilitation.

14. O'Connor and Perreyclear, "Prison Religion in Action," 11–33.

15. Ibid., 30. See also Ellis, "Denominational Differences," 185–98. Ellis found significant differences only between believers and atheists/agnostics in respect to illegal drug use, but not among different denominations. The only religious denomination whose members reported the lowest offending rates in more than one offense category was the Greek Orthodox.

Sociological theories support the positive impact of religious services on the rehabilitation of inmates. The first is the *social-attachment theory*,[16] which holds that the more attached a person is to the major social institutions of life (family, education, work, politics, and religion), the less likely he or she is to commit a crime because he or she has something of value to lose by committing a crime. The *social-learning theory*[17] regards criminality as part of a learned behavior. According to this theory, offenders are able to learn new behavior. Both theories support active participation in religious activities, whether as a way to establish social attachments or as an opportunity for new social learning.

Although more research is needed to understand the impact of religion on rehabilitation, many prison administrators understand that religious programs offer an important service to inmates and help to reduce idleness. Many disciplinary problems have to do with a lack of motivation to change and with the overwhelming tedium of daily routine. They see that religious programs channel inmates' energies and provide opportunities to use their talents in meaningful ways. The various positive effects of religious programs include stress reduction, improvements in the general health, strengthening of prosocial behavior, encouragement to undertake active steps of improvement like studies or creative arts, and many more.[18]

Unfortunately, *many prison authorities only reluctantly create space for religious programs*. The reasons are manifold; the most commonly given reason is the concern about security, though *security* used in the prison context has a wide meaning and can refer to any challenge to the status quo. Another typical barrier to the expansion of religious programs is a claimed lack of staff. Sadly, prison management often fails to realize that a smoothly running religious program can have a long-term ameliorative impact, freeing staff for needs elsewhere. I believe that the deeper reasons for administrative resistance are, first, a lack of understanding; and, second, the feeling of ownership.

Many *prison administrators still understand little about how faith affects behavior* and personal transformation. It is therefore important to remind prison authorities how religious programs and rehabilitation are linked.

16. This theory has been developed by Hirschi, *Causes of Delinquency*. A revision of the theory is presented in Gottfredson and Hirschi, *General Theory of Crime*.

17. This theory has been developed by the American sociologist Edwin H. Sutherland (1883–1950). A central thesis of his theory is that persons become delinquent if they encounter more attitudes supporting delinquency than attitudes opposing and rejecting it.

18. Thomas and Zaitzow, "Conning or Conversion?" 253ff.

Even if the scientific proof is not as straightforward as one expects, it is evident enough that religious activities *are* a successful form of rehabilitation, a form that is by far the least expensive.[19] The *chaplain's role as agent of social change* has continuously been suggested in scientific literature. Research in the United States found that among inmates who attributed their successful postrelease reintegration to a member of the prison staff, one-sixth cited prison chaplains, although chaplains constituted less than 1 percent of prison employees. Chaplains were also the second most frequently cited staff members credited with bringing about inmates' rehabilitation.[20]

Because prisons are total institutions, there is also a *danger that they are run like little fiefdoms* belonging to the prison warden or, in more centralized structures, to the head of the prison department. They are outside public scrutiny. The public gets involved only when a famous criminal is admitted, a spectacular outbreak occurs (which rarely happens in Hong Kong), or prisoners reach the outside world through rehabilitative programs. At these points, the public will measure the success or failure of the prison system. Some prison authorities, therefore, jealously maintain ownership of any positive news or developments emerging from prison. They regard prisoners as their own assets and do not like religious organizations reaping rewards for their own programs.

Before concluding, we should express a note of caution regarding religion and rehabilitation: Although prison ministries should definitely claim positive rehabilitative effects for their programs, visitors should never forget that successful rehabilitation is *not* a criterion for Christian care for inmates. Visits in prison happen not for specific results but for the gift that Christians have received and that moves them to transcend the separating walls of imprisonment. One should equally be critical when measuring success of a religious program by its rehabilitative effects. Christian care in prison happens not to make better citizens, to help inmates adjust, or to improve inmates' morals. All these are possible *by-products* of Christian

---

19. O'Connor and Perreyclear, "Prison Religion in Action," 28, calculate that the *yearly* costs per inmate served were US$150–250, in a context where prison chaplains are paid by the prison department. In other contexts, like Hong Kong, where all religious programs (including chaplaincies) are done on a voluntary basis, the costs are even lower.

20. Glaser, *Effectiveness of a Prison and Parole System* (1964). His findings are quoted in Sundt and Cullen, "Role of Prison Chaplain," 272. The study by Sundt and Cullen also comes to the conclusion that the chaplain's role has not changed substantially since the 1950s.

care. However, the care does not happen for extrinsic reasons but for the glory of God and in response to his calling.

Finally, there is a difference between the individual and the collective. Even where the overall impact of religious activities on the prison population is questioned, it is still obvious that tremendous transformation can happen in individual inmates and that even the seemingly most hardened criminal can change in a profound and lasting way. How this spiritual process happens is the subject of the next chapter.

BIBLIOGRAPHICAL NOTES

In the past years considerable research has been done on the relationship between *religion and rehabilitation*, or more specifically on the effectiveness of religious programs for offender rehabilitation. The *Journal of Offender Rehabilitation: A Multidisciplinary Journal of Innovation in Research, Services and Programs in Corrections and Criminal Justice* 35/3-4 (2002) has dedicated a whole volume to the topic of *Religion, the Community, and the Rehabilitation of Criminal Offenders*. For a comparative review of different empirical studies on the relationship between religious programs and rehabilitation, see J. Gartner et al., *Rehabilitation, Recidivism and Religion: A Systematic Literature Review* (Baltimore: Loyola College in Maryland, 1990). An essay by M. T. Sumter and T. Clear, "An Empirical Assessment of Literature Examining the Relationship between Religiosity and Deviance since 1985" (Paper presented at the Academy of Criminal Justice Sciences Conference, Albuquerque, 1998) similarly offers a comparative review of different studies on religion and rehabilitation. For a summary of their findings see Thomas P. O'Connor and Michael Perreyclear, "Prison Religion in Action and Its Influence on Offender Rehabilitation," *Journal of Offender Rehabilitation* 35/3-4 (2002) 11-33. The study of M. Young et al., "The Impact of a Volunteer Prison Ministry Program on the Long-Term Recidivism of Federal Inmates," *Journal of Offender Rehabilitation* 22 (1995) 97-118, investigates a group of inmates who had received special training by Prison Fellowship Ministries to become religious leaders while in prison. The study finds a clearly positive impact of religious training on long-term recidivism; a similar study is the one by B. R. Johnson et al., "Religious Programs, Institutional Adjustment, and Recidivism among Former Inmates in Prison Fellowship Programs," *Justice Quarterly* 14 (1997) 145-66. I am not aware of relevant studies from the Chinese or East-Asian context. The essay by Jody L. Sundt and Francis T. Cullen, "The Role of the Contemporary Prison Chaplain," *Prison Journal* 78/2 (1998) 271–98, evaluates more specifically the role of the prison chaplain in offender rehabilitation. The research is based on a questionnaire sent to randomly selected prison chaplains in the United States.

On the *impact of religion on prison life* see the highly readable essay by Jim Thomas and Barbara H. Zaitzow, "Conning or Conversion? The Role of Religion in Prison Coping," *Prison Journal* 86/2 (2006) 242–59.

On the *church behind bars* see the discussion in Dale K. Pace, *A Christian's Guide to Effective Jail & Prison Ministries* (Old Tappan, NJ: Revell, 1976), 199–214.

On *reasons for participation in religious activities* see Harry R. Dammer, "The Reasons for Religious Involvement in the Correctional Environment," *Journal of Offender Rehabilitation* 35/3–4 (2002) 35–58; Todd R. Clear et al., "The Value of Religion in Prison: An Inmate Perspective," *Journal of Contemporary Criminal Justice* 16/1 (2000) 53–73. Dammer based his research on interviews and questionnaires with inmates, chaplains, and prison staff. The research of Clear summarizes how inmates understand their participation in religious activities. Both studies refer to the context of the United States; my own experience supports many of their findings for the Hong Kong context.

4

Christian Faith and Spiritual Transformation in Prison

FAITH AND RELIGIOUS LIFE in prison is, primarily, not what people from outside prison do for those inside. It is the spiritual life of inmates: their questions, their struggles, their hopes, and possibly their transformations. Chaplains or regular visitors are in the privileged situation of being able to witness and encourage the inmates' spiritual life, but they are not the primary initiators. To truly support the spiritual growth process and to assist in establishing a church, it is necessary to respect the fact that the inmates *themselves* are the starting points of spiritual growth.

The questions addressed in this chapter follow:

- What is the inmates' spiritual situation, and how does the Christian faith respond to it?
- How does spiritual transformation happen when inmates are touched by the message of the gospel?
- What does Christian faith offer someone in prison?

CRISIS AND SPIRITUALITY: PRISON AS UPSIDE-DOWN EXPERIENCE

Imprisonment is one of the most serious crisis experiences one can imagine, causing high levels of stress and disruption to life.[1] During such periods of extraordinary readjustment to a new situation, previously irrelevant questions start to become relevant. People who never bothered about questions of spirituality may in this moment of crisis reevaluate their previous concepts of life and start to think about what lasts and about what is ultimately important in life.

First, and on the surface, a person entering prison simply settles in a new environment and, similar to moving to a new place, experiences new opportunities. What traditionally kept him or her busy ceases, and new patterns of life can be tried out. Suddenly, a person has ample time for activities that were out of the question in his or her previous life.

However, a crisis experience also carries an ambivalent spiritual potential that can lead either to a breakdown or to deeper life. On the one hand, it is during such periods in our lives that we are reminded of the *fragility of our life*. A crisis reminds us that life is unpredictable, not at our disposal, and not in our control. To distract ourselves from the precarious footing of our existence we have developed sophisticated techniques: structures of meaning and values that lend our life a sense of normality, clarity, and necessity. Many of our collective and individual activities aim at stabilizing our daily life and at defending it from collapsing on its foundation of uncertainty. We establish values by measuring persons according to their professional and social status, or according to the wealth and respect they receive in a socially relevant group. And we aim at achievement and success in order to be able to give and to show generosity instead of being in a status of depending on others. To the extent that these endeavors turn into our foremost concerns and our primordial raison d'être, they prevent us from touching the transcendent, unreachable but constantly effective ground of our life.

In the crisis triggered by the admission to prison, the structures that used to provide direction to our life break down. The yawning void lurking underneath the surface of our life and life's precarious footing can no

---

1. According to a scale of stressful experiences developed in the US, the highest stress level is caused by the death of a spouse (set as stress value 100). Detention in jail or other institution ranks fourth, with a stress value of 63; see Clinebell, *Basic Types of Pastoral Care*, 188–89.

Beyond the Walls of Separation

longer be suppressed. We feel how basically lonely we are in our life, adrift and disoriented. The established strategies to avoid facing this loneliness and the potentially humiliating reminder of our own mortality and limitation fail when the stability of our daily life crumbles.

On the other hand, the moments when our established structures of life crumble can also allow us to touch on a deeper and more sustaining foundation of life. Spiritual specialists like hermits or monks voluntarily withdraw from society as a learning process in order to face the transcendent ground of life more immediately. Transcendent ground: this refers to the recognition that life, during its crucial moments like birth and death, sickness and recovery, joy and sadness, is beyond human control, and a gift of God. These spiritual specialists withdraw from wealth and social status in order to learn to depend on God instead of depending on their status. Similarly, by keeping ourselves busy we avoid facing immediacy in relation to this basis of our life. The withdrawal from the bustle of daily life into silence allows us to recognize the basic human solitude as a fertile ground for a deeper growth in relationship with God, and to overcome its threatening aspect. The Dutch priest Henri J. M. Nouwen describes this as the way from loneliness to solitude, from being threateningly lonely to feeling safe in being alone.[2] In solitude, we discover our being alone as a basic pattern of our existence. Imprisonment *can* be an opportunity to move from loneliness to solitude; the prison *can* turn into a spiritual retreat where a new existential ground replaces the broken structures of meaning of the former life and leads beyond the alienating experience of prison life. Imprisonment *can* offer a person the strict disciplinary framework to reach new spiritual horizons. The crisis experience of imprisonment, the public condemnation, the breakdown of a person's social standing, the disruption in family life, the financial challenges can turn into opportunities to reconnect with life's fundamentals or root experiences, to grow closer to the mystery of life, and to rediscover its essential spiritual dimensions. The breakdown may lead people onto a path where they overcome a wrong pride and discover new dependencies.

At a low point of their life inmates face a nakedness, emptiness, and loss of meaning that they previously—through all sorts of activities, illicit and otherwise—avoided facing. At this point, they may move from

---

2. A good description of the loneliness of the human spiritual situation and attempts to escape it can be found in Nouwen, *Reaching Out*, 3–15, in the section titled "A Suffocating Loneliness."

threatening loneliness to solitude, from the experience of nakedness and exposure to a deep feeling of being embraced by God. On this path, they discover a new and, we could say, spiritual depth in human existence and human relationships:

That love is experienced most purely where we receive it without our achievement;

that love reveals its strength most powerfully where we receive it *against* what we have done;

that forgiveness is indeed pure grace, freely given;

that what we are yearning for is, in fact, very simple—to be loved, accepted, and called by our name;

that the evil we are a capable of doing is not the whole of our reality, but is limited through the love we receive and give;

that admitting weakness can turn into new strength;

that tears are not signs of failure but a victory over a socially or privately imposed concept of one's self;

that feelings must not be suppressed;

that we are not what others told us and taught us that we were, or what we thought ourselves to be;

that losing what one had can lead to more abundance;

that what makes life valuable can be very simple;

that life can be different, even radically so, and still be precious and worth living;

that changes in one's life need not threaten but can hold new promises;

that death can turn into new life.

These *upside-down experiences* are what we call spiritual experiences. They have similar form to the upside-down experiences that the Bible recounts; paradoxical faith statements as the core message of the Bible: God has elected Israel not because of her greatness, but because she was the last among the people (Deut 7:7); the cross, a symbol of torture and oppression, turns into a symbol of salvation; the death of Christ is not the victory of those who killed him, but the victory of God over evil. Spiritual changes and breakthroughs may happen when I discover that the upside-down experiences reflected in the Bible have something to do with me, when I am touched by an overwhelming feeling of what is ultimately important, and when I find myself connected to a history of similar experiences. In such moments we perceive something of the transcendent ground of life that establishes value beyond societal valuation.

When life takes an unexpected and difficult turn, and when inmates, and other people alike, discover a new order of value and meaning, new life emerges from the ruins of the old. In such a moment, a prisoner may experience a *transcendence* and *proximity to God* that he or she has never experienced before: God as "the 'beyond' in the midst of our life."[3] In this way, prisons *can* become places where there is an *abundance of spiritual life*.

Spiritual experiences during imprisonment reflect in concentrated form the experience of modern man and woman and assume as such paradigmatic character. Indeed, both the loss of meaning and the feeling of living in limbo, not knowing what life is about, quite generally belong to a context of modernity, where traditions fail to offer a framework and a stable value system for an individual's existence. An *existential anxiety*, a continuous threat of nonbeing, permeates our whole being. The permanent awareness of our finitude, the awareness of growing older, the knowledge that time ticks away—they play like faint background music in the distance through the whole of our lives. The knowledge that decisions taken and wrongs done cannot be changed looms like a dark shadow over our present. The imposed inactivity of prison life causes mechanisms that were supposed to help us escape the awareness of our mortality to break down. Painful anxiety and feelings of lack of purpose can no longer be withheld through activism or busy life. Many inmates, when experiencing the radical crisis of entering prison for the first time, ask: what is the reason for their continued existence? What is left in the ruins of life? And they painfully realize that they no longer possess the same ample possibilities to avoid the horror of emptiness as when they were outside. However, they may start to learn that this emptiness does not have to be threatening, and that it was in fact the previous life, the one leading them to crime, that lacked orientation and purpose. In such possible spiritual revival, a person in prison can experience a radical reaffirmation of meaning in the midst of apparent meaninglessness, and reconnect with the foundation of our existence: the gift of life.

Inmates experience critical periods at different times of their imprisonment. A first intensive period of such feeling is directly after arrest. The

3. Bonhoeffer, *Letters and Papers from Prison*, 124.

turmoil of the first night in detention is hard to imagine: possibly knowing what kind of sentence they may face, often *not* knowing what kind of life they will encounter, and worrying about family and friends, about unfinished business and open debts. A second period is just prior to and after trial and, to a lesser extent, prior to and after appeal. This is when a decision is coming up, and the inmate realizes that this decision is almost completely outside his or her control. The inmate's entire mind is focused on the upcoming trial or appeal that will be so decisive for his or her life. After trial there is a feeling of closure: something of which one was afraid now becomes a definitive and inevitable reality. A third period is during the first weeks in prison. Of course the slow adjustment to prison life already begins during detention, but the person in detention keeps a distance from reality, hoping that release will come after the trial. Now reality sets in, and the prisoner has to establish his or her life in the miserable environment of prison. Finally, an important crisis experience happens when approaching release. Now all the fears about the future set in. Many inmates cannot repress the fear that they are insufficiently prepared for release, or that being reunited with family may not be as sweet and harmonious as they had always fantasized.

Of course, periods of crisis can also happen spontaneously at other times of imprisonment, often provoked by family developments, sickness of a spouse, the death of a loved one, conflicts with other inmates, betrayal by a trusted friend, or personal failures such as losses, insurmountable debts, or any other dead-end feelings. A crisis experience often occurs when inmates are arrested in prison for violation of internal rules and put under disciplinary confinement. During such crises, the surface of life turns extremely fragile and vulnerable, and questions of despair and hope, of tormenting guilt and possible forgiveness, of death and rebirth become crucial. Crises are turning points in a person's life story, with potential for both the complete breakdown of previous life structures, and the discovery of new potential in life.

EXPERIENCING FORGIVENESS: NEW LIFE AFTER DEATH

Indeed it is often at such a point of crisis that prisoners can hear the message of the Bible and existentially receive it. They hear how the life of Jesus Christ was a life of utmost failure that eventually turned into victory. They can rediscover themselves in the Bible, for what they experience is exactly the same thing: to die, to be dead and buried, and, at the point where hope and acceptance enters their life, to be raised from the dead.

Prisoners in Hong Kong express this feeling of death in their own argot: Stanley Prison is called ancestral hall (*ci tang*)—that is, the house where one's deceased ancestors are venerated; to receive a visit in prison is called going to worship at the graves in the mountains, or (for short) visiting the dead (*bai shan*). Inmates find themselves buried alive; while time around them moves on, their own time has come to a standstill. They can identify with and find proximity to a God who revealed himself, not through earthly glory, but through suffering and worldly failure. They feel close to the small people at the fringes of society who follow Jesus and who start to play a powerful role in the history of transformation that takes its starting point from Jesus. Faith, then, means to experience the movement from death to life in one's own person: to escape death, to enter life.

For people in prison, the message of *forgiveness* is possibly the single most important message to provide comfort and meaning. They hear the parable of the Lost Son (Luke 15:11–32) or the story of Jesus's encounter with the woman caught in adultery (John 8:1–11) and are amazed about such a message of noncondemnation.

Some people react critically to the Christian message of forgiveness and wonder whether it is not somewhat cheap comfort for somebody who has committed a serious crime to receive forgiveness so easily. However, most inmates I have met do not receive this message as cheap comfort that relieves them of responsibility for their crime. Prisoners burdened with self-condemnation outnumber those who take their guilt easily.

> One inmate whom I had known for many years appeared generally rather cool and seemed to show little repentance. He had committed a murder, and his overall expression fitted quite well the image of the hardened criminal. At some point I talked with him about his relationship to his mother and about his past. I thought that our relationship and trust level was strong enough that I could confront him with his past. His reaction mixed a slight feeling of annoyance with generous understanding for my lack of insight: "Look, Pastor, everyone here inside this workshop is deeply repentant for his crime—and not just because we were caught."

However, to admit wrong openly and to show repentance is difficult and unpopular in a context where toughness and manliness count. Many inmates struggle with this message, not because they lack repentance, but because they cannot believe it to be possible. Feelings of guilt have become part of their identity; self-condemnation outweighs social condemnation. For them, the message of Christ that stands in such stark contrast to both society's and the courts' condemnation offers space to breathe: an acceptance where they are not reduced to the single role of a criminal but are seen in a broader light, as a lost son who can experience transformation.

It would be wrong to think that given the gravity of their crimes, prisoners should first be confronted with the evil of their deeds and only then receive comfort through the message of forgiveness. The fear that they could misuse the forgiveness they receive to avoid responsibility is unjustified. For this they would not need the promise of forgiveness. To think that the severity of their crimes causes them to lose the chance for forgiveness is wrong. It is one of the profound scandals of biblical teaching that it repeatedly stresses the forgiveness to the most serious offenders. This is the point in the parable of the Prodigal Son, who by asking the share of his father's estate, implicitly expressed the wish for his father to die. It is equally the point of Jesus's fellowship with tax collectors (Luke 5:27ff; 19:1–10), who through their greed undermined the communal togetherness and severely hurt the lives of their compatriots. It is the scandal of a free grace that precedes all human activity, and the inmates seem to understand it naturally. They experience well enough how condemnation still abounds, but for many inmates the message of forgiveness becomes a turning point in their lives. For possibly the first time they are not approached and identified as failed ones, but as loved ones.

This doesn't mean that there is no room for confronting a prisoner with his past crime, or for encouraging him or her to share feelings of guilt and receive healing through confessing past injuries inflicted on others. However, this step happens later, when a stable relationship of trust has been established. Inmates first need to hear the message of forgiveness and receive the crucial support that gives them strength to face their situation.

Being *valued, treasured,* and *esteemed* is for many inmates a radically new experience. This is particularly an issue in authority-centered[4] contexts like the ones in Hong Kong and China where education is often understood

---

4. Clinebell, *Basic Types of Pastoral Care,* 97–98, uses this word repeatedly to describe nonwhite cultures that have a different understanding of the role of authority than those rooted in the European context. The authority-centeredness of a culture can be measured by the concept of *power distance,* see Hofstede, *Culture's Consequences,* 65ff; see also the table with different values of power distance, ibid., 77.

in a way that undermines healthy self-esteem. The educational emphasis is on correcting wrongs rather than on supporting strengths. This, combined with a superstitious belief in the harmfulness of praise and encouragement, makes many young people lose self-confidence. A negative self-image is common to most inmates. Many inmates have had negative experiences in their education, family, or professional lives. Being valued and treasured radically challenges the image that they developed of themselves, and that other people continuously reinforced. To be seen and addressed as a creation in the image of God is a tremendously new and uplifting experience.

GROWING INTO A COMMUNITY: FINDING NEW BELONGING

Such new understanding of oneself, such a new image of who one is, is not received in abstract form or through an abstract message, but is communicated through the practical experience of joint celebration in the worshiping community. Such fellowship provides a sense of belonging that makes the shifts in self-understanding real. The inmates enter into a community that is based on radically different values to those they have known until that point. They gain a new understanding of what family can be, often in contrast to what they have learned in their past.

> A young inmate, Ah-Luen, approached me when I visited his workshop one morning and quite suddenly poured out his heart to me. He told me about a difficult youth, having his parents divorce when he was three years old, living with his father, and being taken care of by a neighbor until she died when he was eight. From then on, he lived virtually on his own while his father was working. He entered a youth gang and was involved in burglary and brought to a training center. After his release at the age of fifteen, there was still nobody to care for him, and nothing was provided to keep him away from Triad involvement. He again joined the Triads and got involved in criminal activities that ended tragically when the whole group killed a young man. Ah-Luen was sentenced to a long prison term. He had never felt part of a family: his father was already sixty when he was born and didn't allow him to keep in touch with his mother; he never had a sense of belonging—except, in a certain way, as part of the Triad group.
>
> One morning in prison, after a restless night, he was listening to the radio and heard a pastor describe God as a loving father and

invite the listeners to accept this unconditional love. The message immediately touched Ah-Luen, and he connected it with the occasional contacts he had already established with the prison chaplain because there he had felt a similar acceptance. Since then, he has built a stable relationship with the chaplain and Christian volunteers who visit him. He started to study and to develop a positive and constructive attitude towards his future.

The acceptance and the belonging that inmates feel from the Christian faith community in prison allow them to gain a new understanding of who they are. It is from this point that important changes in behavior, values, and self-esteem arise; it is very difficult for such transformations to happen if not supported by the practical experience of being accepted and having close kinship. This is an important point of difference between faith-based healing and psychological therapy. Obviously, both perspectives are aware that these feelings cannot just be communicated rationally. However, faith-based healing can transmit changes in self-esteem, feelings of being accepted, and a sense of belonging *through the reality of the faith-based community*. The more somebody becomes attached to a community, the less likely such a person is to commit a crime.[5] Psychological therapy, in contrast, can facilitate similar processes only through the more narrow interaction *between counselor and client*. Faith groups thus allow not only analysis and deeper understanding of these psychological needs but also the *real experience of belonging* to a caring group. This forms the basis for healthy and holistic psychological development. Many inmates indeed are passionate about belonging to a community of healing. In fact, such therapeutic communities have had positive effects in the rehabilitation of both drug addicts and inmates with personality disorders,[6] and these communities could also reduce problems of inmates' discipline or of recidivism.

CRACKING A CYCLE OF DESTRUCTIVENESS: RESTORING BROKEN RELATIONSHIPS

What many people involved in prison ministry find particularly fascinating is how radically and thoroughly some transformation processes happen. Many inmates experience a spiritual revival that stands in all-out contrast

---

5. See on the social attachment theory chapter 3, Religion and Rehabilitation.

6. For more about these communities, see the bibliographic notes at the end of this chapter and also chapter 5.

to their previous life. This process happens, however, often only hesitatingly. Inmates have so deeply internalized the negative images that society holds about them that they initially find it hard to accept the genuineness of this acceptance. They take the gentleness and the acceptance for a fake. It takes time to establish trust in people who have ample experience with broken promises. However, if trust can be established, it can open the floodgates: the acceptance of the faith community or of its representative cracks the defense shells inmates have built up to protect against deceit and broken promises. Suddenly they can put down the negative images that shaped their self-perceptions and others' perceptions of them. Quite easily, an extensive confession of the former life flows out without much confrontation.

> When I met Dirty—this his telling nickname (recounted with permission)—he was in his early thirties. He had grown up in the turmoil of the Cultural Revolution in China, in the late 1960s and early '70s. What he had learned during his youth, since education was suspended, was how to pick fights and bully authorities. He was an active part of the Red Guards, the groups of young people who looted the whole country and destroyed much of its cultural heritage. As a young man, Dirty moved to Hong Kong and, not having many other resources, soon joined a Triad gang. There he qualified himself as an excellent fighter, brave and loyal to his "big brother." His criminal career ended when he was arrested after a killing in a Triad attack. He was sentenced to life in prison and soon felt at ease in the underworld of the prison.
>
> He continued his lifestyle of swearing and fighting and went in and out of disciplinary confinement. I had known him for several years when I met him once again during one of his many stints in the isolation ward. He had just received the news that his father was in hospital and that his son had been fighting in school, and his mood was accordingly dark. That's when I started to talk with him about his life and his family. It was while he was remembering his son that something broke open: Dirty was reminded that he was not just a fighter, not just a rebellious young man, but himself a father who was now far away from his only son. He remembered a neglected relationship and the need to find reconciliation with his family. That was, according to his own account, when something cracked.
>
> Since then Dirty has undergone a dramatic transformation. He has not only reestablished contact with his son, patiently writing to him, hoping but little expecting a response, until eventually the relationship started to grow. He has also stopped fighting and

Christian Faith and Spiritual Transformation in Prison

hasn't had any further disciplinary record. Besides the healing in his relationships—in his family and in the institutional context—he has also experienced physical healing through quitting a strong nicotine addiction. He became an active member of our worship community and frequently gives testimonies. Unlike common ex-offender testimonies, Dirty's talks focus, not on the evil criminal life before his transformation, but rather on the continuous healing that he has experienced after what we may call conversion. He has tremendously grown in self-awareness and in the awareness of others (for instance, when actively remembering the names and the needs of our volunteers, when writing to them, or when interceding for them in prayer).

Being approached as precious, being seen in the light of God's forgiveness, and learning to see oneself in this light can indeed crack the vicious circle of negative perceptions and subsequent destructive behavior. If such a break happens, it is not unusual that the contrary dynamic evolves: a sense of achievement when long-lasting experiences of failure are interrupted, and positive feedback reinforces the efforts that one has already made. A series of disappointments gives way to improvements in self-confidence, particularly in the confidence that a person is free to do something about his or her situation.

OVERCOMING THE OTHER CAPTIVITY: BEYOND THE BONDAGE OF ANGER

Love and forgiving acceptance can indeed become an encounter with transcendence, even a transcendent peak experience. Such a moment of being in touch with something that transcends all our previous knowledge and imagination, being touched by God, can indeed spur a radical change of mind. This is, as I understand, what happened when Peter met Jesus for the first time (Luke 5:1–10). When Jesus led Peter to an amazing catch of fishes, Peter responded not simply, as could have been imagined, with a feeling of gratitude and amazement, but with fear and with a surprising confession of being a sinner.

I remember inmates who had violent conflicts. Partly they interpreted such violence within the logic of necessary self-defense. Partly they admitted that they felt themselves caught in a cycle that they couldn't break through. It is a feeling of being trapped that comes close to what the Apostle Paul expressed in Rom 7:21ff: "when I want to do what is good, evil lies close at hand . . . but I see in my members another law at war with the law of my mind, making me a captive to the law of sin that dwells in my members. Wretched man that I am!" (NRSV)[7]

Obviously, stories of change do not always last, and it is common that people relapse. Such relapse into violent behavior challenges visitors in several ways. They are reminders that it is not in a counselor's, a visitor's, a prison officer's, or a prison manager's power to cause change, and that even a genuine spiritual change will not necessarily last forever. A once dominant pattern of behavior that has been broken through can at any time regain the upper hand. Another challenge is that at such a point vexing questions arise: Is the support given to relapsing inmates simply a waste of efforts? Or were the previous spiritual expressions only pretended? Are such inmates, as is often suggested by other inmates or by prison staff, simply manipulating religious visitors? Does a relapse happen due to a lack of continuous counseling? I believe such experiences show more than anything else how fragile any process of spiritual and psychological change is, how hard it is to reach firm ground, and, even more, how deeply a person can be trapped in anger, violence, and fear.

Being trapped in such mental or spiritual imprisonment can indeed be more painful than any physical imprisonment. Feelings of anger and unhealed wounds of the past can hold a person captive over a long time span, as the following account shows.

> I had known Ah-Man for nearly ten years and always liked him for his friendliness, his warmth, and his strong ability to express his feelings. He had been part of the Christian community ever since I had known him, but over the years, I witnessed how he had become more actively involved, more outspoken, and firmer in his faith. He was on a life sentence for murder and still had around ten years left until his possible release, when, at one point, I asked him what his Christian faith meant to him and whether he believed that he would be able to sustain it upon his release. At this point and finding ourselves undisturbed, he shared with me how he became who he was. Ah-Man had, as a nine-year-old boy, been sexually abused by his uncle. Although unable to tell his family about it, he believed that they were aware of what had happened to him. Ever since that fateful event, Ah-Man carried a deep anger in his heart and blamed his father for not protecting him better. The innocence of his childhood had fallen apart. He felt

---

7. All quotations from the Bible are taken from the New Revised Standard Version.

disliked by his peers and an outsider in school. As a teenager and as a young adolescent, he repeatedly tried to sexually attack others but, fortunately, never succeeded. When he was about twenty, one of his few friends approached him and asked him to help him take revenge on somebody who had raped his sister. Their revenge turned into murder. Ah-Man, it seems, avenged himself, if not on the one who had previously harmed him, then on the one who harmed somebody close to him.

The subsequent arrest and conviction to a lifelong prison sentence and the experience of being imprisoned was not what hurt Ah-Man most. More painful was to be in the grip of a smoldering anger against his tormenter and against his father that never left him. Countless nights he spent in his cell, crying and cursing, not knowing how to overcome this painful memory. Worse for him, he had grown up within a spiritual framework that regarded what had happened to him as fate and as a natural consequence of what he had done in previous lives. It was through a slow process of personal reading and interaction with visitors and other inmates that something new grew, and that he found an alternative spiritual understanding: one that believed in the ongoing re-creation and reconciliation of God with humans. It did not come as a sudden spiritual breakthrough but as a slow process of growth that led him to a new experience and a new kind of pain: after the first pain of his initial injury and after the second pain of his continuous anger, he began to feel a third kind of pain: the pain of compassion—compassion for his victim, for all his previous victims. It was a pain that brought him close to the compassion reflected in the suffering of Christ on the cross.

A few days after Ah-Man's sharing, the yearly graduation ceremony in prison took place. Every year, this is a much anticipated event because it is the only opportunity for inmates to share a meal with their families and to meet them directly, without a glass screen separating visitors and inmates. Ah-Man was also there, together with his mother and his father, who had come a long way from a faraway place. It was the first time that Ah-Man's father had seen his son since Ah-Man had entered prison. On this occasion, Ah-Man showed unique tenderness and affection to his father who, it turned out, had equally been gripped by feelings of guilt for failing to give affection and guidance to his son. After this graduation ceremony, Ah-Man wrote the following:

"I have to admit that my relationship with my family was edgy and rough, especially with my father. There was a time when I simply hated him for no particular reason. The gap got wider as the years unfolded. I ended up here in prison, and he got stuck in his own. Both were locked up with pain and shame, guilt and hatred. Each time we had the chance to communicate either through letters or phone calls, the clear presence of walls was obviously felt, and both of us were afraid to face each other.

"Every single day of my life here in prison, there was not one moment that I was not surrounded by the pain from my past. There were times when I broke down in loneliness and my real prison seemed thousands of times closer than the walls and guard towers. I tumbled on and swung from one corner to another in search of the purpose of my life. I came across a prison chaplain who told me what became a revelation to me: 'Life is not merely about achieving goals or making huge fortune; it is about what exists in our heart . . . By God's grace, you have been given a second chance; you can put these trials and tribulations to your benefit.' It was the first time I felt my heart growing within me and tears streaming down from my eyes. I saw the light of God's grace shining through the bars of my dark cell and showering me with love.

[At the graduation ceremony] "I held my mom and dad in my arms tightly and let our heart feel each other's love. It was a complete assurance for them of my well-being and receiving. Now, as my father has seen with his own eyes, surely, he will be able to put down his bitter feelings."[8]

What triggered a breakthrough in the spiritual transformation of this inmate is possibly less one specific encounter with a chaplain and the specific words he received in it than the continuous experience of being given a second chance. He experienced this as comfort and as promise of a love stronger than the wounds of the past. This was in itself a liberating experience. Yet something more happened: Ah-Man reached out to his own father in in a gesture of fatherly forgiveness. The lost son turned into a forgiving father—embracing his physical father. The hug of physical father and father-turned-son brought the shadows of the past to an end. The story of the Prodigal Son comes to its conclusion when the son himself becomes the forgiving father.[9]

---

8. This excerpt from the letter is shortened and slightly revised and amended by the author.

9. See similarly Nouwen, *Return of the Prodigal Son*, 120ff, where Nouwen offers a meditation of this process of returning home and turning into the forgiving father.

CONFESSING GUILT: GROWING IN RESPONSIBILITY

During my early experiences as a prison chaplain, I visited an inmate on a life sentence for murder, and during my regular visits to him, he described in detail how he had been sentenced unjustly. I was quite upset about the situation, considering that this man had to face around twenty-five years behind bars for something that, he convinced me, he had not done. Later, I happened to visit another inmate who turned out to be the accomplice of the first one. From him I heard more about the case, and things started to look different. I still don't know the reality, but I learned that many crimes are indeed difficult to face and to attribute to one's own actions. Moreover, many inmates lack the personal strength to face up to their crimes. To emotionally survive the dramatic events of a crime and the enormous guilt resulting from it, a person sometimes needs strong defense mechanisms and quite often represses memories of and feelings related to what happened. Claiming innocence and casting blame at others may show an inmate's inability to cope with the heavy guilt that would otherwise arise.

On the other hand, as we saw earlier, many inmates are aware of their wrongdoing by means of the condemnation they receive from society through the courts. The experience of being part of a caring and forgiving community enables an inmate to move beyond mere awareness and to grow in accepting responsibility for the committed crime. The different stages of healing from guilt—confession, restitution, and reconciliation—are based on an environment that expresses forgiveness and care.[10] Accepting a life situation that (at least at that moment) cannot be changed is a crucial step in the process to constructively handle imprisonment. Only when inmates assume responsibility can they move forward and regard the time in prison not just passively as fate imposed by others but as an integral part of their own lives—obviously a low point, but one that leads to new stages in life. This is also the reason why external factors should never become an excuse for inmates to avoid responsibility. Understanding how social, educational, or economic factors influence a person to commit a crime is important.

---

10. Clinebell, *Basic Types of Pastoral Care*, 142ff, describes how guilt feelings can be resolved through a five-stage process: confrontation, confession, forgiveness, restitution (including changes in a person's behavior), and reconciliation. I essentially agree with this description. However, due to the personality of many inmates and the nature of their crimes, it is in the context of prison rather rare to find the ego strength necessary to start this process with confrontation.

However, if such an understanding relieves a person from taking responsibility, this person gains nothing.

> Ah-Kin was a young man on a life sentence for murder, quite arrogant and demanding, constantly seeking special benefits and constantly expressing his annoyance about other people, be it inmates or even Christian visitors. I had known Ah-Kin for several years. Despite his rebellious character, he had an appealing personality, and he eventually started to join our worship. During one service we played an interactive game. The task was for the groups of inmates to examine several fictitious cases and choose one convicted person from a group for an amnesty. When discussing each case's merits (among them also a murder case) Ah-Kin strongly rejected the idea of awarding the amnesty to this man: after only six years in prison, he hadn't paid the price yet. I then asked him if this also applied to himself. At this point he reacted with a sudden and surprising confession of his guilt. He expressed for the first time how he accepted his imprisonment and the responsibility for what he had done. He then started to share how the moment of being caught after his crime was a huge relief. He had spent the week after the murder profoundly shaken and unable to talk to anyone. When the police finally came to his house to question and arrest him, an unbearable turmoil finally came to an end. At the time of our discussion, Ah-Kin still had to face another eighteen to twenty years in prison, but from that point on he developed a more constructive attitude toward his imprisonment.

When inmates accept responsibility for what they have done, they move towards a new self-understanding, one that transcends the external definition imposed on them through the whole process of criminal trial and various psychological assessments and background reports. At this point, they start to accept a new definition of themselves that understands past wounds both received and inflicted on others as a meaningful and necessary, though painful, process. It is indeed one of the goals of spiritual growth that inmates come to the point where they are reconciled with a past that is sometimes hard to face, and where they can say, "Yes, I am the one who has committed this crime. This is part of my life story, and I will continuously carry this burden with me, but I can hear the message that there is life beyond my guilt, and I can accept that forgiveness also applies to me. I've no need to hide anymore." Or more simply, "Here I stand. God, you know me."

LIBERATING THE MIND: FINDING NEW VALUES

A confession—the outpouring of a story that has not been shared, but that has been in the mind constantly, resurfacing as a nightmare during the long hours of darkness or as painful memory fragments during the day—has a tremendously liberating effect. It can liberate by integrating past harm into a person's present life and by clearing the way towards new ground. A confession frees the mind of a continuous but ultimately vain mental effort to gloss over past failures and to fight the fact of imprisonment. Learning to accept the reality of one's own imprisonment means neither resignation nor fatalistic abandonment of self-value. Rather it means to move away from a negative definition of one's own existence, to see oneself, not in the light of what is lost, but in the *new* light of the qualities of the very now. Inmates still find that life is like constantly bumping one's head in a narrow confinement where desires and wishes are frustrated by strict rules. But they will also discover that despite all restrictions and narrowness, a kind of *good life is still possible*, even behind bars. The values of what makes life good may be very different to what was important in the past. But an inmate may treasure these new values as much as he or she ever treasured the values of life outside. Due to the reality of material deprivation, spiritual values become particularly important—among them the values of peace, equanimity, and reconciliation with oneself, with one's peers and with God, the source of our life. These values provide a purpose that receives strength and inspiration from beyond the narrow confinement of this world. In the words of an inmate,

> The only thing that is lacking in here is freedom of movement and women, but that is only a state of mind. I've seen some guys who don't really realize that they are in prison because it is not the prison that they see, it is the walk with God. Prison doesn't bother them anymore.[11]

Inmates discover a surprising dynamic: The more an inmate focuses on the values of the realm of God, the more the daily frustrations lose their sting. Where previously they became tense, with knots in the heart, they now remain unaffected. Regular visitors to prison sometimes encounter inmates who radiate deep spirituality and equanimity. They have let go and do not pursue (and are not pursued by) the powers of random desires. They

---

11. Quoted in Clear, "Value of Religion," 62.

radiate a dignity, humility, even serenity that stands in sharp contrast to their surroundings.

New values include voluntary steps of self-discipline—to stop smoking, gambling, or using foul language. Christian visitors, who tend to regard these habits as un-Christian behavior, support them in these moves, but the initiative lies with inmates who joyfully try out what is possible on the basis of their new spiritual freedom. More important, the new values of a liberated mind build the seeds of a counterculture in prison, which can lead inmates to rare experiences of success in a place where such experiences are hard to find. These values also lay the groundwork for an active practice of love in prison, sometimes to the point of self-sacrifice.

> Ah-Kiu was a highly educated inmate who was on a long prison sentence for a violent crime. Starting from an attitude of philosophical skepticism, he went through a long process of spiritual transformation that slowly turned him into one of the most important pillars of our prison fellowship. He was a gifted musician and worship leader, and he had a passion for people who took spiritual transformation seriously. He repeatedly pointed me toward inmates with special emotional or spiritual needs, and he had an extraordinary sensitivity for those around him who were suffering. The management equally liked him and was proud of him, as his high educational achievements cast a positive light on the prison's rehabilitation efforts. For these reasons he was granted a privileged work assignment.
>
> Great was my surprise when, one morning upon entering his workshop, I was told that he wasn't there anymore. He had been moved to another workshop that I knew as a Triad stronghold and center of gambling activities. Such a sudden move was unusual for somebody with his overall achievement, and I was instantly worried that something serious had happened. Yet when I found him in his new workplace, he sat there, peacefully, in the midst of a group of inmates from mainland China. It turned out that he himself had voluntarily given up his privileged work assignment and requested the move so that he could teach English and business administration to these inmates. His presence and his fellowship touched a growing number of inmates, who started to join our worship services and abandon their previous gambling involvement. His presence thus increasingly affected the whole of the workshop. However, soon enough I was reminded about how difficult it is to establish a counterculture in prison: after several

months, he had to move on, pressured by Triad threats. His presence had inspired so many inmates to join the Christian fellowship and to abandon gambling that Ah-Kiu had undermined the main source of Triad income and provoked an angry reaction.

A person's conversion touches the whole network of relations in which he or she lives. Spiritual transformation, once begun, perpetuates itself and sets in motion a process that unlocks further capacity for love, and inspires a wider context beyond the individual inmate. Many visitors to prison witness how the spiritual change of one inmate becomes a motor for tangible growth in interpersonal relationships. Inmates who have been touched by such processes start to actively extend pastoral care to yet other inmates. One inmate said,

> "Before [prison], it was all me. Now I know life is also about relationships. I have to think of others and God. If you're serious about God, you have to take on the nature of God, and God cares about other people too."[12]

BREAKING THROUGH GENDER STEREOTYPES: STEPPING ON NEW EMOTIONAL GROUND

One of the most touching transformations in many inmates happens when they start to admit feelings buried in their concept of maleness. The common saying "Boys don't cry" has a parallel in Chinese that expresses this socially shaped role of man: "Men shed blood, not tears," or "Men don't cry when bleeding" (*nan liu xue, bu liu yanlei*)—with the obvious double meaning of one's own blood as well as the blood of others, implying that men are fighters, not criers. The emphasis on toughness and on repressing one's feelings, a typical male attitude, has far-reaching impacts on all society and on the self-understanding and self-expression of men in our societies. Not only does it signify an impoverished image of men, but it also alienates men from being able to express themselves meaningfully. Scholars have noted the individual and social destructiveness of one-sided development (that is, developing toughness at the expense of other qualities). Experts have also pointed out that more balanced personal growth that integrates

---

12. Quoted in O'Connor and Perreyclear, "Prison Religion in Action," 19.

so-called feminine and masculine qualities may be crucial for the survival of our planet.[13]

There are similarities and differences between the Chinese and some Western contexts in how personality development depends on gender. Both contexts know similar stereotypical roles for males and females: achievement, rationality and perseverance for men; caring, sensitivity, and emotion for women. Both contexts also reward and publicly acknowledge masculine characteristics while reserving the so-called feminine characteristics for the realm of private life. However, at least three factors are in play around gender roles in the Chinese and Taiwanese contexts. First, women seem, at least in the context of Hong Kong or Taiwan, naturally accepted in political and economic leadership roles. Second, women in the Chinese context, increasingly also in mainland China, have a high degree of economic independence and subsequently a high social self-esteem. Third, despite a stronger presence for women in economic life now compared to the past, Chinese women seem more conditioned by stereotypical roles: the authority-centered cultural context supports the dominance of males in public life and enhances traditional roles like that of female submission. The result of this somehow contradicting summary is that female submission and male machismo seem stronger—or at least less often questioned—in the Chinese context.

Spiritual growth challenges traditional gender-dependent behavior patterns that repress men's emotions. Jesus's role model includes caring, compassion, tenderness, and responsiveness to the needs of others, qualities typically neglected in societies that identify strength, courage, and the ability to bear pain with masculinity.[14] This integration of traditionally feminine qualities, as well as Jesus's liberated form of dealing with women at the fringes of society, inspires the faith community to broaden socially inherited gender roles. It is an important purpose of pastoral counseling and worship to provide a space where repressed emotions can be released and where such release is accepted as more than an embarrassing one-off weakness, but can become part of a more holistic, more inclusive and balanced person.

> Ah-Lam was in prison for indecent assault. He established a basic relationship with the chaplain and Christian workers and visibly

---

13. Clinebell, *Growth Counseling*, 20; and Clinebell, *Basic Types of Pastoral Care*, 37 and 166ff, with further recommended reading.

14. See Clinebell, *Basic Types of Pastoral Care*, 64.

treasured the visits and the support he got from them. This trust turned into an important lifeline when he experienced a severe crisis: his girlfriend visited him to say that she wanted to break up. He felt deeply depressed and told me that he had thought about suicide but didn't have the guts for it. As I listened to him, encouraging him to pour out his burdensome feelings, he expressed a deep sense of sadness and loneliness. Not only had he lost contact with his mother for more than twenty years, he also felt estranged from his father and had little contact with him. To make matters worse, he had recently heard that his father had been admitted to a mainland hospital. While sharing all his misery, he broke into tears and I held him tightly so that he could cry on my shoulder. In the subsequent visits we followed up on the feelings that he had previously expressed, and I noticed that the opportunity to cry had filled him with genuine gratitude and that the wound caused by the separation from his girlfriend was in a process of healing. Two months later, he received a visit from his father who came all the way down from Guangzhou, a journey of around four hours including a very busy border crossing. Ah–Lam had won the strength to directly communicate his sadness about the neglected relationship with his father, and he apologized to his father for the crime that he had committed. His father responded with tears, and it was the first time that he saw his father—a man from a region in China that is particularly famous for machismo—crying. This whole process was a cleansing experience for both father and son and a huge step in the emotional growth of Ah–Lam, and possibly that of his father as well.

Developing a culture where weakness, tenderness, and gentleness are cherished and where persons are inspired to express their vulnerable and emotional side is one of the important goals of the worshiping and caring community. I have always regarded it as a precious moment when inmates start to treasure this counterculture and shape it in their own way.

It was the worship service after the father of a twenty-four-year-old inmate had passed away. This young man, Ah-Ban, had already been in prison for around eight years—first in a juvenile prison, and after turning twenty-one years old, in adult prison. He was well integrated among his peers and had been baptized a year earlier. The service started in a subdued tone when one of the worship leaders, an inmate from the same work unit as Ah-Ban, informed the community about the death of a parishioner's father. I was deeply impressed by the emotional sensitivity and softness with which the whole group of worship leaders and the worshiping community responded to this sad event and gave comfort to Ah-Ban.

Such a prison congregation then turns into a place that provides basic, if limited, schooling in the love of God, love of the neighbor, and love of oneself. Learning about loving God and loving other persons does not start with telling a person that they should love more and how they should do it. Instead, it starts with the experience of being loved and with the process of learning to integrate emotions that emerge from loving relationships. This process converges with a psychological therapy that is open to spiritual change. In the words of Erich Fromm, a Jewish philosopher and psychoanalyst, "Analytic therapy is essentially an attempt to help the patient gain or regain his capacity for love. If this aim is not fulfilled, nothing but surface changes can be accomplished."[15] If a faith-based community can inspire persons to gain—or regain—their capacity for love and can lead them to unclog their channels to give and receive love, then true transformation and healing happened.

Bibliographical Notes

My descriptions give strong emphasis to basic *spiritual dimensions and existential anxieties* that become particularly pressing in times of crisis. An inspiring discussion of issues of existential anxiety and guilt in pastoral counseling is offered in chapters 5 and 6 of Howard Clinebell, *Basic Types of Pastoral Care & Counseling: Resources for the Ministry of Healing and Growth* (Nashville: Abingdon, 1984), 103–69. Theological writings that show particular awareness of the existentially precarious character of our life and of how they affect spirituality are, among others, Paul Tillich, *The Courage to Be* (New Haven: Yale University Press, 1952) and Dietrich Bonhoeffer, *Letters and Papers from Prison*, (New York: Macmillan, 1972). Recommended for a psychological perspective on these issues is Erich Fromm, *Psychoanalysis and Religion* (New Haven: Yale University Press, 1951).

Some theories on emotional, cognitive, and moral development provide useful background information to *spiritual development*. Most important is in this regard the theory developed by James W. Fowler. *Stages of Faith: The Psychology of Human Development*

---

15. Fromm, *Psychoanalysis and Religion*, 87.

and the Quest for Meaning (San Francisco: Harper & Row, 1981). A shorter version of his theory can be found in James W. Fowler, *Faith Development and Pastoral Care* (Theology and Pastoral Care Series, Philadelphia: Fortress, 1987). Fowler follows the theories of developmental psychology as formulated by Jean Piaget, Erik Erikson, or Lawrence Kohlberg.

Accounts of spiritual transformations that complement the account offered in this chapter can be found in the wide *testimonial literature*, some written by inmates, other material written by prison chaplains. Among the many testimonial books written I like to mention Henry Khoo's *Shoes Too Big: Continuing a Legacy of Hope and Transformation* (Singapore: Armour, 2007) that mainly traces the story of the Khoo family in their ministry to prisoners in Singapore but also offers testimonies of lives touched behind bars. Another one is Chiu Ming Li's *Revival behind Bars* (unpublished, available as draft at the time of writing this book) that similarly offers testimonies of prisoners in Singapore. See also Choan-Seng Song (editor), *Testimonies of Faith: Letters and Poems from Prison in Taiwan* (Geneva: World Alliance of Reformed Churches, 1984). Most prison ministry groups publish testimonies of transformations in their newsletter and anybody related to prison ministry will easily find access to such testimonies. A very different kind of testimony is Dietrich Bonhoeffer's *Letters and Papers from Prison*, edited by E. Bethge (New York: Macmillan, 1972). For an academic study on Christian testimonies as literary act of self-justification and self-explanation see Jamie S Scott, *Christians and Tyrants: The Prison Testimonies of Boethius, Thomas More and Dietrich Bonhoeffer* (New York: Lang, 1995).

On *issues of gender and male identity* in prison see Don Sabo, et al., *Prison Masculinities* (Philadelphia: Temple University Press, 2001).

On a *comparable description of spiritual changes* from U.S. inmates' perspective see Todd R. Clear et al., "The Value of Religion in Prison: An Inmate Perspective," *Journal of Contemporary Criminal Justice* 16/1 (2000) 53–74.

5

Christian Care for Prisoners: Chaplains and Lay Visitors

UP TO THIS POINT we have focused on prisons and prisoners: how they live, how they feel, how they turn to religious life, and how they change. With this chapter, our focus shifts to people *outside* prison who choose to visit those inside. We tell the story of how the ministry of visitation in the modern prison developed and what tensions it brings.

In this chapter we will address the following questions:

- How do prison visitors cope with a context that exerts such radical power and control over those living in it?
- What are the features of chaplains' and lay visitors' ministry?
- How do chaplains and lay visitors relate to each other?
- How do both chaplains and lay visitors relate to other agents involved in rehabilitation?

TWO FORMS OF CHRISTIAN INVOLVEMENT IN JUDICIAL AND PENAL MATTERS

Christians have often had a special care for prisoners and a deep concern for penal matters. Several factors have linked churches to prison affairs. First, imprisonment is an important topic—or, rather, a very concrete experience—in the stories of the Bible. The Old Testament makes several references to imprisonment: Joseph, most famously, was an innocent prisoner in Egypt; Jewish kings spent time in prison when in exile (2 Kings 25:27; Jer 52:31), and prophets were imprisoned (Jer 37:16). In the same way, the New Testament commonly mentions prison. Jesus was obviously a prisoner before his crucifixion, and many of the early apostles experienced imprisonment—and also miraculous salvation (Acts 5:17ff; 12:3ff; 16:23ff). The Apostle Paul wrote several of his letters from prison. Second, throughout Christian tradition there has been a belief in an intrinsic relation between faith and imprisonment, a belief that prisons are special places of revelation, and that prisoners have a particular relationship to God.[1] This idea arose in the last chapter when we described imprisonment as opportunity for spiritual transformation. (We will discuss this point again later in chapter 9.) Paul vividly describes how he experienced his imprisonment as an opportunity to grow spiritually closer to the suffering Christ (Phil 1:19ff; Col 1:24), and he gratefully realized how suffering through imprisonment advanced the gospel (Phil 1:12ff). The early church's visitation of prisoners (Phil 2:25; 2 Tim 1:16–18) happened therefore not simply as a charitable act but also for the dignity and spiritual value of the prisoners. Third, as the Western church from the fourth century on turned into an official state religion, it became a dominant pillar of society and naturally took over much of the responsibility for judicial and penal matters.

The Christian care for prisoners, for prisons as penal institutions, and for punishment as a judicial process—as seen through history—reveals a peculiar double-sidedness. On one hand, the church has, ever since becoming a dominant element of Occidental society, been a *constructing element*, participating in the establishment of a legal and judicial system that controls and exerts power. In this process, and as a central institution of society, the church lost its independence towards justice and punishment. It became increasingly part of a repressive social order and turned into an institution that exerted power. In medieval Europe's legal system of secular and ecclesial courts with overlapping and competing jurisdiction, church courts showed hardly more mercy than secular ones. Some of the most influential magistrates were bishops. With the emergence of canon law in the twelfth century, a code authored by the Roman Catholic Church, the church disposed of a strong justice system that was, in contrast to most secular law, uniform and valid across the whole European medieval world.

---

1. Griffith, *Fall of the Prison*, 138.

Canon law was not concerned only with ecclesial matters but extended to social and criminal matters as well. Christians were equally responsible for running prisons. Medieval prisons first developed from penitential cells established in monasteries for the punishment of delinquent monks.[2] But already from the eighth century on, the medieval community was responding to severe sins of secular delinquents with penitential confinement or incarceration. These early monastic prisons appeared to be more places of retreat than places of punishment, with workshops and heated rooms.[3] Still, what had started as short periods of penitential confinement later turned into extended periods of imprisonment or even imprisonment for life, in dark dungeons without light and warmth, where one found little consolation and spiritual support. The role of the church as a central institution in constructing society and social cohesion did not change with the Reformation, even though the churches abandoned much of their worldly authority and depended on the state to exert political and juridical power. The close alliance of both Luther and Calvin with the civil authorities made them regard church and state as natural allies in holding back lawlessness. The distinction between crime and sin remained blurred, and punishment was meted out indiscriminately for criminal, immoral, or heretical acts. The spirit of Calvinism and later Puritanism shaped attitudes toward justice and punishment for centuries to come and can be felt even today, particularly in some attitudes visible in the United States.[4] If humans are inherently evil, the theory goes, criminals represent simply an extreme of evil tendencies that all human beings share. Strict punishment, even the death penalty, is thus necessary both to protect the community and to deter its members from yielding to ubiquitous temptations. Puritan society understood a need to respond strictly to crime, lest it be seen as being indifferent to it. The strong influence of the talionic (i.e., retaliatory) aspects of Old Testament law is still noticeable in many repressive and vindictive attitudes towards punishment. The social-constructive side of Christian churches is further visible in the public executions of early modernity: clerics allied themselves with secular powers that exerted social control when they prayed with and for the convicted and encouraged them to publicly express repentance. Their role was integral to the spectacle of public execution and punishment.

2. McHugh, *Christian Faith and Criminal Justice*, 21; Duce, "Prison Chaplaincy," 219.

3. McHugh, *Christian Faith and Criminal Justice*, 21.

4. About the judicial and penal tradition influenced by American Puritanism see ibid., 32ff.

On the other hand, there is a tradition of Christians' using imprisonment as a *lens* through which *to see God*. They understand prison as a living parable that points to fundamental experiences in human existence—corporality, limitation, suffering, chains, hopelessness, and death. Prisons reflect and remind us of tensions that define and characterize our societies: the tension between sin and crime and the realization that whereas sin is more destructive and more far reaching than crime, still it is crime that is punished while sin usually remains without sanction; or the tension between law and justice and the realization that law is not neutral and can be unjust or to the disadvantage of some people.

This second tradition stands in critical tension with the social-constructive tradition and, historically, expressed itself in various forms of care, compassion, and solidarity with those in prison. From early times, Christians distributed food and clothes to those in prison. Although church leaders assumed a mostly constructive role in the dominant institutions of society, they occasionally maintained a critical distance to the social and political order and to the growing convergence of the secular and spiritual realms. They confronted the state and spoke out to protect the weak and powerless from the oppression of criminal sanction. Ambrose, bishop of Milan and one of the leaders of the church in the fourth century, for example, criticized a justice system that favored the economically strong and powerful.[5] He recounted how he was accused from within the church after melting down gold to ransom criminals held as prisoners.[6] Augustine, in a case involving his friend who was murdered, strictly opposed the imposition of the death penalty.[7] In medieval times, those who most strongly uphold the early church's commitment to caring for prisoners were small groups within the church; some, like the Trinitarians[8] or the Mercedarians, also called the Order of Captives, witnessed their Christian love by ransoming captives. Although this happened often enough in a crusading spirit to the benefit of Christians held in Muslim hands,[9] it was not limited to them and could occasionally mean that Trinitarian monks would of-

---

5. Ambrose, *Duties of the Clergy*, book 2, in *Nicene and Post-Nicene Fathers*, edited by Phillip Schaff and Jenry Wace (Buffalo: The Christian Literature Co., 1896), 10:59, chap. 21, quoted in McHugh, *Christian Faith and Criminal Justice*, 18.

6. Ambrose, *Duties of the Clergy*, book 2, in *Nicene and Post-Nicene Fathers* 10:136, chap. 23, quoted in McHugh, *Christian Faith and Criminal Justice*, 18.

7. Ibid., 18–19; similar Griffith, *Fall of the Prison*, 145.

8. Walsh, "Trinitarians," 294.

9. Vose, *Dominicans, Muslims, and Jews*, 209.

fer themselves in exchange for captives.[10] Typically, however, the church's ransoming was restricted to noblemen who were taken as prisoners of war. Charitable acts for prisoners were less visionary, simply aiming at the suffering individual. But were it not for the charity of caring Christians, many poor prisoners, who themselves bore much of the cost of their confinement and services during incarceration, would not have survived. The tradition of the Radical Reformation maintained a critical opposition to the secular justice system. Many Radical Reformers had themselves experienced imprisonment during times of persecution. They interpreted the letter of the Bible more literally and rejected Christians' participation in the coercive power of the legal system. Famous spiritual leaders, most notably John Bunyan and the Quaker leader George Fox, experienced persecution and imprisonment and used the opportunity to care for their fellow inmates.

These contrasting Christian attitudes still shape the church's prison ministry, and we find an ambiguity at work when considering the Christian response to crime and punishment. On one hand, churches all over the world are still important voices that shape the spirit of punishment and that play a central role in establishing and stabilizing society. But at the same time, some people still choose to enter prison and thus bridge the dualism of those inside and those outside.

The church is at work not only through different attitudes but also through different agents—both chaplains and lay visitors. At times they stand in tension, at times they go hand in hand; however, we should avoid identifying the different agents with different attitudes, as the next section shall show (for example, chaplains with a social-constructive, stabilizing role and lay visitors with a compassionate, caring role). Both chaplains and lay visitors choose in every moment of their ministry to ally themselves with one side or the other.

THE DEVELOPMENT OF THE PRISON CHAPLAIN'S MINISTRY

The roots of the prison chaplaincy lie in early medieval times and reflect all along the ambiguity of the chaplain's endeavor. The term *chaplain* comes from the Latin *cappella*, meaning "cape," and refers to Martin of Tours, who shared his own cape with the needy. After his death and canonization, his personal articles (not only his cape) turned into relics that were believed to

---

10. Norman, "Trinitarians," 985.

Christian Care for Prisoners: Chaplains and Lay Visitors

carry spiritual powers. Tragically, the first chaplains were those assigned in battle to carry the cape, originally a symbol of nonviolence and care for the poor, to help defeat the enemies through the special power of St. Martin.[11] The ambiguity of the chaplains' ministry remained when, in later medieval times, they assisted, consoled, and accompanied to the gallows criminals condemned to death, or when they were in charge both of offering Eucharist to repentant heretics and of working to convince others of their errors.

The more recent history of prison chaplains as full-time staff effectively starts with the prison-reform movement of the nineteenth century (see chapter 2). Chaplains, although often opposed to Christian prison reformers, were in fact beneficiaries of these reforms. Many prisons started to employ chaplains to encourage prisoners to penitence. Chaplains thus became the first members of prison staff responsible for rehabilitation. It was because of these reform movements that chaplains became a regular part of prisons in Western Europe, in the United States, and—through the British Commonwealth and the spread of Western judicial and penal ideas—in many African, Asian, and Latin American countries. At times chaplains even assumed the post of prison warden, as during one period in Engaland's Millbank Prison.[12] (This close link between chaplains and the prison administration has not ceased: today there are chaplains who have risen to the highest positions in correctional-services departments.[13]) Yet, despite an apparently central role for the chaplain as the person bringing about conversion in inmates' hearts, the reality was often different. Much of a traditional prison chaplain's ministry was not his own to determine. Prison officials used chaplains to assist in whatever the administration had designed as rehabilitation programs. Besides providing basic religious services, chaplains used much of their time to run prison libraries, to do social work, to assist inmates in their studies, to communicate with inmates' relatives, or to create programs for discharged inmates. Chaplains acted as symbols of traditional morality, to strengthen it and give it validity.

At the beginning of the twentieth century, religion moved from the center of penology to its periphery. The role of the chaplain, who until then was the main person in charge of rehabilitation, greatly declined when

---

11. Griffith, *Fall of the Prison*, 157.

12. Pace, *Christian's Guide*, 60.

13. For example, the former president of the International Prison Chaplains' Association, Reverend Pierre Allard served at the same time as an assistant commissioner of the Correctional Service of Canada.

under the treatment model, other professional groups took center stage in rehabilitation. When the prison school was taken over by trained educators, family contacts were handled by social workers and libraries staffed by trained librarians, the chaplain was reduced to assisting other professional groups in the treatment of offenders or simply to a religious and spiritual role. As Sanford Bates, the first director of the Federal Bureau of Prisons in the United States in 1936 thought: "there was nothing else but religion for the chaplain to busy himself about, and that could be done on Sunday in an hour or two."[14]

However, the reduced role of the chaplain turned out to be a blessing in disguise. Freed from playing a central role in rehabilitation, chaplains redefined their presence in prison. Now they could focus on their role as spiritual guides and counselors, knowing that qualified professionals were taking up their previously borne responsibilities for the miscellaneous prison programs. The growing plurality of professionals involved in prisoner care resulted in positive competition between secular and spiritual forms of healing, and the changes in the institutional role of the chaplain turned into an opportunity to develop pastoral counseling. We can observe three stages in this process. In the first half of the twentieth century, most chaplains emphasized the preaching and teaching of God's Word. Counseling was but a special and individualized form of proclamation that culminated and succeeded in the individual surrendering and turning to Christ. Later, counseling became the main emphasis in a chaplain's ministry, and many chaplains started to understand themselves in close proximity to psychology. They deepened their expertise through Clinical Pastoral Education (CPE) or other counseling courses, and prison chaplains' associations set quality standards for government-supported chaplaincies. More recently, pastoral counseling has gained more spiritual independence from psychology. It is now understood as one element in the broader context of pastoral care and as one of the core elements of what Christian ministry is supposed to do: lead people into a spiritual process of transformation and growth.

Despite the reduced institutional importance of prison chaplains under the treatment model, the chaplaincy further evolved as institution throughout the century. By the middle of the 1900s, most prisons in the West ran religious programs and employed prison chaplains. In the 1960s, an important driving force in the United States was the *prisoner-rights movement*, which demanded religious services for a wider variety

---

14. Sanford Bates, quoted in Shaw, *Chaplains to the Imprisoned*, 32.

of religious groups. Traditionally only priests from mainstream Protestant and Roman Catholic churches had been admitted. When prisoners from religious minorities challenged such arrangements through legal means, the administration started to employ chaplains of other faiths or at least invited representatives from other faith groups to care for religious groups beyond traditional mainstream Christianity. The same development happened in other countries as well.

FORMS OF CHAPLAIN'S MINISTRY: EMPLOYED AND HONORARY CHAPLAINS

At present, chaplains' care for prisoners takes different forms. On the one hand, most Western European and North American countries, and also many in Africa, continue to *employ* chaplains. Chaplains employed by the prison department are, at times, expected to assist officers on request and may even be called as reservists in the event of mutiny. They also assume various intradepartmental responsibilities, attending ceremonies and social events, providing pastoral services to prison staff, and participating in departmental committees. An important duty of official chaplains in many countries is to encourage and oversee the activities of various religious groups. This means that many chaplains are less involved in their own pastoral activities than in organizing and coordinating others' pastoral activities and religious programs. Prison chaplains in the United States report, however, that despite being employed by the prison and thus being part of the institution, they still spend most of their time counseling and regard this as their most important activity.[15]

Official chaplains face the difficult task of caring for inmates while maintaining a loyal but critical attitude toward their employers. Having chaplains employed by the prison department (and thus regarding them as staff members) has led to continual frustration about the effectiveness of this approach. This includes frustrated inmates, who think that the chaplain has easy and direct access to the highest levels of management and whose expectations are correspondingly high; likewise, there are frustrated chaplains, who despite a relatively high formal standing are effectively powerless

---

15. Sundt et al., "The Role of the Prison Chaplain," 67. The study, based on a widely distributed questionnaire sent to prison chaplains in the US, lists the following activities in decreasing order of frequency: counseling inmates, coordinating religious programs, supervising volunteers, conducting religious services, and providing religious education.

and play only a marginal role in institutions where safety and financial concerns are the priority. Sometimes both inmates and the wider public reject official chaplains as biased, as bound by the employing institution, or as collaborators in a context of failed penal policies. Overall, however, frustrations and public perception largely depend on (a) the performance and attitude of the individual chaplain and (b) the attitude of the authorities—whether they support the chaplain in maintaining an independent position, or whether they try to control and define his or her ministry.

On the other hand, there is an increasing trend towards *itinerant, visiting* or *honorary* chaplains. These chaplains are not on the payroll of the prison department but are supported in their ministry by a church or religious group. For their admission as chaplain, they go through special screening and are required to accept the overriding rules of the prison department; in exchange, they receive a status that usually gives them free access to all inmates. Honorary chaplains are exempt from departmental responsibilities and can focus more solely on their ministry. They may have less influence on penal policy, penal programs, or even individual cases, but they have higher institutional and spiritual freedom. They may feel freer to assume a critical role and, not being on the payroll, they may be more easily accepted by inmates as genuine in their care. Again, much depends on chaplains' attitudes and on the attitude of the authorities toward them. There are just as many honorary chaplains, apparently free from institutional bonds, who crave institutional recognition and integration, as there are departmental chaplains with a deep commitment for the prisoners and a critical and prophetic attitude toward the prison administration.

In Hong Kong, chaplains were from the very beginning part of prison life. The chaplain was required to attend every religious service in prison and was expected to pray with inmates, preach to them, and visit them in their cells. They also had to tender assistance to all those under sentence of death. The chaplains served on a voluntary basis until 1974 when the prison department integrated one Roman Catholic priest as a prison chaplain into its regular staff. At present, this head chaplain leads a team of around thirty honorary chaplains, most of whom only serve a small part of their workweek in prison ministry. Chaplains traditionally belonged to the Church of England or the Roman Catholic Church, but since the late 1990s, pastors from other Christian churches have also been appointed. There are still no chaplains from non-Christian faiths.

Christian Care for Prisoners: Chaplains and Lay Visitors

In the literature about prisons one will find plenty of *critical comments* about chaplains. Traditionally, it was seen as ignoble to serve among prisoners; the opinion was that "any needy priest of damaged character was . . . good enough to minister among rogues."[16] A chaplain's image is also linked to the unique position of standing between inmates and prison management, with both sides often finding it hard to accept the values that a chaplain represents. The administration regards the chaplain as naïve: easily conned by smart inmates, generally too soft, and not seeing the whole picture. Frontline officers see the inmates around the clock and know things the chaplain does not: how prisoners who talk sweetly and piously before the chaplain turn around and forget their Christian morality when the chaplain leaves the prison. Inmates, on the other hand, may see the chaplain as a stooge of the warden and vent their anger on this weakest and most easily accessible link of the prison structure. In contexts where chaplains are perceived as part of the prison staff, they have even been caught in physical attacks.[17] The way chaplains respond to the ambiguity inherent in their role may further affect their image. For any chaplain, it can be painfully contradictory to share the good news of Jesus Christ in an environment that he or she has to support, at least formally, while constantly witnessing how it causes harm. Many chaplains struggle with the mission of standing up for values of love and forgiveness in a context of bitterness and hatred. They quickly lose the strength to insist on discovering power in weakness in a context where power is so unevenly distributed.

TENSIONS IN THE CHAPLAIN'S MINISTRY

Chaplains, whether employed or voluntary, are caught in several dilemmas: Should the chaplain focus solely on caring for the neediest inmates? Or is the chaplain's responsibility rather to the prison staff? Should chaplains focus on positively influencing their attitudes, hoping that if they do so, then the inmates will reap long-term benefits from atmospheric changes in prison? Or should chaplains instead concentrate on senior managers who decide important administrative policies, in which case chaplains risk being seen as too friendly with management and, subsequently, losing credibility with the inmates? Different chaplains may come up with different answers. Some communicate more easily with management, who are usually closer

---

16. Clay, *Prison Chaplain*, 101, quoted in Pace, *Christian's Guide*, 75.
17. Shaw, *Chaplains to the Imprisoned*, 99.

to their own social position; others feel more at ease with inmates. Obviously, there is a need to find the right balance between caring for inmates and pleasing the staff. However, with many others, I am convinced that ultimately the allegiance of the prison chaplain is with the inmates, for two reasons.[18] First, and pragmatically, the inmates have no other place to go for spiritual guidance, while prison employees have the opportunity to find other counsel. Second, and theologically, the Christian faith perspective is linked to a perspective of powerlessness. God chose to reveal himself on the cross, in the abyss of powerlessness. In a situation where power is distributed as unevenly as it is in prison, Christians naturally stand with the powerless. We will return to the topic of this partiality later, in chapter 9. Taking prison ministry seriously will always bring the chaplain into tension with the administration. Too different are the goals and the value frameworks of the two sides. Chaplains need at times to assume a prophetic and advocacy role, although much patience and wisdom is required not to overuse this. Chaplains must always be aware that somebody else is running the place, and that experiencing limitations will ultimately bring them closer to the inmates.

One may wonder why religiously neutral governments still maintain the office of the chaplaincy: Why is religious care for prisoners not simply left to religious volunteers? The prima facie reason for having chaplains is that religion is a basic human right, guaranteed even during imprisonment. Prisons are obliged by international law to give prisoners free access to representatives of their faiths.[19] Employing official chaplains from major faith groups helps the prison administration avoid the spiritual anarchy of each individual claiming his or her own clergy or spiritual director.[20] The employed chaplain is equipped with the necessary authority to help the prison administration filter and select from the various religious groups who seek to work in prison. Probably a more important reason is that the presence and official inclusion of chaplains lends some legitimacy to the authorities. The prison administration welcomes chaplains because they have

---

18. See for instance Schilder, *Inside the Fence*, 70–71.

19. The basic rights of prisoners are laid down in several international instruments, most important the "Standard Minimum Rules for the Treatment of Prisoners," regarding religion particularly Art. 41; further the "Convention against Torture and Other Cruel, Inhuman or Degrading Treatment or Punishment," the "Body of Principles for the Protection of All Persons under Any Form of Detention or Imprisonment," and the "Basic Principles for the Treatment of Prisoners."

20. With Shaw, *Chaplains to the Imprisoned*, 11.

a pacifying function. They make inmates feel better and ease tensions.[21] Where chaplains reject such a narrow and purely spiritual role the prison management will swiftly remind them of their core duties and their spiritual responsibilities.

Chaplains usually understand their ministry in *inclusive* terms. This applies particularly to chaplains employed by the government, who have an official responsibility to care for members of various religious groups beyond their own spiritual affiliation. But it also applies to honorary chaplains, although they are to a higher degree indebted to their sponsoring church or religious organization. In prison, employed and honorary chaplains should show restraint and respect in their relation to people of other faiths, knowing that not all faith groups have the privilege of having their own chaplains. Respect towards people of other faiths and towards chaplains representing those faiths is an expression of spiritual humility and a very practical example of what Christian love means.

CARE FOR PRISONERS AS A LAY MINISTRY OF THE CHURCH

Missionary outreach to those in prison has long been a responsibility of the Christian community as a whole. In the late eighteenth century, a significantly new period began. By then, various missionary and evangelistic associations emerged that regarded mission not as something to be left to clerics and specialists but as something for every individual Christian.[22] This voluntarist spirit had a strong impact on the care for those in prison. The eighteenth-century revival movement, led by the Wesley brothers, already included a deep spiritual and pastoral concern for those in prison that found expression in visitation programs. From the very beginning, women played a prominent role, one of the earliest being *Sarah Peters*, who died of jail fever (typhus) only one month after she started her visits. From the nineteenth century on, lay groups of Quakers organized activities within prisons, setting up committees and arranging regular schedules for visits. Elizabeth Fry established the *Association for the Improvement of the Female Prisoners* (1817), which inspired numerous ladies' prison associations and female visiting groups. Other lay organizations caring for

---

21. Pattison, *Pastoral Care and Liberation Theology*, 201. The whole of Chapter 14 offers an in-depth discussion of the commonly conservative role of chaplains.

22. More about this development in Bosch, *Transforming Mission*, 327ff.

prisoners followed, among them the *Salvation Army* (founded in 1865) and the *Volunteers Prison League*, founded 1896 by Maud Ballington Booth, the daughter-in-law of the founding couple of the Salvation Army. Both groups visited prisons to preach the gospel; they worked with inmate families and helped those released from prison.

Important features of later lay- or volunteer-based prison ministry are already visible at this stage. These early female visitors trusted that a unique combination of personal contact and the power of faith should bring about transformation. They worked on a one-to-one basis, allowing lasting relationships to grow, and they invited the released inmates to keep close bonds with the visitors and to fall back on the advice and patronage of the visitor whenever needed. The relationship of the visitor and inmate or ex-inmate was typically modeled on that of the female head of a large household and the servants. Visitors provided a role model, giving direction to the inmate.[23] At the same time, they moved beyond individual care and actively tried to influence senior prison officials to implement improvements while diplomatically maintaining a distance from the formal prison hierarchy.

Since then, further groups have emerged. Besides Christian lay groups, they include groups of other religious origins, and secular or not explicitly Christian groups, like the National Association of Official Prison Visitors and Prisoners' Friends Association.

A particularly strong *growth in lay-based prison ministry* can be observed since the 1960s. Several factors caused this growth: First, cultural changes led to an overall shift from a clergy-based to a more lay-based church life. Second, pentecostal spirituality has since the 1960s strongly influenced historical and traditional churches and has led to their rediscovery of lay ministry. This shift to a more participatory church is evident in pronouncements of all the historical mainline churches.[24] Third, many prison-ministry initiatives are linked to revivalist Christian traditions, both evangelical and pentecostal, which are low-church movements and have always laid great emphasis on lay ministry. Finally, the past fifty years have seen a revival in missionary activities. Traditional churches had, in contrast to revivalist churches, often cared little about mission. Since the 1960s, they are rediscovering it as a core element of Christian existence, realizing that

---

23. Zedner, "Wayward Sisters," 300.

24. For the Roman Catholic Church see the Documents of the Second Vatican Council, especially the Decree *Apostolicam Actuositatem*. On Protestant and Orthodox side, the World Council of Churches has adopted the rule of a quota of at least 40 percent lay delegates in all their committees and assemblies.

pagans are no more the faraway others, and that a mission-minded church can find plenty of missionary opportunities in the traditional heartland of Christianity. They find prison ministry an obvious opportunity for missionary outreach.

Many local prison-ministry initiatives have formed national prison-ministry associations, and these in turn have linked together in the Prison Fellowship International (PFI), an international nongovernmnetal organization (NGO) that now brings together national ministries from around 110 countries. The prison ministries that gather under the umbrella of PFI have always been strongly driven by volunteers from various walks of life but most prominently from two different backgrounds. On the one hand, there are former offenders who became Christians while in prison and who continue to care for those among whom they used to live. On the other hand, there are businesspeople who underneath their success in the world, realize that Christian existence calls them to the radical other side of society.

In Hong Kong, a proper lay-based prison ministry started in the early 1970s when a group of theology students visited juvenile inmates in the Sha Tsui Detention Centre. This ministry led in 1978 to the foundation of the Hong Kong Christian Kun Sun Association, a group dedicated to caring for those in prison. Since then, others have followed, among them Buddhist groups and those without a specific religious affiliation, like the Prisoners' Friends Association. The partnership between the various NGOs and the Correctional Services Department has steadily grown since then.

From the very beginning of lay-based prison ministry, the volunteers caring for prisoners encountered *conflicts* with prison chaplains, as did Elizabeth Fry and the group of visitors she led. An animosity between chaplains and Christian volunteers has, in some places, remained to this day and still has to do with competition and mutual suspicion. Both sides can claim a deeper understanding of the inmate and higher effectiveness in the reform of prisoners. The chaplain usually argues that he or she is more constantly in contact with the inmates and thus has a deeper knowledge of the institution. The volunteers counter that their approach is unbiased and not driven by institutional constraints. But the animosity may have more to do with differences in theology and spirituality: Chaplains usually come from more inclusive churches while volunteer groups often stem from revivalist and partly more exclusivist traditions. The chaplains' inclusive and ecumenical attitudes often contradict the evangelistic commitment of many volunteer groups. Volunteers find it hard to understand the chaplain's role of being a religious coordinator and broker for religious programs of other faith groups. Some inmates use the dichotomy between chaplains and volunteers for their own benefit and try to play one side against the other and thus exacerbate the tension.

The challenge for today is to find a balance and means of cooperation between the historical and institutional ministry of the church in prison and the more revivalist prison-volunteer movement. Any competition between the two sides, both of which represent in one form or other the continuous care of Jesus Christ for those in prison, affects the unity of the body of Christ and harms the Christian witness. Obviously, both sides can benefit from each other: Through the presence of volunteer groups, the ministry of the chaplain is revived, and his or her solitary ministry turns into a ministry of the whole community. Volunteer participation allows chaplains to reach many more inmates than they ever could alone. Prison ministry understood as ministry of the whole community has better resources to reach out not only to the inmates but also to their families. An example of this outreach is the Angel Tree project where volunteers deliver Christmas presents to prisoners' children. On the other hand, volunteers can benefit from the chaplain's deeper understanding of the structures and routines of the prison and from his or her wider awareness of the needs of inmates. The humility necessary for such mutual recognition is the best testimony of what it means to be transformed through Christ.

APPROACHING A NEW PERIOD: CHRISTIANS AND PRISONS TODAY

At the beginning of the twenty-first century, there is a revival of *faith-based initiatives* for rehabilitation of criminal offenders and for persons with mental health problems or histories of substance abuse. A very interesting development is the emergence of faith-based prisons or faith-based prison units.[25] This initiative evolved in Brazil where since the 1970s the prison in the Humaitá district of Rio de Janeiro introduced principles of spirituality and faith. The success of the project, also known as APAC (Association for the Protection and Assistance of the Convicted), had a deep impact on churches and judiciaries far beyond Brazil and led 1976 to the Kairos initiative in the United States. Today we find similar initiatives not only in Latin

---

25. A comprehensive and independent description of projects within this development can be found in Burnside et al., *My Brother's Keeper*.

America and the United States but also in Europe, Asia (Singapore), and Oceania (Australia and New Zealand). The first faith-based prison unit of Europe opened in February 1997 in HMP The Verne in Dorset. Faith-based prisons can be realized in various forms, as halfway houses, as rehabilitation centers for young offenders, or as whole prison or as prison units. They have in common that they are entrusted to a religious group that leads the inmates through a spiritual and life discipline. Non-Christian religious groups have equally begun to develop care programs for people in prison. They offer meditation courses or other faith-based improvement programs, among them the Buddhist Vipassana meditation, a ten-day intensive silent-meditation retreat successfully organized in prisons all over the world.

Faith-based programs for and with prisoners show broad variety depending on the different contextual needs, the interests of those involved, and the abilities of supporting volunteer groups. Some initiatives take their inspiration from the tradition of the therapeutic community or from self-help groups like Alcoholics Anonymous. All the projects of faith-based prisons, therapeutic communities, and self-help groups, mostly run by volunteers, are promising and effective when holistically including different levels of transformation:

- *Spiritual* transformation, or growth in faith and trust: surrender to God;
- *Cognitive* transformation, or changes in ways of thinking, shifts in perception, overcoming negative perceptions and low self-esteem;
- *Emotional* transformation, or growing awareness of own and others' feelings and improving ability to express emotions appropriately;
- *Moral* transformation, or the establishing of a firm, responsible, and nonexploitative moral code;
- *Relational* transformation, or growth in interpersonal skills;
- *Behavioral* transformation, or changes in communicative patterns, the use of stimulants, and eating habits;
- *Educational*, *vocational* and *life-skill* training, or preparing for a life without crime, addiction, or other harmful behavior.

Faith-based initiatives stress the healing effect of a fellowship or (residential) community approach to harmful behavior. *Community* is both context and method in this change process.[26] Healing and learning

26. De Leon, *Therapeutic Community*, 85.

occur communally, through therapeutic relationships with peers in similar situations when individuals learn that they can be helpful to others, and that they are not alone with their problems.[27] The community approach commonly provides a family-style setting that corrects injuries from past family experiences.[28] Ex-offenders, often former addicts, play an important role as peer-counselors and role models. Lay participation in these programs is crucial, as they rely on a diversity of skills difficult to provide through institutional means but easily found in a religious community. Volunteer participation allows the achievement of a holistic width within these programs.

Despite widespread excitement about these developments, one should caution against too much enthusiasm. The history of imprisonment and of Christian participation in the care for prisoners amply shows how good intentions can have bad outcomes, and how the coercive context of prisons has undermined many efforts for the rehabilitation and transformation of inmates.

Bibliographical Notes

Since the 1980s, the *link between religion and law* and the impact of religious factors on law and criminal punishment has received more scholarly attention. Important contributions come from Harold J. Berman and from Michael W. McConnell. See Berman, *Faith and Order: The Reconciliation of Law and Religion* (Emory University Studies in Law and Religion 3, Atlanta: Scholars, 1993); and McConnell, Michael et al., *Christian Perspectives on Legal Thought* (New Haven: Yale University Press, 2001), a collection of essays. It is also in this context that the *Journal of Law and Religion* was founded.

The *Christian contributions to the evolution of penology and criminal law* are well described in Gerald Austin McHugh, *Christian Faith and Criminal Justice: Toward a Christian Response to Crime and Punishment* (New York, Paulist, 1978). McHugh reaffirms Christians' responsibility to confront contemporary penal practices. Lee Griffith's *The Fall of the Prison: Biblical Perspectives*

---

27. See the discussion of the impact that group psychotherapy has on the therapeutic community in Manning, *The Therapeutic Community Movement*, 66–67.

28. See De Leon, *Therapeutic Community*, 26ff for further definitions, conceptions, and theories of the therapeutic community.

on Prison Abolition (Grand Rapids: Eerdmans, 1993) provides many insights about churches' participation in prison and justice. His history offers interesting information about the dissident and prophetic tradition of the church. His overall aim is, as the title suggests, reminding the church of Jesus's prophecy that the captives shall be set free. A broad variety of references to the history of Christian involvement in law and punishment can be found in many chaplains' or prison-ministry handbooks.

More particularly on the *development of the chaplaincy* see the *Journal of Offender Rehabilitation* (Vol 35, Numbers 3/4, 2002). The whole volume is dedicated to the topic of *Religion, the Community, and the Rehabilitation of Criminal Offenders*. Among the articles see especially Jody L. Sundt et al., "The Role of the Prison Chaplain in Rehabilitation," 59–86, which offers a concise description of the role of the prison chaplain during different periods in the twentieth century; see also Jody L. Sundt and Francis T. Cullen, "The Role of the Contemporary Prison Chaplain," *Prison Journal*, 78/2 (1998) 271–98. On the relationship of Christian prison chaplains in Great Britain and the United States to inmates of other religious faiths see James A. Beckford and Sophie Gilliat, *Religion in Prison: Equal Rites in a Multi-Faith Society* (Cambridge: Cambridge University Press, 1998).

On the different aspects of the *ministry of the chaplain* and the roles, challenges, and difficulties of the chaplain's ministry see David M. Schilder, *Inside the Fence: A Handbook for Those in Prison Ministry* (New York: Society of St. Paul, 1999). His view of the prison chaplain is rather traditional and hierarchical, but he covers in a holistic manner all the different areas of chaplains' responsibility. Another good account is Richard D. Shaw, *Chaplains to the Imprisoned: Sharing Life with the Incarcerated* (New York: Haworth, 1995), which gathers the views of prison chaplains in the United States through a questionnaire. Shaw's book offers a good discussion of diverging roles of prison chaplains, tensions in their ministry, and difficulties with inmates or with prison administration. More recently, the book by Dennis W. Pierce, *Prison Ministry: Hope behind the Wall* (Binghamton, NY: Haworth Pastoral, 2006) shows contextual sensitivity in describing the punitive trends in the United States. Pierce describes the needs that chaplains can fulfill, particularly the creation of niches that help inmates to cope with their incarceration, and that give them a sense of belonging.

On the *historical background of the emerging voluntary and lay-based ministry* and on the missiological significance of lay-based ministry see David Bosch, *Transforming Mission: Paradigm Shifts* in *Theology of Mission* (Maryknoll, NY: Orbis, 1991), 327–34; 467–74; Ralph D. Winter, "The Two Structures of God's Redemptive Mission," in: Ralph D. Winter and Steven C. Hawthorne (eds.), *Perspectives of the World Christian Movement: A Reader* (3rd ed. William Carey Library, Pasadena California 1999), 220–30; Andrew F. Walls, "Missionary Societies and the Fortunate Subversion of the Church," in Winter and Hawthorne, *Perspectives*, 231–40.

On *faith-based prisons*, Jonathan Burnside et al., *My Brother's Keeper: Faith-Based Units in Prisons* (Cullompton, Devon: Wilan, 2005) offers precious insights. The book is particularly valuable as it is based on a scientific study commissioned by the British Home Office to assess faith-based prisons. The book places this assessment in a broader context by telling the story of the origins and developments of these units. The study does not gloss over the failures of some projects, as with the Kairos-APAC project in England and underlines what can be learned from them: the need of close monitoring and supporting of ex-offenders and of transparency in communication and in finances, as well as the importance of a strong and well-prepared local volunteer base. The overall positive conclusions serve as precious basis for future developments of faith-based prisons in other parts of the world.

On the *therapeutic-community movement* that is part of the background of faith-based initiatives see George De Leon, *The Therapeutic Community: Theory, Model, and Method*, (New York: Springer, 2000). De Leon's comprehensive resource book presents the history, conceptual framework, and practice of the therapeutic community as a self-help community. He emphasizes the use of the therapeutic community approach particularly in the treatment of addictions. Nick Manning, *The Therapeutic Community Movement: Charisma and Routinization* (International Library of Group Psychotherapy and Group Process, London: Routledge, 1989), tells the story of therapeutic communities in the field of psychiatric care and underlines the importance of group experiences as medium of change. He neglects, however, communal religious groups that are important precursors of the movement. On the restorative-justice and community-justice movement, see Gordon Bazemore and Mara Schiff (eds.), *Restorative Community Justice: Repairing Harm and Transforming Communities* (Cincinnati: Anderson, 2001).

6

A Communication Guide to the Visiting Ministry

WHAT DO PRISON CHAPLAINS or lay visitors actually do when they visit those in prison? And what do they need to learn to become effective prison visitors? The following two chapters introduce practical aspects of prison ministry, a kind of handbook of how to do it. Chapter 6 focuses on attitudes and communicative acts of visitors, and chapter 7 turns to the question of how inmates are affected by the context of inequality and the roles that visitors assume. For this discussion, we largely abandon the distinction between chaplains and lay visitors. The difference in their roles is gradual, not categorical, and most of what follows (if not specially designated) applies equally to both, so we will use the general term *visitor*.

Visitors have an immediate and important impact on spiritual life in prison. They are *a lifeline* to the outside world, representing crucial ties to outside society that help mitigate the pain of imprisonment. The chance to talk to somebody from outside offers relief and reduces the strong sense of being forgotten by society. Visitors *normalize* the prison experience and break through inmates' sense of isolation. They add skill, knowledge, and variety to church activities in prison. They act *as role models* through their faith life, through their ministry, and through their communicative behavior. They give important *support* and help *reinforce changes* that are happening. When inmates see how faith has impacted the lives of visitors, they may be inspired and receive guidance. In the encounter with visitors, the inmates have a chance to verify and adjust their transformations and to receive feedback from them. Visiting church groups allow inmates to participate in a fellowship from outside. Finally, visitors *create* a sense of *social attachment* and provide a setting for new social learning[1] and thus have an impact on rehabilitation. Visitors connect inmates with constructive and life-affirming sources of behavior, and bring motivation to change.

The chapter considers the following questions:

- What personal and spiritual qualifications do prison visitors need for their ministry?
- What are important tools of counseling and pastoral care that visitors should understand?
- What are distinctive forms of visiting and communicating with inmates? What purpose(s) do they have?

THE STARTING POINT: BEING, NOT DOING

If one asks about a starting point for prison ministry it is this: *the personal readiness of every visitor not to transform but to be transformed.* A prison visitor should ask if he or she is ready to receive rather than to give, to change rather than cause others to change, to be touched rather than to touch others, to be challenged in what one thinks was right and wrong rather than to challenge others. Entering prison with such an attitude ensures that the visit will *also* have an impact on those in prison.

This first and most basic precondition for any prison visitor is both difficult and easy at once. It is *difficult* because it goes against natural inclinations. We have seen how many volunteers in the Prison Fellowship movement are entrepreneurs or businesspeople; many visitors come from backgrounds where achievements and goals count. It is natural that they maintain a similar achievement-oriented attitude of active service when ministering to those in prison. It is remarkable that people offer their precious free time, often a weekend afternoon—or possibly a whole day, including the long journey to remote prisons—to inmates whom they at first hardly know. Some even take a day off work. Not surprisingly, visitors expect to see a return on their investment; they expect results from their visit. Still, visitors need to learn that their encounter may not yield the

---

1. See above, chap. 3.

results they expect upon entering the prison. The outcome of relationships with inmates is often vague, not as visitors would have liked, and visitors do not know how their presence and care has been received.

However, it is also easy, at least once visiting has started. The most common feeling visitors express when leaving the prison is joy and gratefulness for what they have received, rather than pride about what they were able to give. Visitors realize that the warmth of the inmates' reception, the joy of the joint fellowship, and the depth of the sharing and the mutual trust go far beyond what a visitor imagined to give. The mutuality of the encounter and the experience of being on a joint spiritual pilgrimage transcend the purpose-driven mindset that many visitors bring into prison.

If we stress that the visitors themselves need to be ready to be changed and to experience rather than to cause spiritual transformation, the visit can happen as much for the sake of the visitor as for the sake of the inmates. Such an approach is, first and most directly, a *pastoral* necessity: a visitor who wants to bring change without accepting his or her own need for change opens a gap that tangibly prejudges the inmate as the one in need of change. It also projects an image onto the inmate that forecloses any room for surprise about who he or she truly is.

Second, it is a necessity related to the communal character of the church. We could call it an *ecclesiological* necessity because its mutuality is what distinguishes those engaged in Christian fellowship from other groups that aim at rehabilitation. The awareness of being of the same quality and nothing better, part of a fellowship of sinners, creates potential for growth in visitors that an attitude of "service here, transformation there" would spoil.

Humility is, third, a *missiological* necessity or a necessity related to the mission of the church: a one-sided encounter undermines the fellowship and togetherness that is the basis for a genuine missionary encounter. Inmates may feel turned into objects of the missionary, evangelistic, or spiritual agenda of the visitor and turn away, because they reject the imposed passive position of being only recipient. This is in both mission and pastoral care generally wrong; it is worse in prison, where inmates are already overwhelmed by feelings of uselessness and involuntary passivity in most aspects of life. Instead of offering empowerment, it reinforces an attitude of dependence.

Finally humility is a *theological* necessity because it reflects Christ's attitude of living among men and women in brokenness. This is what theological language usually describes as *kenosis*, referring to Phil 2:5–11, the process of self-humiliation and the attitude of radical humility, in which Christ emptied himself of all divine qualities to become fully human. This attitude affected the way he related to the people around him, living among them as an equal, not pretending to be better. The genuine character of this attitude is something that we can only strive for: To follow Christ in his process of self-humiliation and to truly give up the feeling of being spiritually, psychologically, or morally superior to those we visit is a challenging task for every Christian visitor.

Thus, engaging in prison ministry has first to do with the readiness to sail off on a journey of encounters where the destination is not known. Such an attitude is possibly the only significant precondition for starting to visit those in prison because it prevents visitors from overestimating their role. The visiting ministry in prison is important, but its function is only auxiliary to the initiatives that arise from inmates' own spiritual lives. Any Christian or other religious program that is too much concerned with its own goals and already knows where it wants to lead the inmates is destined to fail.

Pastoral care requires becoming a particular kind of person, rather than simply applying certain pastoral techniques. Pastoral care, in prison or elsewhere, is less an activity that reaches certain goals than a status of being. The motto is, "It is not what you do, it is the person who does it."[2]

KEY QUALITIES OF A VISITOR: A HEALING PENTAGON

The focus on being rather than doing, on personality rather than techniques, on a specific attitude rather than a specific set of skills, is supported by developments in pastoral care and twentieth-century psychology. Characterizing both disciplines is the rediscovery that the most important qualities for a therapist or counselor are a set of attitudes that shape the encounter between counselor and client. Carl Rogers, founder of so-called client-centered therapy, taught that a therapist needs three basic qualities: genuineness, respect, and empathy.[3] Since then, this set of qualities has become known as the *therapeutic triad*. These are not confined to specialists but apply to all visiting ministries that aim at healing and restoring relations.

2. Pattison, *Critique of Pastoral Care*, 14.
3. Rogers, *On Becoming a Person*, 47–49.

I suggest a slight modification of this therapeutic triad in the context of prison ministry, adding humility and compassion to construct a *healing pentagon* for a visitor. These five qualities reflect the starting point we introduced above: All avoid orientation towards goals, problems, and solutions, while instead describing the psychological and spiritual maturity of the visiting person.[4] Together they prepare the ground for an open encounter, focused not only on dealing with inmates' problems but also on the visitor's role as a fellow pilgrim on a spiritual journey. The five key qualities are closely related and mutually define each other: genuineness without respect turns hostile, without empathy turns superficial, without compassion turns biased, and without humility turns arrogant.

The first key quality is *genuineness*, or, as Rogers called it, congruence. Genuineness is also described as honesty or authenticity; it refers to an attitude of openness that does not hide a person's true feelings, thoughts and values. A genuine person transmits the same message through verbal and nonverbal expressions, communicates feelings appropriately, is direct and approachable, and is spontaneous in communication and in the expression of feelings. In short, such a person simply tries to be him- or herself—as the expression goes, "comfortable in his or her own skin." Genuineness is not a learned skill but an expression of spiritual maturity, a person's trusting in his or her communicative expressions while accepting and being aware of his or her own limitations and weaknesses. When briefing first-time visitors to prison, I usually remind them to relate to inmates as they would to any other person in their congregation.

The second key quality of a visitor to prison is *unconditional positive regard*, also described as respect, acceptance, or nonpossessive warmth. It is an attitude characterized by love, affection, friendliness, and sensitivity. Respect finds expression in concrete acts of behavior like reliability, faithfulness, and an active interest in the lives of inmates. An unconditional positive regard has a strong theological basis (more about this in chapter 9): It is what Christians describe as *grace*, which does not need to be earned and is present before we are aware of it. It is the unconditional love through which God encounters humans in the person of Jesus Christ, and it is a *positive bias* that rediscovers a reflection of God's image in the most distorted person. Ideally, such a positive bias is a natural part of a visitor's inclination and his or her way of relating to other people. However, most people

---

4. On a discussion of key characteristics of counselors or pastors see also Clinebell, *Basic Types of Pastoral Care*, 416ff.

preparing for visits in prison, and even those who have made frequent visits, are naturally affected by the dominant prejudices about those in prison. Most visitors therefore need to actively counter the negative images surrounding those in prison and consciously establish an attitude of positive bias, a constant alertness that discovers where our natural or original bias towards those in prison affects us. A common question that inmates (if they dare) like to ask visitors is, how did you see us before coming here? This is an attempt to find out about society's prejudices and how they affect visitors. Such an attitude of positive bias is what sets visitors most strongly apart from many prison officials, who commonly have a negative image of inmates. At the same time, it is a powerful attitude for encouraging new life to grow. The love dispensed through unconditional positive regard is like water to a plant. It awakens life in a person in the same way that parental love awakens life within a child. The child encountered with negative bias will wither as his or her potential shrinks, and confidence wastes away; distrust becomes a self-fulfilling prophecy. In contrast, unconditional positive regard fills a person with power and strength. It affirms the importance and underlines the value of the other person.

The third key quality is *empathy*, the ability to feel what the other person feels, to see the world through the other person's eyes, and to assume the perspective of the other person. Empathy is a form of active listening that is sensitive to feelings and thoughts communicated through verbal and nonverbal means, and that suspends its own judgment. Even though there is an element of skill involved (more about this below), it is foremost an attitude, namely, of switching the focus from one's own person to the other, being concerned less about oneself and more about the other. It is an attitude that expresses appreciation for what it means to be in the other's situation, acceptance towards the other, and trust that the other's perspective is meaningful and worth being taken seriously.

The fourth key quality, *compassion*, is closely related to empathy. Compassion is an attitude of joining in the wounds of another person, becoming vulnerable together. The word comes from Latin and means "to bear with" or "to suffer with." In compassion, I do not simply try to assume the perspective of the other person, as in empathy; rather, the other

A Communication Guide to the Visiting Ministry

person's suffering becomes my own. The pain of the other touches on my own vulnerability and fragility and helps both sides of a caring encounter discover a deep togetherness in pain. This attitude relates to the image of the *wounded healer* introduced by Henri Nouwen.[5] The image encourages an understanding of suffering and failure as a way through which a deeper level of sensitivity and spiritual awareness grows. There, at the very point where I am touched by the despair or loneliness of the other person, it is no more just the other person, but I join him or her in the midst of it. I feel an affinity that turns pain into a joint experience of our mortality, our basic existential condition. It reflects the basic Christian pattern, where the world's pain becomes Christ's, and it hints at Christ's identification with the hungry and the thirsty, the naked and the stranger, the sick and the one in prison (Matt 25:35–36). There, at the point where they suffer, we see not them but Christ.

Finally, the fifth key quality of a visitor is *humility*. This quality is particularly important in the context of prison visits, for many inmates struggle with the gap between visitors' apparent successfulness and their own apparent failure. As a visitor, you must present yourself in humility, aware that indeed nothing makes you better than those you visit. The world may think of you as successful and full of achievement, and you might have enjoyed a different upbringing, received different gifts, or gone through a different spiritual transformation. But there is as much darkness in you, as much potential for destruction, as in anyone you visit. There is the same loneliness and alienation, the same despair and fragility in you as in the person you meet. Humility thus is an attitude expressed verbally and non-verbally that makes an inmate sense your awareness of failure, limits, and the destructive potential in your own life. Humility is necessary for theological and for psychological reasons: we should be humbled by the radical sin of our human nature and by the experience of how destructive potential has lain hidden in so many seemingly promising persons. Humility means accepting and enduring our weaknesses and our own tendencies to fail, for "if we cannot endure failing and being weak, and being seen to fail and be weak, we are not yet in a position to love and be loved."[6]

---

5. Nouwen, *Wounded Healer*. The image is often referred to in pastoral care literature and has been further developed by, among others, Campbell, *Rediscovering Pastoral Care*, chap. 4.

6. Maria Boulding, *Gateway to Hope* (1985), 9, quoted in Pattison, *Critique of Pastoral Care*, 168.

Visitors who enter prison with these five qualities will spontaneously have a deep impact on inmates.

THE BASIC ACT: A MINISTRY OF PRESENCE

After discussing the basic attitudes and key qualities for a visitor, we now look at the actual prison visit. What happens in a prison visit? How is it done? Prison ministry starts as a ministry of simple presence. A visit reflects the Christian belief that God has taken the first step in inviting everyone to receive his love.

The ministry of presence applies differently for chaplains than for other visitors. A chaplain shows presence by regularly visiting all wards of a prison, thus easily allowing every inmate to get in touch with him or her. Such ambulant ministry (walking through all parts of prison) is a simple and, at the same time, powerful form of communicating value and acceptance to every inmate. The chaplain thus acts as a *low-threshold counseling opportunity*. In the Hong Kong context (and in contrast to most chaplaincies in Europe or the United States), this ambulant form of presence is made easier through the lack of a chaplain's office. If chaplain and inmate need privacy for a more genuine encounter, they usually have to find a quiet corner away from the hustle and bustle of the workshop. I usually make a point of at least once per month visiting every ward of the two or three prisons that I serve. Such an approach is tiring and time consuming, leaving actually too little time for individual in-depth encounters. However, if the chaplain does not want to limit the focus to a small number of interested and spiritually active inmates (often the strongest in relationship building) but hopes to reach out to the prison population as a whole, such or a similar form of continuous presence is indispensable.

The ministry of presence is a ministry of *precounseling*.[7] The chaplain walking around in a workshop is a constant reminder of an opportunity, an invitation to engage in an encounter that might lead to spiritual change. The inmates may find no need for such an offer or may reject it as irrelevant, but they know that the offer is there, and they may turn to it as to something familiar when the need arises.

The ministry of presence is also a simple way of *introducing basic values* of the chaplain's ministry and, more broadly, the Christian faith. One of these values is to project a nonjudgmental image that regards conflicts—or

---

7. The term *pre-counseling* has been used by Hiltner, *Pastoral Counseling*, 128ff.

A Communication Guide to the Visiting Ministry

disciplinary and relational problems—not as moral but as pastoral problems. If, for example, the chaplain regularly encounters an inmate in disciplinary confinement, the chaplain should interpret this not simply as a lack of adjustment or as expression of a rebellious character but as pointing to a deeper unease that prevents an inmate from finding a more peaceful way to deal with the present reality of imprisonment. Projecting a nonjudgmental attitude is particularly important in prison, where people live already under society's judgment. Another value similarly introduced is an acceptance independent of results: The ministry of presence does not aim at effectiveness but trusts that presence is valuable in itself; changes may come, but they might happen in other ways and at other times than expected.

A slow and patient process of getting inmates acquainted with the values and work principles of a chaplain thus prepares the ground for the necessary trust to further develop the relationship. If the chaplain is perceived as judgmental and coercive, or if the counseling offered appears threatening, the inmate will be less likely to turn to the chaplain for help. The chaplain is always aware that the privilege of free access to all parts of the prison and his or her status within the prison reflect a chaplain/inmate imbalance that should never be exploited. The proactive preparation of a relationship for deeper counseling encounters distinguishes a prison chaplain from the clinical psychologist or other professionals involved in counseling. The ministry of chaplains has a low threshold; chaplains are easily available, actively reaching out to the inmates and establishing relationships with people remote from church life.

The ministry of presence becomes particularly important for the care of those in *solitary confinement*. Visiting the solitary-confinement block can consume much time and energy. I usually stop in front of every cell, greet the inmate, ask in a gentle and low-key way about how he feels, give some words of encouragement and try to evaluate quickly whether there is a genuine need for a longer encounter. Due to time limitations, this evaluation often happens rather randomly; it may well be that many inmates would appreciate a longer stop. Nonetheless, I hope that the regular visits, short as they may be, are meaningful and supportive. With a number of inmates I experienced crucial breakthroughs only when they were in disciplinary confinement and removed from normal association.

> Ah-Kwan was an inmate I had known for several years, and despite repeated attempts in the normal ward to find a quiet moment for an opportunity, I didn't really get close to him. He remained

defensive and withdrawn. All I observed was that he had difficulty expressing himself, stammering when talking and overly clinging to persons who cared for him, but still not revealing much about himself. He was a loner and expressed little warmth. One day when I met him in disciplinary confinement, I shared with him my impression that there were actually more things that he wanted to share with me, but that he couldn't find the right way. I encouraged him to open his heart and not worry. At that point, he finally started to talk about a long-hidden pain of past wounds and abuse. Detached from his usual surroundings, he found the confidence to touch on subjects that he usually avoided.

On the other hand, visitors other than chaplains express the ministry of presence differently, most important through *continuity* and *reliability*. A regular visit helps the inmates develop trust. Many inmates have experienced a lot of betrayal and injuries in personal relationships in their past, and visitors who brave adverse conditions and meet the inmates despite hectic daily lives send a powerful message by the pure fact of their visit. Many volunteers I met have visited individual prisoners or inmate groups for many years. For many inmates, this reliability has become a strong source of comfort and an inspiration for spiritual change.

The ministry of presence can consume a good deal of time for both chaplains and lay visitors. It includes low-key supportive acts like helping find resource books for studies, looking for information only available in the outside world, or handing out reading material. Requests for information equally belong to precounseling: many inmates approach the chaplain or a visitor first with questions about the Bible, church life, or an issue of public life. These questions are usually a simple test to find out more about visitors, about their way of thinking, and whether it is worthwhile to further pursue a relationship. The ministry of presence is a time to establish friendship with inmates and to build up confidence that the visitor is reliable and genuinely cares for the inmate. Many encounters do not develop beyond these more random, informal, and often interrupted encounters. Yet their value cannot be overestimated, as they most basically communicate Christian faith and values. From them the more lasting relationships and deeper counseling encounters develop.

COMMUNICATION IN THE VISITING MINISTRY: FROM UNDERSTANDING TO GROWTH

We now turn to other elements of how visitors can shape their encounter with inmates to support understanding and spiritual growth. The elements of communication are introduced in order of rising levels of intervention, starting with the least interventionist and ending with the most active. The various elements refer to different periods and to different needs of an encounter.

The following remarks present a *short introduction* into some *skills of counseling* that should be helpful for all kinds of prison visitors. Strategies of *brief pastoral counseling* are particularly useful in a context where visitors face a large number of inmates, a constantly changing prison population, many inmates with obvious needs for counseling, and constraints that make encounters short and somewhat random. Also useful is the so-called *A-B-C method of crisis counseling*, recently promoted in pastoral counseling for those in crisis. The *A-B-C* method entails the following steps: achieve a relationship, boil down the problem, cope actively with the problem. The different steps of the *A-B-C* method can easily be traced in the discussion below, and references for both counseling resources can be found in the bibliographical notes at the end of the chapter.

Listening

Many visitors meet inmates with the intention of sharing the good news and talking about their faith. This is the root for a common misunderstanding: proclaiming the gospel is usually understood as an act of speech by the visitor, sharing and connecting the inmate with the liberating message of the Bible. However, what is needed in a context of constant noise and all-pervasive loquaciousness is a visitor who is not talkative, and for whom the use of words in proclamation is secondary, auxiliary, and used only when needed. The evangelistic practice is too often speaking before listening and answering before hearing (Prov 18:13). Silence can be the most powerful form of expressing the good news of Jesus Christ. The wisdom of St. Francis of Assisi applies today as ever: "Proclaim the gospel! If necessary, use words." God's revelation does not need to come through earthquakes; it can come through a gentle whisper (1 Kgs 19:12). Or, in the words of Dietrich Bonhoeffer,

> Many people are looking for an ear that will listen. They do not find it among Christians, because Christians are talking when they should be listening. He who no longer listens to his brother [or sister] will soon no longer be listening to God either . . . One who cannot listen long and patiently will presently be talking beside the point and never really speaking to others, albeit he be not conscious of it.[8]

Listening is the most basic form of communication. It is a skill that is closely related to the attitude of empathy and is often referred to as empathic listening. It has several purposes: most directly, to reach an understanding of the other person, to establish a relationship of trust; or, more indirectly, to convey value and acceptance. Of course, an encounter does not really start with listening, for many inmates are shy and do not talk easily about themselves. They are not used to the setting of a quiet and focused encounter where both visitor and inmate share about their lives and what is important to them. Many inmates are simply not accustomed to or skilled in oral conversation. A conversation thus starts where visitors take an active interest in the inmates' lives and involve them in a conversation—not just about spiritual issues but about anything in daily life, for through the way they are viewed, all these issues can receive a spiritual quality. Once the conversation has started, visitors keep it flowing through open-ended questions that encourage the other person to continue. Empathic listening expresses its desire to genuinely understand by asking back, seeking clarifications, verifying if one has understood well, and reflecting feelings and summarizing central themes. Listening presence is underlined through eye contact and through a body posture that leans toward the conversation partner. Empathic listening refrains from responding and from expressing understanding too rapidly. It avoids stereotypes that make a person feel categorized rather than understood and avoids talking about one's own similar experiences because this deflects attention from the other person.

Empathic listening is nondirective, nonjudgmental, and nonconfrontational: It refrains from overpowering the other person with wisdom not rooted in experience. It is patient and allows the cleansing stream of a sharing to become effective; the basic attitude should not be one of activism

---

8. Bonhoeffer, *Life Together*, 97–98, quoted in Clinebell, *Basic Types of Pastoral Care*, 72.

but of patient presence. The most common pain arises from situations that cannot immediately be changed, like sickness, death, separation, or, in the context of prison, imprisonment. Empathic listening refrains from reacting to the pain of reality by verbal, practical, or spiritual activism.

Being a good listener does not mean accepting or believing everything, but it does mean showing trust that what a person says is meaningful and has value. The goal is to come to an understanding of both *the feeling and the content* expressed by a person. A visitor should not only recognize the other person's feelings but also determine what is causing a person's pain or what is preventing that person from developing more fully. A most obvious cause of pain for those in prison is the fact of imprisonment, but below that surface other pain may be hidden: the separation from loved ones, worries about one's children, feelings of guilt, or material concerns. When a person feels stagnation in his or her life, it is important to listen for hints of hidden causes, any unresolved issues like personal conflicts, gambling debts, or addiction problems, that need to be addressed before further development can happen. Empathic listening alone (without the subsequent steps) may leave a person only understood but not guided. Yet it is a necessary first step to establish a stable relationship from where the visitor can move on to guidance and confrontation that may, in the further process, complement empathy.

Comforting

When somebody shares feelings of sadness or despair, we naturally want to comfort. A common mistake in such situations is to respond too quickly or with too much activism. If comfort happens too early, it interrupts the crucial, ameliorative effect of a person releasing feelings of sadness, of anger, or of guilt. When somebody listens patiently, comfort is already there and warmth emerges from it. That said, there are ways of expressing comfort that are sensitive and do not interrupt the cleansing stream of a sharing. What is an appropriate reaction depends on what kind of feeling and difficulty is being addressed, and what personality the visitor encounters.

When there is a given reality that is simply sad, is difficult to bear, and cannot be changed, comfort and close presence are essential. Sharing in the speechlessness of an inmate who just received notice that his appeal against his life sentence was rejected is probably the most sensible reaction, and accepting the numbness that such a prospect causes is the most compassionate response—not walking away but staying with the inmate and, if sufficient trust is established, holding him, because physical contact is the best possible comfort. If a person has already found some emotional distance to the source of pain, comfort could consist of giving positive strokes (for example, expressing appreciation for a person's ability to face the situation). A *stroke*, a term used in Transactional Analysis (see more in chapter 7), means a communicative response that implies recognition of the other person. Positive strokes express value and encourage a person to continue in the flow of conversation.

Many people in prison have strong *dependency needs*. They strongly attach themselves to other people and seek their recognition. Some live in a relational void, without immediate family or close friends, and they have little opportunity to receive positive feedback and positive strokes in their life. Visitors from outside are key in filling this void. They can become as important as family members, and they easily see the inmates more often and more closely, with fewer time limits and without the normal separating screen present in visit rooms within high-security prisons. The prison environment amplifies dependency as inmates unlearn independent ways of resolving problems. Some inmates' personalities have little ego strength: they have difficulty coping with frustrations, are pushed by impulses, and are not willing to organize their lives in the ways responsible, adjusted adults would.[9] Visitors sustain such inmates by offering encouragement, appreciation for their achievements, and a fellowship that supplies much-needed human contact. The pattern of interaction between visitors and inmates with dependency needs may hardly change, even over the long term, and some visitors grow frustrated to constantly assume the role of an encouraging elder friend. Still, continuity of encouragement and fellowship may be all that help such inmates find stability and strength to cope with the reality of their imprisonment in more constructive ways.

Sometimes inmates feel so overwhelmed by their present confinement that they lack the spiritual freedom to look beyond the present. They see the reality of a long imprisonment ahead, they see all the damage done, and they just cannot imagine how anything positive could emerge from such a mess. When visitors respond to such feelings and try to convey hope and meaning, they need to avoid the impression of taking the pain too lightly.

---

9. Clinebell, *Basic Types of Pastoral Care*, 174ff, offers a list of characteristics of ego weaknesses.

A Communication Guide to the Visiting Ministry

The visitor can do this if he or she refrains from directly expressing hope or meaning but puts the response in question form:

> "What, among all the things you have shared with me, do you find most difficult to face?" Or, "I can only imagine a bit of how difficult it must be in your situation. However, is there anybody that you find you can still rely on?" Or, "Who, during all these difficulties, has become important to you?" Or possibly, "I understand that, recently, not much positive has happened. However, was there anything that made you happy?"[10]

Something like the first question can help identify core issues to be looked at in a future conversation. The latter questions can have the effect of subtly shifting the focus from the overwhelming negative feelings and turning to positive resources. Such questions can also be group exercises during worship. The participants are invited to look at their past time in prison and think about what was most difficult to face and what some positive experiences were. They may, for example, write three positive and three negative experiences on a sheet of paper and, depending on the level of mutual trust, share the experiences in small groups together with visitors from outside, or put the pieces of paper in the middle of the room so that all may be read, or give the pieces of paper to the worship leader to pray for the issues mentioned. Many inmates react with surprise when asked to identify positive experiences because often it has simply not crossed their minds that even in an adverse situation, reflecting on positive experiences is possible.

> Sometimes visitors encounter *inmates who claim to be innocent*. How to comfort them? On the one hand, a visitor should never reject the possibility that justice has erred. Legal history offers ample examples of such errors. On the other hand, visitors need to be aware that a claim of innocence can stand in contrast to factual evidence. Yet denial does not simply happen for lack of morality. Sometimes the claim is due to a lack of legal understanding on the side of the inmate. (For example, transporting drugs is illegal even if the transporters have no idea what they were doing). Denial can also be a protest against a legal code that is hard to accept. More challenging are cases where an admission of responsibility would place a too heavy burden on a person: he or she is just not (yet)

---

10. Stone, *Strategies for Brief Pastoral Counseling*, 95, follows De Shazer, *Putting Difference to Work*, in calling such an approach "looking for exceptions."

ready to cope with it and needs the claim of innocence to psychologically survive.

Visitors must provide a supportive, comforting presence in order not to add to the inmate's feeling of being trapped. They should take seriously what they hear and should avoid pushing inmates to admit guilt. In the case of somebody being effectively innocent, such pressure adds to a continued victimization. This happened in the biblical story of Job when his friends tried to convince him that somehow he must be guilty but just lacked awareness of it. Even if the inmate is guilty, visitors pressuring inmates to admit guilt forfeit the uniqueness of an encounter that should be different from the overall pressure to admit guilt. Unless a visitor has legal knowledge, a lot of time, or possibly enough finances at hand, I recommend *not* entering into legal activism. Instead visitors may point the inmate to legal resources and, for the rest, accept that they may never know what in fact happened.

Guiding

Guidance happens when the visitor helps *shift a person's focus* from the pain to the resources that offer hope for new beginning and healing: people who still care, skills that an inmate still has, or positive memories that give strength. Visitors may assume the role of visionaries who can see beyond the present confinement and limitations of a person. Again, it is important that the visitor does not impose his or her own vision on the inmate but proceeds softly, tentatively proposing or presenting suggestions in the form of questions. Guidance is happening already when persons engage in conversation, because, by so doing, they naturally broaden their horizons and integrate perspectives and thoughts of the conversation partner. It happens next through positive feedback that reinforces achievements and strengthens inner resources. Guidance happens further in the process of listening and understanding. If visitors clarify a paralyzing confusion of feelings and fears through focused listening and asking, this process may identify priorities that an inmate can address. Understanding the main issues of a given situation helps overcome a threatening vagueness. This is what counseling calls step *B*: "boiling down" a problem into elements with which a person can actively cope.

A more interventionist way of guiding, as through the questions given above, leads an inmate to experience *cognitive shifts* or *shifts in perception*.

A Communication Guide to the Visiting Ministry

Such shifts happen when people start to regard reality not as categorically bad but as neutral, having the potential for both positive and negative. Sensitivity and trust are necessary to lead an inmate toward discovering positive experiences in a reality that is usually conceived only in negative terms. Questions that encourage cognitive shifts are

> If you imagine yourself ten years from now, what would you like to see had happened today? Or, try to imagine the person you are in ten years' time: what are you like? A similar but more concrete form of the question is, imagine yourself one month from now: what could you imagine having done? Or at what point would you be?

Posing a question like this encourages a person to truly look into present resources and opportunities. It can come as surprise for an inmate that even in a place of complete confinement, as in a high-security prison, options are available.

Related to these questions are individual or group exercises that attempt to imagine the future:[11] Writing a letter assuming a positive development from the present reality, using the perspective of three months or a few years later; imagining being a grandfather and telling grandchildren a story of a positive development starting today. In the context of prison, it is helpful to discount the most common response to such exercises, when inmates simply hope for a retrial with a release or a sudden general amnesty. Guiding in this context means actively developing hope that recognizes positive opportunities in the present reality.

> Inspiring for communicating hope are the findings of Viktor E. Frankl (see bibliographic notes), who developed the concept of *logotherapy* based on his personal experiences as prisoner in the concentration camps of the Second World War, a context of extreme hopelessness similar to that of many inmates. Analyzing his own and other prisoners' survival, Frankl found that a purpose and perspective for one's future made the most crucial difference and enhanced chances of survival. Anything could be a purpose for the future: finishing an academic project, carrying on responsibility for one's family, and so forth. From this experience, Frankl derived a therapy that focuses on the future and on practical perspectives rather than on the past and on analysis of the roots of neurotic behavior. Orientation toward the future is a useful approach for

---

11. Lester and Stone, "Helping Parishioners Envision the Future," 49ff, offer a variety of methods how a person can be helped to develop hope.

pastoral counseling, particularly brief pastoral counseling, and distinguishes it from many psychological therapies. Much of traditional psychological therapy is focused on the past and stresses the need to understand and heal the roots of neurotic behavior. In contrast, pastoral counseling is more occasional, is often less structured than secular counseling, and happens more randomly. Its informal character makes it necessary to give important impulses for change in short periods of time.

Cognitive shifts happen also through *reframing*, which assumes that the way we look at reality has a direct effect on how this reality shapes us. A key element in reframing is that it has a self–fulfilling element, like a student who learns in the first driving lesson to focus on the direction he or she wants to drive. When we focus on an obstacle we will naturally move towards it: if we focus on failure, we will fail. If we focus on the reality of imprisonment, we will see only bars all around us. The positive direction of thought uncovered by reframing releases a strengthening energy that turns an originally narrow reality into one that is dynamic and full of potential. Everybody knows simple ways of reframing (for example, regarding a given reality not as a problem but as an opportunity, or regarding a failed exam not as a failure but as a positive reminder of what still can and needs to be learned). Reframing happens through questions like, what is possible now? that seek positive potential in a given situation. Reframing includes introducing opportunities and giving support to pursue them. If an inmate is not able to discover anything that could be done at present, the visitor may simply suggest, "What about writing to me?" (Of course, this is only appropriate if the visitor is committed to responding through letters.) Often, I ask inmates at an appropriate time in the encounter if they would like to write to one of the volunteers of our prison-care group. Many groups have some kind of letter ministry. I attach importance to inmates' taking the first step, but I assure that they will receive a response. A visitor may suggest simple steps of action that boost confidence and lead to positive feedback. A minor step or change in behavior patterns can have a huge energizing effect and become the seed for future steps. Small changes in behavior can give the experience of not being completely helpless, positively influencing the persons' own situation and combating feelings of paralysis. Many inmates discover quitting smoking, gambling, or swearing as behavior changes applicable to life in prison. They equally recognize that success in achieving such goals strengthens confidence.

One form of reframing happens when inmates say that their arrest has actually been a blessing in disguise, for instance:

> "If it were not for being here, I might have already been killed."
> Or: "Imprisonment saved me from going further down the road of drug addiction."

Such reframing, although at times appearing a bit exaggerated, has an autosuggestive effect and turns the primarily negative experience of imprisonment into a positive experience that allows new direction or that may even have saved one's life. Typical forms of *religious reframing* are

> "It is God who brought me to prison so that I would be saved." Or, "God has showed me a way to learn about him and get close to him through encountering Christ behind bars."

If such a proposition comes from an inmate, it is his or her active and successful way of reframing a painful experience. It gives significance to an experience of distress, and meaning to a time usually seen as void of meaning. It is, however, crucial *never to impose reframing* on others. It can be very cynical when a visitor says: "At least by going to prison you have met the Lord Jesus Christ." Such a statement—and I have heard it many times—extends the image of a punishing God, gives legitimacy to punishment, and is insensitive to the reality of suffering involved in imprisonment.

Another form of cognitive shift, which we will further discuss in a later section, happens in worship when people sing against the darkness around them. I have learned to appreciate charismatic forms of worship in prison because the extended singing and the bodily involvement have an energizing, strengthening, and reframing power on many inmates.

> During a period of time a charismatic preacher helped me to lead the worship services in prison. The services he led included patterns with clear reframing effects. For example, he invited people to respond with shouts of hallelujah, and he led in prayer and invited people to speak after him. Such an expressive worship turns into a training ground for people to learn alternative language and perception patterns. The worship has a collectively reframing effect and can cause real transformation by disseminating alternative patterns by which to perceive reality.

However, collective or individual reframing and effecting change through encouraging cognitive shifts have the potential for both abuse and manipulation. A visitor should neither use such an approach with a quick-fix attitude nor introduce any vision of change in a triumphalistic way. Commitment does not guarantee success, and a person who envisions new behavior patterns and new steps may fail. Change should emerge from the striving of an inmate and not be the activist project of a visitor.

Confronting

Confronting usually has an image reminiscent of conflict and animosity. However, well-applied confrontation need not be threatening and narrowly focused on people's inadequacies and sins. Confronting a person is part of a mature, honest, and respectful relationship: It complements empathy and allows for enlargement of self-understanding.[12] Challenging an inmate can be a form of showing confidence in his or her ability to cope with reality. The task is offering forgiveness and witnessing to the values of justice while at the same time identifying a form of confrontation that maintains a supporting relationship without undermining self-esteem.

When challenging an inmate, caution is needed. First, visitors representing the wider church community do well to remember that too often the church has buried compassion and love under a pharisaic moralism. Second, confrontation only makes sense when mutual trust has been established: a visitor needs to earn the right to confront. The more a relationship of love and respect is established, and the more an inmate feels secure and loved, the more confrontation is possible. Third, confrontation needs to happen in gentleness and without the slightest pride: many inmates are unsettled, feel insecure, and have little self-confidence, even while hiding their insecurity under a surface of strength. Finally, it is a basic error to think that people should first be broken through confrontation, be led to a breakdown of their old self, so that from there they can rebuild their lives. This pattern, traditionally used in evangelistic sermons, does not apply to a caring relationship, and applies even less so to the prison context, where people have already experienced the fundamental breakdown of their lives. It is what Bonhoeffer calls "to run man down in his worldliness" and "clerical sniffing around after people's sins in order to catch them out,"[13] a pastoral obsession with people at their weakest.

---

12. Pattison, *Critique of Pastoral Care*, 49. This is also the main thrust of Underwood, *Empathy and Confrontation*.

13. Bonhoeffer, *Letters and Papers from Prison*, 347 (letter from July 8, 1944).

Confrontation, then, is an element in an encounter that continues spiritual and relational growth through a positive twist. For example, confrontation might entail reminding people of their potential or broadening their awareness of other perspectives—the perspectives of the family suffering with them, of their victims, or of the wider society. A soft form of confrontation happens when one reminds a suicidal person how his parents emotionally rely on him and need him to stay alive, that they want to look into his eyes, and that it will be a joy for them to discover joy in his eyes.

A common issue when visiting inmates is to hear complaints about staff, other inmates, the judiciary, or even about other visitors. Inmates are very isolated and have little opportunity to critically discuss relationships with a third party. It is therefore important to allow a cleansing expression of complaints, but it is just as important at some point to mirror reality and confront inmates with the simple fact that they can hardly ever change other people, only the way they look at and relate to them.

Here is another example: An inmate, who feels depressed after a split in a relationship with a girlfriend or wife first needs strengthening support. At some point, however, a visitor may gently lead him to imagine (a) how this girlfriend or wife suffered equally during the turmoil of the past months or years, or (b) what the inmate would have done in the reverse case: "What if your wife had been sentenced to several years in prison?"

Confronting somebody can, in contrast to what we have said up to now, become the start of a relationship.

> I remember Ah-Pang, a inmate on a life sentence living in the isolation ward and hiding from normal association due to the nature of his crime. For many years he had just mumbled a greeting and waved me on whenever I stopped in front of his cell, indicating that he wasn't interested in talking to me. At one point I stopped and confronted him: "I have been passing by your cell for several years now, and you have always just waved your hand without talking to me. I think that is now enough. Look, I just wonder what you think about all day long." He grinned and answered, "I think about how I could die." I asked what made him want to die. His short answer was: "Life is ugly. And I don't have anything to hope for." He even felt sad about his inability to commit suicide. I asked him to tell me more about how he grew up and what went wrong. Although completely out of practice talking at length, he reluctantly started to share his story of quite a good upbringing in a middle-class family. Things turned bad when his family migrated to the US and left him behind for some time. Among other

> wounds, he also experienced sexual abuse as a young boy. After listening to his sad story and confronting his strong desire to die, I strongly affirmed the value of life. I reminded him that there had been a time in his life when somebody loved him. Before all the pain that he must have experienced, there was a moment when he had a mother or a father or some relative who hugged him and nurtured him. The conversation only kept going through my continuous insistence, but it was a significant change compared to years of silence. After that he would talk to me more actively each time I visited him. I regarded it as a small breakthrough when, on my last visit before I departed on a longer furlough, he asked for my address so that he could write to me (which he didn't).

Another way of confronting a person happens when a visitor reflects on an ongoing relationship.

> Ah-Kee was on a long prison sentence. He was at times very attached to me but at other times withdrew and avoided any contact. At one point he shared with me deep feelings of guilt toward his family about legal costs and his failure to contribute to them. I pointed out that even though he could do little for his family from prison, at least he could show them that he was learning responsibility. I told him that in many ways his unstable behavior, reflected also in his relationship with me, was the behavior of a teenager rather than that of a twenty-seven-year-old man.

An important issue is the *confrontation with past crimes*. Some inmates freely talk about their crime in moments of emotional turmoil or spiritual change, and this then is part of a cleansing confession. However, particularly inmates in Asia rather avoid talking about it, and visitors should approach this topic discreetly, for several reasons. First, inmates in public discourse are too often already reduced to and identified with destructive acts of their past. But the criminal act is not the whole of a person, despite what people tend to say. Also, the crime may date back several years and may already have been dealt with appropriately. As prison visitor, one should remember that one is likely not the first visitor in the life of an inmate. Finally, a person needs a strong basis of trust to be willing to talk about a sensitive and embarrassing part of the past. With this in mind, and if the conditions are right, to ask inmates about how they see their past crime(s) does help their growth. I usually address it when inmates prepare for baptism or as one topic during regular encounters when a stable relationship has been well established. It can be an opportunity to discuss what has changed, what has not changed, and how the crime affected other people, and it provides an opportunity to speak out about feelings of guilt, not just to harbor them in the heart. Giving voice to such feelings makes more real the process of change that has happened.

Confrontation with past crime can also happen indirectly through the *story of a third party*. This can give an inmate the necessary space to reflect on his or her own past crime without being pushed to do so directly. Such an indirect encounter with a crime victim can be part of the reconciling process of restorative justice (see more in chapter 8).

> In one of our worship services, a visitor shared the story how her father was killed in a murder when she was a young girl. She recalled the pain and grief that she experienced and how this event had affected her life, as she had to grow up without her father. Most of the inmates listening to her sharing had themselves committed a murder, and the visitor's story had a deep impact on them. It was the first time they had a chance to hear directly the pain of a victim's relative.

To some degree, confrontation is easier in a more authority-centered context like the Chinese one. A pastor or a senior visitor is assumed to have authority to point out wrong behavior and to guide people on the right path; those who are not in a position of authority are expected to respond with obedience and submission. This distinctive allocation of authority and obedience to separate sides has the positive effect of clearly structuring society and individual lives, but it has a more important negative effect of undermining self-confidence, amplifying feelings of inadequacy, adding to repressive forces within the personality, and deepening feelings of guilt and failure. Therefore, it rather hinders growth. For these reasons, due to the specific authority-centered context, and also because prisoners usually already have ample opportunities to encounter people who assume the role of moral authority, I use this approach only conservatively. To overly rely on authority can have an effect contrary to the desired effect.

> Ah-Tak has for several years been in self-chosen isolation due to the nature of his crime, a situation I generally regard as harmful. Ah-Tak was, although full of anxiety in his everyday life, a devout Christian and regularly studied the Bible. At some point, therefore, I assumed my pastoral authority and repeatedly challenged him to

take the step of leaving isolation confinement and joining the normal association with other inmates. I was confident that despite the inevitable initial difficulties, he could adapt and interact better, including meeting Christian visitors during worship. However, the only effect of my authoritarian insistence was a growing alienation between us. Ah-Tak increasingly avoided me and stopped confiding in me about other issues in his life.

Confronting somebody does not happen by imposing a complete set of opinions and values on a person but by inviting this person to consider and imagine on his or her own behalf. Always ask if you would be ready to be challenged by the person you are planning to challenge; this is a good measure of maintaining mutuality in a relationship. Be aware that many people already judge themselves more severely than anyone else would. Confrontation happens successfully on the basis of genuine noncondemnation, as Jesus showed in his encounter with the woman caught in adultery (John 8:1–11).

Celebrating

A final element of communication is celebration. Communication happens not only in one-to-one encounters but also (and often more strongly) in collective activities such as worship or other celebrative activities, which can be opportunities for inmates to express themselves differently and present themselves in a new light.

Sometimes visitors and inmates find it difficult to engage in meaningful conversation in individual encounters. In the worshiping fellowship, or in the informal group gathering, they experience a kind of convergence when care transcends the one-to-one dimension, takes on a cumulative effect, and affects large parts of a prison community. The worshiping fellowship is a place where both visitors and inmates grow together and overcome the separation between inside and outside. If such collective convergence takes off, it can turn a group of individual prisoners and visitors, each one alone in their loneliness, into a healing community.

What is more, communication happens as much through nonverbal means. Pain is, in part, resistant to language and cannot really be shared. In the words of Elaine Scarry, "whatever pain achieves, it achieves in part through its unsharability, and it ensures this unsharability through its resistance to language."[14] Although we regard the chance to express pain verbally as an important element in a healing process, we must constantly be aware that pain ultimately separates the one having pain from those only hearing about pain. Pain resists not only communication but empathy as well. Visitors of those in prison need to constantly remind themselves that ultimately they cannot really grasp what it means to be in prison. It is a sign of professional deformation when this is forgotten.

Worship transcends verbal and one-to-one communication. It touches on the different aspects of human life, spiritual and bodily. The singing and the movement of the music contrast with the overwhelming dullness of prison. Some of the most powerful experiences for visitors are connected to joint worship that offers a radically alternative experience to the overall atmosphere of prison: the power of a group of male basses singing together, the silence of a meditative worship, a prayer where individuals jointly address God. All are spiritual peak experiences that bring participants in touch with transcendence.

How can worship become reviving? One of the goals of worship in prison should be to create an environment that encourages the admission of failure and brokenness, this constant experience of not measuring up to what one would like to. A simple method of creating such an atmosphere can be to invite participants—visitors and inmates alike—to give testimonies about their experiences of brokenness and grace. The task of the person in charge, the group leader, is to steer the testimony in a way that avoids triumphalism and instead in a way that underlines the continuous struggle. A triumphalistic testimony can add to rather than relieve feelings of frustration and failure because it emphasizes success in transformation and may stand in contrast to the reality of many inmates, who experience transformation in more hesitant and ambiguous forms. The visitors and preachers who have the deepest impact are those who admit the less glorious sides of their life, who share them with those they care for, and who do not hide their wounds.

> During a worship service, a visitor shared his own history of alcoholism and what made him overcome it and grow from there. What made his sharing particularly moving was that he was not looking back on a remote past but reflecting on issues that he still

---

14. About pain and pain's resistance to language, see Scarry, *Body in Pain*, 4ff. See also Haney, *Reforming Punishment*, 9–10.

struggled with. Although he had experienced God's grace in being transformed, his sharing lacked any victorious triumphalism.

A visitor who frankly admits wounds moves closer to the inmates than somebody who appears surrounded by an aura of glory. The same applies to ex-offenders who share the stories of their journeys. Seeing an ex-offender in the role of a visitor, integrated in the life and ministry of the church, allows inmates to get a glimpse of what is possible also for them. Seeing how an ex-offender has successfully changed his or her life gives hope.

Another way worship becomes reviving happens when the leadership of the worship remains as much as possible with the inmates. Worship that is prepared, designed, and conducted by people from outside for those inside remains alien to the inmates, no matter how well planned it is. It is a service for the benefit of the inmates and turns them into recipients. On the other hand, worship where the planning and the leadership belong to the inmates turns them into subjects and gives them ownership over what they plan. The content and style of such worship will naturally reflect the concerns and questions of the inmates. The responsibility of visitors is to assist where the inmates need it: training in techniques of how to lead or assisting with music or taking up the responsibility for preaching. When inmates join together to plan and conduct worship, they enter into a community of like-mindedness that allows them to see their situation in relation to other people and experience something of normal life. Any program that treats inmates as subjects and counters the norm of disempowerment will revive inmates and strengthen their subject status. Among the programs that can have empowering effects are

- Alpha Courses where the small discussion groups are led by inmates
- Listeners' programs where a few inmates are trained to offer counseling support to their fellow inmates
- Peer counseling designed along the successful model of Alcoholics Anonymous

A reviving communication finally points to the fellowship in the *eucharistic celebration*. Sharing the sacraments can be a tremendously powerful and reviving experience. Nowhere have I experienced the contrast between the sacramental celebration and the surrounding context more strikingly than in prison. The silence during the celebration; the humility when receiving the bread and the cup; the fellowship of equality with all participants in a circle, including those just joining out of curiosity, who receive a short blessing instead of bread and wine: the silence contrasts with the ubiquitous noise, the humility with a context of self-preservation and assertiveness, and the fellowship with the hierarchical system and the ultimate loneliness of most inmates (and possibly also of visitors). Again, the special character of this celebration and the kind of holiness that surrounds it has a reviving effect. The universality of the eucharistic celebration, the fact that it happens equally in different locations, breaks down the inside/outside dualism. Although an aura of holiness surrounding the celebration adds to its uplifting effect, it is important that the eucharistic celebration does not appear too holy and thus alienate participants. The way the Eucharist is conducted should make it a uniting experience, including for newcomers and not-yet-believers in the body of Christ.

> **PRINCIPLES OF COMMUNICATION (I)**
>
> - *Change*—Be ready to see your own need for change instead of seeing it only in other people.
> - *Goals*—Enter prison not with goals you want to achieve but with an open mind, ready to be surprised.
> - *Positive bias*—Develop a positive bias of trust and confidence and be aware of areas where negative prejudice still prevails.
> - *Effectiveness*—Trust that your visit has an effect on the other person even without you seeing it.
> - *Beyond the small circle*—Make yourself available to those at the fringes and to the less articulate. They equally need to establish relationships.
> - *Reliability*—Be reliable, regular, and consistent in your visits and in your promises.
> - *Listening*—Remember that listening and silence can be the most powerful form of speaking and of sharing the good news.
> - *Non-Interventionism*—Seek understanding rather than solutions and refrain from activism. Changes come through God working in the inmate, not through the visitor's intervention.
> - *Trust*—Take seriously what you hear and refrain from judgment, even if the story sounds unlikely.
> - *Comfort*—Ask questions that focus on positive events and available resources.
> - *Cognitive Shifts*—Prepare the way for cognitive shifts to happen. Support inmates in identifying and pursuing opportunities.
> - *Beyond Words*—Be open to interaction that transcends verbal communication.

Bibliographical Notes

For *general information* on counseling see Howard Clinebell, *Basic Types of Pastoral Care & Counseling: Resources for the Ministry of Healing and Growth* (Nashville: Abingdon, 1984). For the context of prison, chapters 7 to 9 are particularly valuable. Further Stephen Pattison, *A Critique of Pastoral Care* (London: SCM, 1988); Alastair V. Campbell, *Rediscovering Pastoral Care* (Darton, Longman & Todd, 1981); Robert J. Wicks et al., eds., *Clinical Handbook of Pastoral Counseling*, Vols. 1 and 2 (New York: Paulist, 1993).

A good introduction to *brief pastoral counseling* is offered in Howard W. Stone, ed., *Strategies for Brief Pastoral Counseling* (Minneapolis: Fortress, 2001). See further Gary J. Oliver et al., *Promoting Change through Brief Therapy in Christian Counseling* (Wheaton, IL: Tyndale House, 1997). Brief pastoral counseling has developed since the early '90s and stresses limited objectives, the use of homework, and a counseling sequence of not more than six sessions. The experience of brief pastoral counseling is that a change in one or a few central issues of suffering can trigger change in secondary causes of suffering.

On a discussion of the *A-B-C method of crisis counseling* see Howard W. Stone, *Crisis Counseling*, (Philadelphia: Fortress, 1976); Clinebell, *Basic Types of Pastoral Care & Counseling*, 205ff. Clinebell offers an extended *A-B-C-D* method, where *D* stands for "develop an ongoing growth-action plan."

On *counseling and compassion* see Henri J. M. Nouwen, *The Wounded Healer* (New York: Doubleday 1979). The book offers a deeply spiritual guide for people in ministry to recognize the sufferings of their time and of their counterparts in their own hearts.

A short introduction to Viktor E. Frankl's *logotherapy* is available in Viktor E. Frankl, *Psychotherapy and Existentialism* (New York: Washington Square, 1967), 5–14. Frankl's most famous work, in which he recounts his experiences in the concentration camp, is *Man's Search for Meaning: An Introduction to Logotherapy*. The book is available in many different editions.

On *confrontation* see Ralph Underwood, *Empathy and Confrontation in Pastoral Care* (Theology and Pastoral Care Series; Philadelphia, Fortress, 1985). Underwood emphasizes that empathy and confrontation don't stand in opposition to each other but are linked through respect.

7

Roles and Relationships: Visiting in an Unequal Context

THE LAST CHAPTER INTRODUCED elements of visitors' communication with those in prison. We highlighted how successful communication emerges from specific attitudes rather than mere skills. We underlined the importance of presence as the most basic form of communication. We showed how the interaction has different levels of involvement: listening, comforting, guiding, or confronting. And, we learnt how the joint celebration in worship and Eucharist revives and transcends verbal communication.

This chapter addresses a further aspect of communication that has been only implicitly present up to now: Both the context of interaction and the communicative behavior affect visitor-inmate relationships.

The context of the encounter between visitors and inmates is one of inequality. Inequality must not always be bad. Quite often it is a natural part of human relationships. Sometimes we may not want (or are not able) to remove the inequality in a relationship, but we should be aware of how it affects our relationships and our counterparts' spiritual growth. Equally, visitors choose specific communicative behaviors by assuming specific roles and, by doing so, impress a complementary role on their counterparts. The roles and the established relationships can either alleviate the inequality between visitor and inmate or exacerbate it, thus hindering an inmate's spiritual growth.

Experiencing inequality and being defined by other people's role choices can disturb the liberating and reconciling power of what visitors are trying to communicate. Pastoral care and the ministry of visitation aim at restoring broken relationships—between people, or between people and God—and at helping people to know love, both as something to be received and as something to give.[1] These aims are ultimately incompatible with inequality, but in the present situation the presence of inequality is part of the given context and needs to be taken seriously.

This chapter deals with the following questions:

- What are roles that prison visitors can assume or that may be attached to them?
- How do specific roles shape the counterpart in an encounter?
- How can visitors avoid communicating a condescending attitude that hinders growth?
- What are sensitive issues of which visitors should particularly be aware when ministering in a context of inequality?

VISITORS IN DIFFERENT ROLES

Some clarification is needed at this point. Speaking about different roles might appear to lack genuineness. We may think that if somebody is genuine, he or she is just what he or she is, nothing more: "role free." However, looking at daily life, we soon realize that genuineness and multiple roles are not mutually exclusive: My role is different when I am talking to my wife than it is when I am talking to my parents; it's again different when I am relating to my children, to friends, to students, or to people I visit in prison—and still I try always to be genuinely myself. A person is a complex combination of images and roles that are self-chosen and of images, roles, and expectations that are projected from outside. A role is a comprehensive set of communicative patterns linked to typical models. Understanding the diversity of roles that one has and that one receives is part of a visitor's growth in self-awareness, and it includes an element of humility and self-relativization. We are never just what we think we are. The way other people see us is different from how we see ourselves, and ultimately, a person's composite identity is surrounded by a mystery known only to God.

---

1. See the definition of *pastoral care* in Campbell, *Paid to Care?*, 1.

Roles and Relationships: Visiting in an Unequal Context

The discussion about the different roles of a counselor has several backgrounds. It is closely related to the discussion about the different roles of the pastor in general. Different times brought varying concepts of the role of the pastor: theological specialist, communicator of social values, mediator between the divine and the worldly realities, helping companion in times of crisis, or prophetic actor and political activist. These different roles of the pastor appeared not only successively but also simultaneously and representing competing interests of those involved in church life.

Two further sources inspire reflection on roles in pastoral care. On one hand, the theological tradition distinguishes different offices—or, we could say, roles—of Christ: prophet, priest, and king. The church tradition subsequently distinguished different ministries or basic functions of the church; a classical distinction is the one of four parts, namely, worship (*liturgia*), witness (*martyria*), service (*diakonia*), and fellowship (*koinonia*).

On the other hand, some psychological theories explain patterns of human behavior by referring them to roles. Transactional Analysis (TA),[2] for example, explains behavior patterns as a dynamic interaction of Parent, Adult, and Child states, with Adult representing the ideal state of the ego. In human interaction, we actively assume one of these roles or states and by choosing a specific role impose a counterrole on our partner(s). For example, when addressing somebody as a child, we activate the other person's child role, although he or she may respond in a way different from the one suggested. Insights from TA have brought awareness of how roles imply specific reactions by the counterpart in an interaction.

Visitors use different roles, some more appropriate, some less. We should be aware of which roles we *like* the most, and which *fit* us best. The two categories are not necessarily identical, and neither role is necessarily the best response to inmates' needs. Here the aim of introducing different roles is to raise visitors' awareness of the implications, strengths, and weaknesses of common roles in Christian ministry. When one thinks about possible visitor roles, many come to mind: some are more formal, some more personal; some are more aloof, some more friendly; some focus more on conveying content, some more on establishing relations. The following list does not claim to be complete:

---

2. Transactional analysis (TA) has been developed by Eric Berne and became most famous through his book *Games People Play* (1964). For a short presentation of the principles of TA, see Clinebell, *Basic Types of Pastoral Care*, 382–87.

- Auntie/uncle
- Brother/sister
- Father
- Mother
- Relative
- Friend
- Big brother
- Confidant
- Advocate
- Animator
- Entertainer
- Social worker
- Caregiver
- Pastor
- Preacher
- Teacher
- Listener
- Counselor
- Intercessor
- Messenger
- Lifeline
- Healer
- Fellow pilgrim
- Spiritual director
- Role model
- Assistant
- Advisor
- Life teacher
- Servant
- Guest

Each role has distinctive connotations and provokes specific images. Some roles stem from family relations, others from the religious realm or from the cultural context of inmates. Most roles either reflect social patterns known to inmates or religious patterns that visitors and religious inmates like to apply. Some roles have negative connotations for visitors, who might reject them. Yet inmates might impose them on the visitors and see them in light of such a role. For example, the role of big brother suggests inmates' Triad-like dependency on a visitor, who is elevated to a questionable level of authority, but this role also exudes warmth and implies loyalty and friendship. Similarly, visitors may not like to be simple entertainers, but some inmates see them as such. In contrast, visitors usually see specific Christian roles as purely positive. However, inmates might see things differently and find that such roles express a distance that contrasts sharply with their cravings for relationship and warmth. Some roles are very broad and include various aspects: for example, the role of the pastor integrates nurturing, guiding, and caring roles. In the following paragraphs we will discuss only a few particularly common and important roles of Christian prison visitors.

Nurturing Roles: Father and Mother

The role of a father has in Christian tradition become a common epithet for church leaders, although this stands against the message of the Bible (Matt 23:9). In the Catholic Church, priests are commonly called *Father*; Protestant chaplains in countries that follow the English chaplaincy tradition are often equally called so. The father role is ambiguous, particularly in traditional, authority-centered and paternalistic contexts. Assuming a fatherly role can undermine the autonomy of the other person, pinning him or her in the eternal role of a child. In terms of Transactional Analysis, the father has an authoritarian image and is in danger of activating the other person's child role. Children, indebted to the father's care, always remain subject to his authority, and they respond to the father's care, material support, and protection with continual obedience and reverence. This does not end when the children become fathers themselves. When inmates see visitors as fathers, they place visitors in a position of honor and authority that can stifle the inmates' growth.

A fatherly role has, on the other hand, a nurturing aspect, responding to dependency needs that are particularly acute in times of crisis. When everything around a person breaks down, it is strengthening and reassuring to rely on a fatherly presence. A father can reprogram a negative father image in a son's (or daughter's) mind, and the visitor can introduce a different father model than the existing one: not an authoritarian, punishing, aloof father, but a caring father who is not shy to share his emotions, and who integrates aspects of motherly care.[3] A motherly role is thus not restricted to female visitors.

We have described the importance of the mother in the emotional life of inmates (see chapter 1). This applies also to visitors who assume a motherly role. The image of the mother is as much shaped by gender stereotypes as the role of the father, but it avoids hierarchical, patriarchal, and growth-stifling connotations. Here, the stereotypical images rather work to the advantage of emotional liberation, as many male inmates talk more easily about their emotions to women, who stereotypically are seen as experts in matters of the heart. The motherly role revives much of what we treasure in Christian care: nurturing and life giving, unconditional acceptance, or forgiveness. Some of the strongest visitor-inmate relationships are built on the basis of a visitor assuming a motherly role in an inmate's life.

> A young inmate from the South Asian subcontinent deeply missed his faraway mother. He asked me to introduce an elderly lady who could be like his mother during the time of imprisonment. The relationship subsequently established gave him many years of steady support, both educationally and emotionally.
>
> Another inmate facing a very long sentence had no outside relatives or friends other than his mother, who was too old to visit

---

3. A good description of a fatherly ministry is the short text of Madsen. "Power of a Father's Blessing," 48–50.

him. One of our visitors became his surrogate mother, and he always affectionately addressed her as such.

Many inmates have very traditional understandings of gender roles. Visitors should be aware of these stereotypes and correct them: in the case of a motherly role, this means including assertiveness and determination; in a fatherly role, it means avoiding traditional paternalistic behavior patterns and showing the strength of openness to one's emotions. Role models of manhood and fatherhood presented in the Bible (e.g., the father in the story of the Prodigal Son or some Psalms' descriptions of Yahweh) offer ample inspiration for revising stereotypical gender roles.

Teaching Roles: The Preacher and the Teacher

The ministry of preaching and teaching, also called the ministry of the Word, is one of the basic functions of Christian existence and is traditionally linked to a position of authority (such as a pastor or elder) in the church. Even in lay-based prison ministry, it is a role most popular with pastors, clerics, or full-time ministry workers. The role of preacher and teacher finds expression in worship settings or in individual visitor-inmate encounters that focus on teaching and proclamation. It includes the teaching of biblical knowledge, biblical doctrines, and (possibly more challenging) moral issues in the Christian tradition. Inmates who have grown to a mature spiritual level quite naturally want to learn more about faith and actively approach visitors or pastors to learn how to read the Bible and how to understand biblical themes. However, visitors who take the initiative of assuming a teaching role without being asked to do so often alienate inmates. They are imposing a hierarchical relationship, because this is how teaching is understood in authority-centered contexts. Here, the teacher-student relationship is similar to a father-son relationship: the former gives care and support while the latter responds with obedience, respect, and submission. Put into the subordinate role of a student, the inmate becomes a recipient. Visitors who assume teaching and preaching roles risk imposing issues for which the listeners are not prepared, or that do not correspond to their questions. Talking about issues that do not matter in the inmates' life can lead to frustrating feelings of powerlessness for the inmate.

Teaching and preaching is often linked to confrontation, for instance when the preacher or teacher expounds on general principles of what he (indeed this is mostly a male behavior) believes and on values he stands for.

Roles and Relationships: Visiting in an Unequal Context

What we have said about confrontation applies also here: Visitors need to earn the legitimacy to teach. Preaching is an imposition of authority that needs to be preceded by the inmate(s) having developed trust. Inmates can be quite critical of somebody who assumes the authority implied in teaching without being asked to do so: does he really have the proper understanding of inmates' life, needs, and suffering to be able to share knowledge of the Bible and insights about God in a manner relevant to those in prison?

When one assumes a teaching or preaching role, it is important to remain as closely linked to the experiences of inmates as possible and when preparing a message to constantly ask how a topic looks from the perspective of an inmate. A visitor does not need to abandon his or her own perspectives but should present them with humility and in a form that allows or invites contradiction. Values or issues are ideally presented in a personal and dynamic form rather than through rational discourse. If a visitor addresses issues that really concern inmates and that are within their experiential realm, an individual encounter or a worship service can become lively and challenging. Issues that are relevant for inmates include anything that relates to daily life and does not seem to come from the study of a preacher or teacher. Ethical questions and issues of crime, if presented in an open and (of course) anonymized way, can stimulate strong interest.

> Visitors may consider discussing issues and impressions that they come across during their visits (for example, the difficult question of Christian existence and prison subculture). But these discussions should take the form of a dialogue, rather than a monologue. A highly relevant topic is the issue of sexual offenders and their treatment in prison: talk about the bias that each person suffers and that each inflicts on other people. Bible studies can become relevant when inmates are invited to identify with a specific character in a biblical story. I once experienced a fascinating worship discussion with a group of inmates asked to identify with any one of the characters in the story of the Good Samaritan: the robber, the victim, the Samaritan, the innkeeper, the priest, the Levite, or even the donkey. In a second round, they were invited to think which character represented Jesus. Finally, they were asked to consider how and in what role Jesus, if he entered the room, would see each one of them.

Mediating Roles: Intercessor and Advocate

Intercession in the context of Christian faith usually refers to the interceding of Christ on our behalf or to the interceding prayer of Christians on behalf of others. Inmates most commonly pray for themselves and for their families; to extend this interceding concern to people beyond the narrow area of family and friendship is a significant step in spiritual growth and in the growing awareness of others. Visitors function as role models when praying with and for inmates and when taking up their needs in prayer. A prayer touches on experiences at the boundaries of rational life and at the limits of what can be expressed in words. Prayers, in general, mediate transcendence. They are a powerful form of talking to God—and, for those joining in prayer, of interacting with others. A prayer transforms the quality of the moment and makes transcendence present in the profanity of prison life. Intercessory prayer establishes a triangular relationship where visitor and inmate gather in a joint relationship to God. In the interceding prayer, visitors forward the prisoner's (their partner's) needs and sadness to God, and an inmate may thus find relief. This spiritual dimension of Christian visitors points to an important difference between psychological therapy and Christian healing: in psychotherapy the client experiences the relationship with the counselor as a mirror that reflects the client's own thoughts and needs; in Christian healing, a person finds a window to a transcendent reality—a window through which the wind of another reality blows. Christian visitors can trust that even without being overtly religious, they bring this triangular relationship into an encounter. They have a role and a spiritual dimension that mediates transcendence and thus naturally has a transforming impact. I am particularly aware of this mediating role during visits to the block of solitary confinement or, as frequently happens, when I meet inmates who simply ask me to pray for a special need they have.

On the other side, visitors also assume another mediating role that appears in contrast to spiritual mediation but effectively reflects the indissoluble unity between the vertical and the horizontal, or the spiritual and the worldly vision of Jesus: Intercession happens in worldly form when visitors intercede on behalf of inmates—with prison authorities, with government offices, or with judicial boards. Intercession can take several forms: (a) intercession *on behalf of individuals*, most commonly through supporting letters to parole boards but also in cases where inmates are at a special disadvantage: for example as a single Spanish speaker among a group of Chinese speakers; (b) intercession *on behalf of a group of inmates* who face a particular problem: as minority groups (e.g., because of their native language), as sexual offenders, who are segregated from other inmates in a special workshop and denied privileges that other prisoner groups are granted; or as inmates of a workshop who feel threatened by other specific inmates; and (c) *on behalf of prisoners as a whole*, when addressing general penal issues.

This horizontal form of intercession is better known as *advocacy*. Advocacy is a difficult but inevitable role for visitors, especially for chaplains. A visitor needs to adopt a basic bias in favor of those in prison, even if inmates are also active perpetrators of injustice. This demand first arises from what we described in the last chapter as key qualities of visitors; and, second, it arises from an approach that understands crime not purely in individualistic terms but as a result of the brokenness of our society and linked to a wider political, economic, and social context.

Though chaplains are often the only ones available to intercede for prisoners, advocacy is risky because it threatens the relationship with the prison administration and implies that those advocating change know better. Many chaplains indeed know a lot, at times even things concealed from senior management. Yet frontline officers, in daily contact with inmates, know more. Advocacy is an intricate balancing act: by interceding on behalf of individual inmates, groups of inmates, or even the whole prison population, chaplains take a stand against the prison administration. This is at least how most prison administrations perceive any intercessory intervention or advocacy. Such a step, then, can in the long term undermine a chaplain's credibility, good standing, and working relationship with the administration. A chaplain who is marked as a troublemaker opposing the administration will, in the long term, find many impediments to work and will probably achieve less than might have been accomplished with a toned-down approach. Even in cases of suspected violence perpetrated by prison staff against inmates where reports come from reliable sources, it is very difficult to intervene.

> In my earlier years there was a situation when I confronted the prison warden with worrying information I had received about a case of staff violence against an inmate. In the discussion with the warden, I realized that there was no proof. I should have known better. Either the violence did not happen, or if it did, the perpetrators knew how to avoid the view of the installed closed-circuit TV cameras. Nowadays I usually tell inmates frankly what my, and

more so, their possibilities are. I encourage them to seek justice, but I remind them that they are facing an uphill battle, and that their attempt to find justice will have its costs.

Often the most significant result of intercessory intervention is a bad reputation for the chaplain and added burdens on an already difficult diplomatic relationship with the prison administration. Chaplains face similar challenges when they decide to make public statements about penal policies. Prison administrations expect the same loyalty and submission from chaplains as from all other staff, even if chaplains are not on the government payroll. A public expression of opposition to penal policies is seen as a breach of confidence and is most strongly condemned.

Experienced chaplains warn about too much eagerness in assuming the role of the inmates' advocate, although they agree that it is an indispensable role for themselves and for visitors.[4] We will discuss in the next chapter why the ministry of visiting those in prison still has a social and prophetic dimension. Visitors should always be aware that they cannot refashion the prison system; they cannot circumvent rules even if the rules appear inhuman and degrading. However, the intercession on behalf of inmates, if done in humility, has a further spiritual dimension. When visitors intercede on behalf of others and, as usual, just run into brick walls, they participate in the continuous experience of weakness and powerlessness that characterises the inmates' own lives.

Connecting Roles: Friend and Guest[5]

The roles of friend and guest provide what many inmates most yearn for: a fellowship of mutuality and support. Assuming the role of a friend implies an equality that is a standard of our new fellowship in Christ: "I do not call you servants any longer, because the servant does not know what his master is doing; but I have called you friends because I have made known to you everything that I have heard from my Father" (John 15:15). Encountering inmates as friends describes the relationship as a bond between equal

---

4. Pederson, *How to Establish a Jail and Prison Ministry*, 111; see also Shaw, *Chaplains to the Imprisoned*, 127.

5. For a wider discussion of the role of friendship, its applicability and its ambiguity in pastoral counseling in general and in the context of prison in particular, see Brandner, "Seelsorge und Freundschaft," 184–200.

Christians on a joint spiritual journey,[6] and it avoids all connotations of condescension that hamper growth and obstruct genuine relationships.

The role of guest points even more strongly to conviviality as the basic form of Christian life in fellowship. Conviviality is the togetherness of Christians that includes mutual support, learning in partnership, and fellowship in celebration.[7] In fellowship, Christians share not only the word of God but also their lives, or in the words of St. Paul: "So deeply do we care for you that we are determined to share with you not only the gospel of God but also our own selves, because you have become very dear to us" (1 Thess 2:8)

The role of guest is ambiguous, as it implies that prison is the home of the inmates, who host the visitors. Prison never fully becomes a home to inmates; if it does, they have become institutionalized to an unhealthy degree. On the other hand, prison is a temporary reality, and maintaining a constant rejection of one's life environment is equally unhealthy. I regard the role of guest as one of the most sensitive ways of approaching inmates. If visitors come as guests, they express the highest level of respect and value to their hosts. A guest accepts the rules of the host and enters the alien prison environment as somebody who wants to learn and understand what it means to live in such an environment and about the spiritual challenges of such a place. Guests come with questions rather than with answers and solutions, with a healthy curiosity, and with respect for the local culture. A friend's care and a guest's relatedness reach beyond the moment of togetherness. Inmates recognize and acknowledge the genuineness of the connecting roles if they see that the connecting bond goes beyond a one-time encounter. Showing reliability, continuity, and memory of what a person has shared are important ways to express friendship and respect.

> It is helpful to keep a record of visits and to consult it before the next encounter. Such a record is also a useful device for intercessory prayer between visits. If visitors repeatedly ask the same question, they are perceived as not really paying attention and not caring. Inmates will feel frustrated if they share their deep concerns with a visitor and, upon the next visit, find out that the visitor has forgotten all they had said. Another useful way of expressing ongoing care and friendship is through a short note or

---

6. See Moltmann, *Church in the Power of the Spirit*, 314ff.

7. The term *conviviality* is important in Latin American liberation theology, where it is often referred to with the Portuguese *convivência*. See Sundermeier, "Konvivenz," 49–100, especially 51–59.

letter as feedback to an encounter or as encouragement on issues addressed during the encounter.

Up to now we have introduced different roles that visitors typically assume and that impress complementary roles on those visited. The roles discussed so far have in varying degrees implied mutuality or inequality. The following section discusses more explicitly how inequality affects the communication of the gospel.

COMMUNICATING THE GOSPEL IN THE CONTEXT OF INEQUALITY

The reality of prison ministry is that visitors and inmates stand in a relation of radical inequality and one-sided dependence. No matter how much we emphasize mutuality and equality in prison ministry, the reality of this inequality cannot be denied. Visitors can come and go as they like, while inmates are bound to stay. Visitors can choose to render certain services or not, while inmates have little to offer in reciprocity besides their affection and gratitude. Visitors can initiate encounters and all kinds of programs, while inmates depend fully on steps taken by visitors.

Moreover, ministry in prison involves another inequality that is possibly more significant: an *emotional inequality*, or a *relational dependency*. Dependency between the caring person and the one receiving care is a common problem in pastoral care, exacerbated by the context of prison. Visitors gain excessive relational power as they turn into important sources of love and warmth in the lives of inmates who, deprived of their previous nurturing networks, yearn for close relationships and acceptance. Inmates strongly respond to the visitors' presence and their offers of help, and they willingly believe in order to deepen a friendship that has become so vital when deprived of loving and caring mutual relationships. Evangelism is, in this light, understandably easy.

This inequality is not something visitors can actively shape. It is part of the reality they encounter. Visitors should, however, be aware of it, be sensitive to the potential for abuse, and adjust their communicative behavior to this imbalance. People in crisis (as many people in prison are, at least for some periods) are highly receptive. They are less defensive, more vulnerable, more accessible to help from outside, more willing to enter into dependent relationships, and more open to new ways of coping with problems. This emotional state can, as we have seen, be an asset. It can be an opportunity to discover new spiritual dimensions and new mental and emotional ways of coping with hardship. But the heightened vulnerability and accessibility can also be exploited when visitors take quick advantage to turn inmates to Christ, or when they lead people into deeper dependency and into regressive forms of faith. When proclamation of the gospel overpowers inmates and fails to take into account the imbalance between visitors and inmates, the liberating and life-giving power of the gospel is spoiled. Such evangelism turns the biblical message of the cross upside down. It expresses a mentality of conquest and extension of one's own empire, and puts the inmates in a situation of sink or swim. Structurally, it is not much different from Triad recruitment. Insensitive evangelism makes inmates feel that their relational bond with visitors is conditional on positive reception of the Christian faith.

The inequality in the visitor-inmate relationship is particularly striking when one visits those in solitary confinement—an issue for chaplains but not for other visitors. Walking through the isolation ward, going from cell to cell, peering through the bars of the door, and greeting the inmate, who has no prior notice of such a visit, represents an intrusion into the inmate's small private realm without being directly invited. The intrusive effect is mitigated by the fact that a good number of people come by in the course of a day: food distributors, senior staff or justices of the peace making inspections, or prison guards making random tours. Still, the setting of the encounter between chaplain and inmate stands in contrast to the intention of a caring and equal visit. In such a situation, when intruding upon the privacy of the inmate, a chaplain should refrain from dominating the content of the encounter.

The relational inequality naturally has an impact on the method of preaching in the context of imprisonment, as it renders certain theological categories inappropriate. One of them is the wrath and judgment of God. Obviously, it is part of the Christian faith tradition to believe in the final judgment of God, and in God's revealing himself not only as loving and forgiving but also as wrathful. However, if a visitor challenges an inmate to face the wrath of God, this happens from an already existing power imbalance. Proclamation unaware of the relational one-sidedness, blind to the reality of inequality, is a form of spiritual corruption that imagines spiritual processes to happen in purely spiritual realms.

CHRISTIAN CARE AND PROPAGATION OF FAITH

Throughout this and the last chapter I have been speaking consciously about Christian care (or simply the ministry of visitation) rather than about prison evangelism. There are several reasons for a cautious approach to evangelism in prison. First, as has been seen above, a deliberate strategy of evangelism that directly aims at conversion neglects the uneven power relationship between visitor-evangelist and inmate. The Christian evangelist comes from outside prison, from a position of having, from a position of liberty; to evangelize people in prison from this standpoint turns them into recipients instead of respecting them as subjects. Such evangelism fails to respond to their deepest spiritual need: receiving full personhood and acceptance into a fellowship of mutuality.

Second, evangelism happens more effectively through other inmates —person-to-person evangelism within the same people group—than through people from outside. The prime task of visitors is instead to be an inviting community. This means (a) to communicate invitation beyond mere words through an invitational lifestyle of the community, and (b) to establish an environment that enhances evangelism and an atmosphere that encourages Christian inmates to extend the invitation to other inmates.

Third, when visitors propagate faith during an encounter and aim at conversion, the encounter often becomes a kind of contest where inmates are persuaded of the truth of Christianity and pushed to admit or accept it. Such an evangelistic approach is unlikely to be sustainable and will not be the beginning of a creative relationship in which genuine spiritual growth happens. The visiting and care ministries should engage those in prison not on the level of arguments about faith but on the level of their existential questions and conflicting feelings.

Fourth, visitors who propagate faith in prison and engage in prison evangelism commonly aim at a response, a transformation and conversion on the side of the inmates. Such an attitude neglects the fact that conversion is not a one-off event but a lifelong process. Also, true conversion is not a one-way communicative event that aims at change only in the target of evangelization; it involves both sides of an encounter. It includes processes on the side of the visitors—shifts in perception of the inmates, or increased attention to remaining prejudices—as much as it calls for a process of repentance and transformation on the side of the inmate.

Fifthly, and most important, allowing inmates to witness the principles of Christian faith and life at work attracts them more than any solely cognitive propagation of Christian faith. Sometimes visitors focus on the cognitive content of faith to the neglect of the relational aspect. The living encounter with Jesus Christ through the experience of being accepted and valued is a direct, practical, and emotional way of teaching what Christian faith means. When the visitors' message is too word centered, the evangelistic invitation turns into its opposite and frightens people. This is especially the case when one shares the Christian faith among people with low levels of (or little interest in) literacy. Partly for this reason, pentecostal missions have been successful: their services are less word centered; their language is less abstract and closer to the people. Propagation of faith that focuses only on the cognitive level ignores the fact that the visiting ministry already is evangelism, in practical and experiential form. Evangelism is not the proclamation of objective truth but the *truth actualizing itself* in the encounter. To be visited and thus to be valued, to be cared for and thus to be loved, is indeed the best possible news. It is the most powerful way that the gospel, the good news of Jesus Christ, can substantiate itself. A nonverbal invitation that manifests itself through Christian presence, through deeds, or through witness ultimately reflects the incarnational character of what we invite to: God incarnate.

RELIGIOUS LANGUAGE IN PRISON

A related cautiousness applies to the use of religious language in the encounter with inmates. It is a misunderstanding to think that frequent use of religious language makes an encounter more spiritual. The spirituality of an encounter does not lie in the use of specific vocabulary but in its overall quality: whether an encounter builds a bridge to basic experiences of Christian faith, whether it is transparent to the experience of God's loving and forgiving presence, and whether it communicates the values of the kingdom of God. Religious language as such has no intrinsic value; it only tries to interpret, indirectly and on a secondary level, the primary religious experiences of people who have been touched by the presence of God in the midst of their lives. Giving comfort without using religious words is a completely valid form of spreading the gospel.

Having said that, I note several situations when religious language obviously adds value to an encounter. A first, obvious place is the worship, where implicit spiritual experiences can find explicit interpretation. Worship services are, among other things, training grounds to explore and learn the use of religious expressions. Another appropriate opportunity is when somebody gives a public testimony and shares about faith experiences. The religious expressions highlight and interpret these experiences for an audience less familiar with religious language. To introduce biblical themes in individual encounters can be a way of consolidating and summarizing a conversation that was, in the first place, centered on personal experiences. When visitors help inmates link their own experiences with those of the biblical tradition, they underline the relevance and validity that transcend the present moment. Religious expressions can further have a powerful reframing effect, as has been seen above. Sentences like "It was God who arrested me," or "I am in prison, but I am free," if spoken from the perspective of the inmate and not imposed by visitors, transform the inmates' very reality. Therefore, religious language turns from a secondary event that describes reality to a primary one that causes and shapes reality. Finally, prayers similarly use religious language. To conclude an encounter with a prayer may be a genuine need for a visitor, more so than for the inmate. It will be helpful if the prayer is simple and short—this can give the inmate an idea of what prayers sound like. A prayer that is too verbose will alienate a person who is less used to religious language.

Overall, visitors need to be aware that using spiritual expressions, biblical words, or theological interpretations in a real-life situation can block a conversation. Hasty introduction of religious language and the use of heavy theological words will have a divisive effect, excluding those who are not familiar with biblical words or theological terms or phrases. Many inmates will not feel comfortable enough to admit that they do not understand religious words, and some inmates will feel constrained to model their personal sharing after the biblical pattern. Religious words only make sense if both sides in the encounter understand the framework.[8]

PHYSICAL CONTACT DURING A VISIT

A final issue that deserves short mention is the reality of physical contact between visitors and inmates. What I am referring to in this section is physical contact between persons of the same gender. When men visit female inmates, additional factors come into play, not least the exacerbated power imbalance between visitor and inmate because of gender power

---

8. For some guidelines for the use of religious language see also Clinebell, *Basic Types of Pastoral Care*, 122–23.

inequalities. What gives added delicacy to the ministry of male visitors to female inmates is that many women carry wounds from the past or have experienced abuse that will interfere with a caring relationship. On the other hand, women visitors to male prisons should be aware that their mere presence in an environment where inmates are deprived of heterosexual encounters carries connotations not at all spiritual. This should not be a reason for women to avoid visiting male prisons. On the contrary, assuming a nurturing and motherly role, helping inmates connect with their emotional lives by building up a balanced relationship to persons of the opposite gender, or simply being role models and showing another image of womanhood (different from what many of the inmates know)—all these are crucial contributions for women to make in prison ministry. However, since public physical contact between persons of different genders is generally avoided in prison, this obviously applies equally to the religious setting, even if at times the warmth and the togetherness of the fellowship interfere with cultural codes. Physical contact beyond the simple and ritual handshake is misleading and best avoided.

There are different forms of physical contact between persons of the same gender, some more ritualized or formalized, others more casual and ordinary. A ritual touch, like the laying on of hands when praying, is common. It underlines on a physical level the spiritual link that emerges when people join in prayer and meditation, and it transmits warmth and strength nonverbally. The handicap of such ritual touch is that it allows little reciprocity. The physical nature of the encounter can be distracting, and adjustment in case of unease happens less casually and may take on added meaning. Ordinary physical contact—through holding hands when walking or through handshakes, hugs, or taps on another person's forearm, shoulder, or back—is more important and more natural.

Physical contact is an important form of communication and is a strong expression of care. It reflects the holistic character of our ministry that includes healthy relationships to our bodies. Physical contact can assume different meanings; most simply it is communication where our usual word-based communication fails or is unavailable.

> Ah-Hung was an inmate who had suffered an accident that caused minor damage to his brain. He had difficulties communicating verbally, although he seemed to understand what happened around him. His communicative difficulties caused frequent disciplinary conflicts that brought him into solitary confinement.

> There I met him and, unable to engage in meaningful communication, I stretched my hand through the bars of the door and felt how he gripped it and started to massage it in a tender and loving way. The several minutes of speechless physical encounter belong to the most intense moments I have experienced as a chaplain.

Physical contact is an important form of expressing acceptance, friendship, and fatherly or motherly love, and it transcends the inside/outside separation. Against our common perception of Asian people as physically distanced and controlled, I have discovered that if there is a good level of trust, most inmates are at ease with close physical contact—not only among their peers, but also with the chaplain or with staff. It is common for inmates to walk in the courtyard holding hands, or to sit together in close physical contact.

> Ah-Lam was a young inmate on a life sentence for murder. For many years, he had been confined to the psychiatric prison because he was regarded as suicidal. After his transfer, he soon started to join our worship. He was glad to find somebody familiar when he met me again in this new environment. In the process of a growing relationship, he went through a strong spiritual transformation and confessed his past guilt. Eventually he asked for baptism. During the baptismal worship, he publicly shared what he had gone through in his life. Our long hug after the baptism was like the peak of a father-son relationship, like the conclusion of a life that had gone terribly wrong, and like the signal for the start to a new life.

Physical contact can also provide a way of understanding. A handshake that is overly stiff or other signs of physical unease can point to hidden wounds or past physical abuse. People with a history of having suffered physical abuse usually spontaneously assume a body posture that keeps other people at bay. It needs sensitivity to grow in awareness in physical interaction, as I myself learned when an inmate with a history of having suffered sexual abuse withdrew from my touch. Persons with such a background will easily experience any physical contact beyond a simple handshake as a violation of their boundaries.

Visitors will do well to be attentive to such signs, but they should equally remember that while we are usually more trained in awareness of verbal communication, physical communication carries plenty of ambiguity and a great potential for misunderstanding. This is particularly the case in communication with people of different cultural backgrounds, whose body language and cultural code we spontaneously often fail to understand. A tap on the shoulder or touch on the forearm can express equality and togetherness as easily as superficiality and condescension.

> Walking through the prison workshops I habitually shook hands with many inmates. Alternatively, when people were busy and did not have their hands free, I used to communicate by a slight touch on the upper arm or shoulder. I did the same when meeting people busy holding cards during card games. Only after many years did some inmates point out to me that a tap on the arm or the shoulder of a person gambling is believed to expel good fortune and to bring misfortune in gambling.

PRINCIPLES OF COMMUNICATION (II)

- *Roles*—Assume as much as possible roles that increase equality between you and your counterpart.
- *Respect*—Be a guest and behave accordingly: Meet the culture and life context of the inmates with respect.
- *Sharing the gospel*—Remember that the simple fact of your visit is the most powerful form of communicating the good news of Jesus Christ.
- *Religious Language*—Be conservative in using religious language: The spiritual potential of an encounter does not depend on it.

BIBLIOGRAPHICAL NOTES

> I am not aware of any specific study on the *different roles in pastoral counseling*, far less on such roles in the context of prison. Obviously, what role a visitor likes to adopt depends, besides the factors mentioned above, especially on a person's understanding of what pastoral counseling is. The highly readable compendium of Doris Nauer, *Seelsorgekonzepte im Widerstreit: Ein Kompendium* (Stuttgart: Kohlhammer, 2001)—unfortunately only available in German—describes different concepts of pastoral counseling. Introducing each of these concepts, Nauer also critically reflects on each concept's articulation of the pastoral counselor's role. The book gives insight into the diversity and the strengths and weaknesses of different pastoral roles.

The writings of Henri Nouwen, especially "Creative Ministry" in *Ministry and Spirituality* (New York: Dayspring Edition, 1998) and *Reaching Out* (Fount Paperbacks 1998[1975]) give profound inspiration to the idea of the *visitor as friend and guest*. Nouwen has inspired a good number of pastoral counselors to further develop this concept, among them the German theologian Rolf Zerfass in *Menschliche Seelsorge* (Freiburg: Herder, 1985). Sallie McFague's *Metaphorical Theology: Models of God in Religious Language* (Philadelphia: Fortress, 1982) develops the idea within a more systematic-theological framework and discusses the idea on the level of the image of God by arguing for the use of the metaphor of friendship to express a mature relationship with God. Further discussion of the pastoral role of friendship can be found in Tobias Brandner, "Seelsorge und Freundschaft: Pastorale Rollenvielfalt und Rollenambiguität in der Gefangenenseelsorge," in Ralph Kunz and Isabelle Noth, eds., *Nachdenkliche Seelsorge—Seelsorgliches Nachdenken: Festschrift für Christoph Morgenthaler* (Arbeiten zur Pastoraltheologie, Liturgik und Hymnologie 62; Göttingen: Vandenhoeck & Ruprecht, 2012), 184–200 (available in German).

8

Prison Ministry as a Social Ministry

THE PREVIOUS CHAPTERS DESCRIBED inmates' transformations and spiritual changes and how the communicative and role behavior of visitors enhances such changes. The focus was firmly on those inside prison. This chapter shifts attention to the *effect of prison ministry on those outside*— on the church, and on society at large—and asks about the impact on the visitor. We will distinguish different levels of how visitors—and, through them, society—are affected. First, prison ministry touches visitors *spiritually*, as the encounter with inmates' pain helps them rediscover dimensions of their lives that had been buried under the dominant rationality of everyday life. Second, it affects visitors *socially*, as they connect to an alien social reality and, through the encounter with those in prison, learn about the social dimensions of crime and punishment and about the social conflicts in which crime happened. Third, it affects visitors *politically*, as they are drawn into seeing how justice is exerted in our society and how it causes harm to those on the receiving end. The visitors' sociopolitical learning process thus leads them to alternative visions of justice and of changes in the politics of punishment.

The chapter considers the following questions:
- What does prison ministry contribute to visitors' spiritual growth and to the church community at large?

- What impact does the presence of prison visitors have on prison administration and penal affairs?
- How do prison visitors affect penal policies in our society?

THE CHURCH INVOLVED IN PRISON MINISTRY: BEING CHURCH TOGETHER

Inviting church members to join the ministry in prison happens not only for the sake of inmates but also—and equally so—for the visitors themselves. The visit is not a one-way (outside to inside) event: it revives the visitors and, through them, the church as a whole. It builds up the church and provides an opportunity for Christians' relational, spiritual, and theological growth, transcending the simple one-to-one encounter and assuming a social dimension.

The involvement of Christians and church groups in prison ministry affects the whole body of Christ in several ways, two of which begin with the individual. First and very directly, witnessing transformations in prison, celebrating together with people the dramatic shifts in their lives, participating in powerful revivals, "seeing God at work"—all these are greatly reviving experiences for visitors. This is what shapes many chaplains' or prison visitors' accounts of their encounters in prison: the joy of witnessing the power of God in a place of darkness. Second, many volunteers come from demanding professional backgrounds where they find little opportunity for reciprocity. They find it hard to shed the attributes important in their professional lives—strength, domination, success—when participating in normal church life. In the context of prison, however, many visitors find it easier to admit hidden aspects of their lives. They discover that those in prison, apparently so different, are at the same time yet so similar. Visitors and inmates are not as far apart as public opinion and dominant definitions paint them. What makes the prison visit an event that bears so much healing power for visitors is the obvious fellowship of brokenness. The loneliness that many churchgoers experience among all the neatly dressed and well-balanced people is gone, and they realize that they are not alone with their own brokenness and wounds. A visitor gave the following account of how she experienced healing through prison visits:

> What first brought me to visit prison, I cannot recall. All I remember was taking Matthew 25:34 quite literally. I wanted to be the

sheep, and so I took steps to give a glass of water to the thirsty, clothe those who were naked, visit the sick, and the imprisoned. Only the Lord knew that the one imprisoned was myself, and I realized that during the first sermon I heard about forgiveness (through the story of Zacchaeus). I walked out of the prison gate having a few faces in my mind—the faces of my father, my biological brothers, and a few people more. My father was by no means bad. He worked like most fathers did. He gave us food. He never had an affair. He never spanked us. But he simply was not present. We lived in the same house, but like strangers. I seemed transparent to him, all of us did. I always tried very hard to erase the resentment I felt against him, and yet I failed. Now I realize how my struggles with food have so much to do with that. Since my first visit, the question of forgiveness has not quite left me. And if I had to come up with one thing I am most thankful for since visiting prison, it would be the forgiveness God has given me—it is this that allows me to be free from resentment I have held for years. He has taught me to forgive people who have hurt me deeply, and to forgive myself. The moment I made a decision to forgive, the manipulative force of food just vanished.

When walking into the prison chapel for the first time, I had no idea that I was so broken, withholding so many things. My years of experience with males, guys at home and guys I wilfully squandered my youth with, made me fear them more than anything else. Strangely there I was, in a male prison. Perhaps that's the irony. In that group of male prisoners, I discovered gentleness I am not familiar with, acceptance, joy, humility, and simply love. Perhaps the very fact that they are all locked up gave me more assurance: "Don't be afraid; they won't hurt you." So, prison has been a place of healing, a place of love, a place of search and a place of encountering God.

In prison, I find no pressure to be anyone but myself. Why? Perhaps the love, the brokenness, the redemption, the resurrected life and the humanity of the fellowship are the very elements that create a place to feel safe. With my middle-class, professional church friends heading toward a life of marital and monetary prosperity, and with my other friends rolling in the mud of a vicious cycle of sin-confession-sin-confession, I find the little chapel in prison the place where I don't have to pretend to be strong *or* weak. Together, we love and learn to be loved. Together, we let God's healing love and forgiveness fall. Together, from the little love we have, we see hope, and with little hope, faith becomes possible.

This is an account of an individual, but prison ministry has implications that go beyond the individual visitor and shape the church at large. First, it makes the church more inclusive, breaking the narrow bonds of social adjustment and including people at the fringes of society. Many churches are aware of how much they have become a social club for the well-adjusted and relatively successful middle class, but they do not know how to transcend those social boundaries. Becoming a church with those in prison makes the church more whole and more inclusive. A church that partners with prison inmates will be enriched and find itself more fully reflecting the diversity of God's children.

Second, prison ministry changes the image of church, projecting less the image of a victorious communion of the saintly and more a fellowship of sinners standing under the cross. Understanding the church as a victorious communion is not wrong but may create problems. Many ordinary people do not feel qualified enough to be part of such a fellowship; they think church is only for those who are already sufficiently transformed, not for those still bound in sin and brokenness. In contrast, understanding the church in prison as fellowship of sinners turns it into a *low-threshold church* that welcomes people at different points of their spiritual journeys who communicate their wounds and their needs for healing quite visibly.

Finally, a church that includes those in prison will experience an atmospheric change. The visitor quoted above felt safe enough to admit her own need for healing only when she entered a place of broken dreams and broken hopes. What we have said about compassion (see chapter 6) affects the church as a whole. Where the church participates in the suffering and hopelessness of inmates, there it is about more than the other people's suffering—it turns into a joint experience. Others' and one's own suffering are no more hidden and suppressed but more easily admitted and jointly addressed. We are a fellowship that groans with the whole creation (Rom 8:22–23) and that partakes in the pain of those who wait in hope for their wounds to be healed.

PUBLIC INVOLVEMENT IN PENAL MATTERS: UNCOVERING INMATES' INVISIBILITY

Prisons are social institutions that evoke plenty of images. Ever since the public spectacle of corporal punishment gave way to imprisonment, punishment has been largely removed from public view and hidden behind

Prison Ministry as a Social Ministry

thick walls. While inmates' privacy was safeguarded, prisons turned into objects of imagination and, naturally, public anxiety grew around what was unseen. The word *prison* became a metaphor with a broad range of meanings, attracting images of moral evil, social marginality, educational failure, and plenty of other negative connotations. People are at once repelled and fascinated by the reality of a counterculture where other rules are thought to apply. Prison visitors frequently experience how eager people are to hear stories from behind these walls of exclusion and to learn what kind of dreadful figures are confined there. The reality of prison has turned into something invisible. Many traditional cultures associate prison with negative spiritual energies. In superstitious faiths, prisons are believed to be sources of bad luck.

> A young participant in an evangelistic meeting recounted how he was worried about failing to wake up in time and being late for prison ministry. He knew that his mother would not wake him up, as she strongly discouraged him from joining. Even though she knew that he was part of a church group, she was sure that a visit to prison would bring him bad luck.

The invisibility of what happens in prison is in many cultures—and possibly most strongly in Asian cultures, with their strong sense of face—exacerbated by a psychological effect of imprisonment that surrounds it with shame. The condemnation of the evildoer extends to members of the prisoner's family, who are equally shunned. The invisibility cloak[1] that surrounds prisoners is achieved by various means: by the remoteness of most prisons; by security fences that create or support a negative image of those inside and present them as wild animals who need to be locked up for the protection of society; by thick walls, which project an image of danger; by difficult entry procedures that underline the separation of inside and outside.

Establishing contact with those in prison is, therefore, a basic step that contradicts public strategies of shunning them. It uncovers their invisibility and breaks through the isolating walls that bury them under imaginary negative metaphors. Or, more simply, visits make prisoners real, demythologize them, and make it possible to see them for who they are.

This uncovering process has several dimensions that build the social character of prison ministry. First, for many visitors, the encounter with the

---

1. See the presentation given by Youngquist, "Youth and the Criminal Justice System," 4ff.

reality of prison is an eye-opener. The encounter with real people—and the discovery that they are not monsters but merely other human beings who happened to respond to individual, familial, or social problems with wrong decisions or destructive impulses—makes visitors recognize how not only people but, together with them, their social problems have been hidden behind thick walls. The growing sensibility for the inmates' lives and social reality of inmates naturally broadens visitors' perspectives and sharpens their awareness for the social context of crime and punishment. They begin to see the crime-producing factors in our society: the dominant culture of getting rich quickly and of playful material obsessions—whether in casinos or stock markets—that inevitably turn serious; a sexist culture that presents women as readily available and subordinate to male authority; unemployment and an economy that allows hard-working people to remain poor; and, as in the case of Hong Kong, the extreme scarcity of living space that easily leads to family violence. Listening to the stories of inmates helps visitors understand that crime does not happen in a vacuum as the choice of a lone individual who considers how to satisfy greed or other evil impulses. Visitors instead recognize crime as one element in a social conflict of intersecting individual decisions and social factors. The visit leads to a deeper understanding of this social conflict and raises visitors' awareness for the healing needs not only of individuals but also of society as a whole.

Second, visitors learn to balance the tension between individual and communal responsibility. A crime is always a personal act: not everyone in hardship turns to crime. By treating offenders as responsible moral agents, we uphold a positive image of humans and assume that each individual is able to make moral choices. At the same time, standing in the biblical tradition that emphasizes communal responsibility as part of Israel's covenantal relationship with God,[2] we regard the individual as part of a social network that has failed, and we seek to redress those shortcomings.[3] Recent theology, influenced mainly by theologies of liberation, recognizes how the Christian tradition has overemphasized the individual dimension of sin. Christian participation in prison and justice, in turn, naturally grows in the

---

2. Marshall, *Beyond Retribution*, 120–29, especially 124. Marshall discusses the retributive theories and shows how the obvious retributive elements are to be understood as part of Israel's covenantal relationship. Punishment thus happened with the goal of restoring the community. See also Hoyles, *Punishment in the Bible*, 99ff.

3. Haney, *Reforming Punishment*, 133ff, shows how childhood events and developmental contexts, or what he calls sociohistorical factors, increase the likelihood of adult criminal behavior.

Prison Ministry as a Social Ministry

awareness for the corporate dimension of sin. Visitors who reached a deeper understanding of the inmates and of what caused them to be what they are will perceive them not only as sinners but also as those sinned against.[4] To balance individual and communal responsibility lays the ground for a social response to crime that insists on morality but transcends the narrow, individualized scapegoating of people who have committed crimes.

Third, Christian visitors break through the isolation not only of inmates but equally of prison staff. Many unhealthy and destructive dynamics stem from the joint isolation of inmates and frontline staff, who both establish a corporate identity in contrast to the other. A classic psychological test, the Stanford Prison Experiment of 1971, showed how good people can do bad things when placed in an environment designed to elicit mistreatment, and how the prison environment creates specific and oppressive behavior patterns.[5] Visitors break through this harmful dualism—a collective folie à deux—and normalize the prison reality. They help both inmates and the administration to dissolve the black-and-white construction of their reality.

Fourth, the presence of people from outside—not only in the visiting room but also in the chapel, the core of many prison buildings—is a natural form of community involvement in a sensitive area of society. Visitors are able to see what the wider society does not. They acquire basic knowledge of an otherwise invisible area of society. This applies even more to the chaplain, who is not part of the prison administration, and who can walk through all prison wards. This special insight (some may call it a supervisory function) does not need to become explicit and should remain low key. Prison visitors hardly have the means to directly address problems of the prison system, but their mere presence has a reconciling effect. A total institution left on its own, without community involvement, tends to foster abuse. Too often prisons are seen as sovereign territory of those in charge where the administration controls even the official supervisory channels. Volunteer participation in prison ministry counters such temptations and moves the closed area of a total institution into the public realm, where it belongs. It reminds administrators that prisons are part of the social and communal realm.

---

4. The expression of the "sinned against" goes ultimately back to the Lord's Prayer —see more in chapter 9. In the penal discussion, it has for example been used by Menninger, *The Crime of Punishment*, 19.

5. See bibliographic notes to chapter 1. The Stanford Prison Experiment has gained new relevance in the wake of the abuses at Abu Ghraib.

Finally, the prison experience equips visitors to become an important resource for community involvement in rehabilitation and care for ex-offenders (see chapter 3). In addition, prison visitors also become low-key, lay experts in matters of prison and criminal justice. They prepare the ground for a more community-based punishment, to which we now turn.

PRISON MINISTRY AND PENAL REFORM: SEEING JUSTICE FROM THE INSIDE OF PRISON

The ministry of presence and of communion with the inmates, the compassion and empathic listening, all lead to a growing ability to see the world from the perspective of those behind bars, the recipients of punishment.[6] Visitors will discover that justice is obviously a central issue in the life of inmates, and they will recognize the need to face issues of justice in the larger context of social justice.[7] With the inmates they experience how prison-based punishment, in its attempt to repair the harm caused by crime, fails to repair it and instead causes new and more harm.[8] It leaves many inmates with anger, self-centeredness, and distorted personalities, which easily lead them to renewed crime; prison-based punishment destroys the social network on which inmates had previously depended for a life without crime. Removing people from their community and keeping them in special places of punishment hinders their later reintroduction into society. For one thing, ex-convicts may face an inability to adjust to the outside world. For another, the wider society harbors negative attitudes toward them. According to Nacro, a British charity that works to prevent crime and resettle offenders, 60 percent of ex-offenders find their work applications rejected specifically because they have been in prison.[9] Prison stays also harm the families of those in prison, although they are innocent of the crimes committed: children who lose a father or mother, spouses who are left as single parents, or parents who lose the support of a son or daughter. Prisons are a huge expense of public funds with little positive return and still fail to repair the harm done to the victims of crime.

---

6. Pattison, *Pastoral Care and Liberation Theology*, 235, comes to the same conclusion for a sociopolitically aware pastoral care in the context of the mental health sector.

7. See also Welch, *Ironies of Imprisonment*, 23.

8. See the more extensive description in Consedine, *Restorative Justice* (chapter 1).

9. See Thompson and Cavadino, "Role of Non-Governmental Agencies," 5.

Prison Ministry as a Social Ministry

This is where restorative justice comes in. As doubts grow about current policies of punishment, penologists and penal practitioners have started to focus on alternative approaches to crime and punishment. Restorative justice has become one of the key answers in this search and a central concern of NGOs like Prison Fellowship International. A growing number of penal practitioners and academics, frustrated by the dead ends in the present justice system, are devising ways to reform the present penal system. Dead ends in the system can affect judges, legislators, and prison administrators. For instance, judges may have no choice but to impose harsh sentences even though they may be expensive and counterproductive. During their annual budget debates, lawmakers may confront rising costs in the penal apparatus (even as crime rates fall[10]). Prison administrators face a high number of repeat offenders returning to their supervision. The 2001 retirement speech of the British chief inspector of prisons, Sir David Ramsbotham, gives us a glimpse of how deep the awareness of systemic failure is among those running prisons, even if thorough reforms have not materialized:

"If prison worked, there would be work or education for every prisoner.

If prison worked, we would be shutting prisons, not opening more.

If prison worked, judges would not be seeing in the dock the same people over and over again.

If prison worked, we would not be imprisoning more people than any other European country except Turkey.

If prison worked, fewer mothers would be in prison and fewer children would be in care.

If prison worked, we would be saving billions of pounds with fewer prisons, fewer care homes and fewer court cases."[11]

Restorative justice has several *key characteristics*. First, it places *victims at the center* of justice. Victims are of course those who have been

---

10. Todd R. Clear, a professor in criminal justice, in a foreword to Consedine, *Restorative Justice*, ix. Clear states that since 1975, there has been almost the same number of years of declining crime rates as years of increasing crime rates in the US. However, prison populations have gone up every year. See also the numbers and a chart about the growth of imprisonment in Blomberg, *American Penology*, 224–26 (chart on page 225).

11. Ramsbotham, *Prisongate*, quoted in Catholic Bishops' Conference of England and Wales, *Place of Redemption*, 1. The words actually came from the chief inspector's wife, who had watched her husband struggle with the lamentable state of Britain's prisons.

harmed by a crime, yet in the current retributive system they receive no compensation and experience no healing. Restorative justice takes the concerns of the victims seriously. It is a common but wrong assumption of retributive justice that victims are helped most by toughness against offenders. To be sure, a tough punishment can give a certain satisfaction to a victim. However, what victims need more is transparency in the legal process, channels for their voices to be heard, assistance in healing the wounds of crime, and, where applicable, compensation. Restorative justice aims at healing the harm done to victims while at the same time restraining them from unlimited personal revenge.

Second, restorative justice is *community based* instead of state based. Most traditional societies regard crime as a violation of communal relationships requiring restoration.[12] An understanding of crime as a violation of an abstract code of law and of the state's authority is a later development. Only in medieval Europe did crimes turn from violations of a person or a community into violations of the king and the royal order.[13] Then the response to crime became more abstract and lost the element of reconciliation between offender and victim. Restorative justice recovers this communal dimension by including all affected parties: victim, offender, families, the community, police, and judicial representatives. Government and local communities work together to make sure that the interests of all involved are dealt with appropriately.

Third, restorative justice *involves the offender* by placing responsibility for an offense in his or her hands. In a traditional judicial process the offender faces judge, jury, and witness as a passive recipient of punishment. In a community-based judicial setting the offender faces the pain of victims and families more directly. This can prompt offenders to recognize the harm done and prepare them to become actively involved in finding ways to repair it.

Fourth, and particularly important for us, restorative justice is *biblical*. This is the overwhelming consensus of both biblical and restorative-justice scholars.[14] The biblical justice tradition seeks restoration of just relation-

---

12. Consedine shows this with reference to the Maori tradition of Aotearoa (New Zealand); see Consedine, *Restorative Justice*, 161; Van Ness shows it with reference to ancient law and the tradition of the Old Testament, see Van Ness, *Crime and Its Victims*, 64–65 and chapter 10.

13. Van Ness, *Crime and Its Victims*, 66–67.

14. See Hoyles, *Punishment in the Bible*, 28ff; Marshall, *Beyond Retribution*, 45–59; Consedine, *Restorative Justice*, 147–56; Van Ness, *Crime and Its Victims*, 103–39.

ships, a *shalom* justice, rather than simple punishment. It aims at reconciliation between victim and offender and regards sanctions as simply one (rather than the most important) part in the process of healing the wounds of crime.

Various *models of restorative justice* have successfully been tested and applied: community-service projects, restitution programs that aim to pay financially for a crime, victim-offender reconciliation programs, family or community group conferences, community-based supervision programs, and many others.[15] A lasting and successful program is the *Sycamore Tree scheme* run by a number of Prison Fellowship groups. In this program, prisoners hear from volunteers who have been victims of crime, with the aim that offenders' awareness of the victims will be raised.

Restorative justice has two further consequences. First, punishment becomes less prison based. The widespread dependence on prison-based punishment is like a doctor prescribing the same medication for every kind of bodily pain. Restorative justice does not reject prison-based punishment but reduces its dominance in the justice system. The growth in imprisonment rates is particularly acute in the United States, where by the beginning of 2008 the incarceration number for the first time crossed the critical threshold of one in 100 adult US Americans.[16] A trend toward higher rates of incarceration and more prison construction can be observed in other places as well. Custodial punishment is the most expensive and, as we have seen, the least effective way of responding to crime; yet, as Norval Morris, a scholar in the history of prison, points out, "the irony is that the less effective the prisons are in reducing crime, the higher the demand for more imprisonment."[17]

Restorative justice instead reserves custodial punishment for offenders who are unwilling to participate in or fail to positively respond to restorative-justice forms, as well as for recidivists and for the minority who, due to their violence, pose a danger to the community. Restorative justice uncovers the ineffectiveness and harm of much prison-based punishment, most particularly in the case of short sentences that do not allow enough time for serious rehabilitative programs. Restorative justice reduces the harm that results from prison-based punishment and that leads to the

---

15. For an overview of successful initiatives and programs see Church Council on Justice and Corrections, *Satisfying Justice*; see also Van Ness, *Crime and Its Victims*, chapter 12.

16. See footnote 20 below.

17. Morris, "Contemporary Prison," 229.

destructive cycle of repeated offending: broken relationships, disrupted lives, or professional disqualification. Alternatives to prison-based punishment include intensive supervision, suspended sentences, fines, home confinement, periodic (night or weekend) imprisonment, boot camp, or restriction orders. Examples from the history of alternative justice methods support the argument: in France, a rise in suspended sentences reduced the prison population by half between 1887 and 1956.[18] In Sweden during the 1960s it became official policy to use prisons as little and as painlessly as possible.[19] During the same period most European states successfully introduced noncustodial sentences for first-time offenders without an adverse impact on the crime rate.[20]

The second consequence of restorative justice is that it aims to normalize the prison context and advocates reforms that reduce the harm emerging from imprisonment.[21] Restorative justice favors making prison environments as much like the free world as possible and removing unnecessary hardships. In many cases, prisons with less supervision and more internal autonomy for inmates are the best means of returning offenders to society as productive citizens[22] without jeopardizing the security of other inmates. In a restorative-justice framework, rather than being kept (at a high cost) in high-security prisons (a scheme that risks fostering their criminal potential[23]), first-time offenders are assigned to low-security prisons or prisons without walls.

This has been only a short summary of what restorative justice is. This book is neither about restorative justice nor about penal reform, and those who want to learn more can easily find the relevant information (see the bibliographic notes). What we are trying to show is that *prison ministry and*

---

18. O'Brien, "Prison on the Continent," 189.

19. Ibid., 197.

20. Although this is not sufficiently supported by methodologically satisfactory studies, we can responsibly claim that alternative punishments do not appear to lead to an increase in crime or in recidivism; see Morris, "Contemporary Prison," 229. Equally, no serious research has been able to demonstrate a positive link between a higher rate of imprisonment and a reduction of the crime rate.

21. Haney, *Reforming Punishment*, 308ff.

22. O'Brian, "Prison on the Continent," 196–97, with further historical examples.

23. Slosar, *Prisonization*, 128, shows in his sociological research how inmates who had been less involved in a life of crime (as measured by the number of previous offenses) were significantly affected by the restrictive organizational climate and were prisonized by adopting behavior patterns of prison.

Prison Ministry as a Social Ministry

the restorative-justice movement are closely related, not just random partners. The ministry of visitation, the real encounter with those in prison, builds a background and gradually moves the penal and judicial movement towards restorative justice. Christians who have experienced the transforming and reconciling power of forgiveness will carry this experience from the realm of the individual into the corporate realm and call for a justice that moves beyond retributive punishment to one that fosters reconciliation. They will naturally apply faith-based principles in their quest for a judicial and penal system that allows true healing and change. They will join attempts to move away from mere punishment and toward the restoration of broken relationships. Both prison ministry and restorative justice share the same spirit and principles, which stand in contrast to retributive punishment. Both express a form of power with instead of power over those to be punished. In a restorative-justice model an offender does not passively receive his or her punishment from an authoritarian judge. Rather, the judge or an appropriate community representative and other concerned parties (or their representatives), together with the offender, seek a way to heal the harm caused by crime. The first step in a reconciliation process is the visitors' affirmation of the inmates' subject status.

To conclude, whenever people visit prisons, this act goes beyond the individual encounter and turns it into a social ministry: Visitors go through a sociopolitical learning process that leads them both to a growing understanding of the social role of prison and criminal justice, and to an empathy toward what it means to be at the receiving end of penal policies. This learning process connects restorative justice and prison ministry. Visitors discover the prison as an institution at a social intersection: the values of a society set in stones, in law codes and in penal practices—or, as Fyodor Dostoevsky put it, "The degree of civilization in a society can be judged by entering its prisons."[24] By entering prison neither in captivity nor as part of the paid staff, visitors learn about strategies and policies of punishment, about structures of social control, and about the values defined by the politically, socially, economically, or culturally dominant elements in a society. This learning process teaches visitors about how our society works, how it punishes, how it excludes and includes, how it distinguishes right and wrong—and it is as basic to Christian education as to know the Bible. Visiting those in prison is, for those who are willing to do it, a simple

---

24. Dostoevsky, *The House of the Dead*.

education in the values and the functioning of our society and therefore an integral part of Christian learning.

Getting in touch with the perspective of the recipients of punishment equips Christian citizens to critically face politicians who call for tougher punishment or to wisely inform people ignorant about the length, the reality, and the pain of imprisonment. Visitors will point to contradictions in penal practices and ask, is passing new criminal laws (or maintaining existing ones), thus creating new prisoners, the most appropriate way of dealing with social problems?[25] Or, why does distributing or using certain drugs lead to lengthy imprisonment while distributing or using other drugs (not necessarily healthier ones) increases corporate profits? Christians asking these questions will emphasize that legal tenets and penal practices—what constitutes a crime (and what does not), how crime is punished, and how people are treated during punishment—are not God given but change through history and mirror the dominant values of a society at any given time. Questioners realize, as Erik Wright stated, that "the punishment of crime is a political act."[26]

Building bridges between the inside of a prison and the outside world equips visitors to understand that prisons do not survive because they were effective, but because they have successfully linked contradictory social roles and justifications for punishment (deterrence, incapacitation, retribution, and rehabilitation), and because the socially established dichotomy of inside and outside the law, and inside and outside prison, remains an instrument of social control. The visiting ministry rejects this logic and negates through its very action the great divide.

Bibliographical Notes

> On *restorative justice* see Charles Colson and Daniel Van Ness, *Convicted: New Hope for Ending America's Crime Crisis* (Westchester, IL: Crossway, 1989); Daniel W. Van Ness, *Crime and Its Victims* (Downers Grove, IL: InterVarsity, 1986). These two books give a solid introduction into the topic of restorative justice.

---

25. It is interesting to note that in one particular year half the criminals arrested in the US were held for violation of legal precepts that had not been crimes fifteen years before, see Tannenbaum, *Crime and the Community*, chapter 2, quoted in Hoyles, *Punishment in the Bible*, 101.

26. Wright, *Politics of Punishment*, 22.

Daniel Van Ness is Director of the Center for Restorative Justice that is sponsored by Prison Fellowship International. In this position, he is one of the important advocates for restorative-justice reforms. Jim Consedine's *Restorative Justice: Healing the Effects of Crime* (Lyttleton, NZ: Ploughshares, 1995) explores the crisis of the present retribution-based punishment and introduces alternative restorative approaches as presented in the biblical account and as tested in traditional precolonial communities in Australia, New Zealand, and the Pacific nations. A report from the British Bishops' Conference Department for Christian Responsibility and Citizenship and published by the Catholic Bishops' Conference of England and Wales, *A Place of Redemption: A Christian Approach to Punishment and Prison* (London: Burns & Oates, 2004), offers a thoroughly researched and well-argued call for justice reform. It contains very practical political suggestions for steps to be undertaken. The British bishops are not known for their radicalism. The document of this group represents an impressive voice that calls for changes on the sociopolitical level. It has international relevance as British law and penal policy still have a wide impact through the common-law system and the commonwealth.

On *biblical concepts of justice* see J. Arthur Hoyles, *Punishment in the Bible* (London: Epworth, 1986); Howard Zehr, *Changing Lenses: A New Focus for Crime and Justice* (Scottdale, PA: Herald, 1990); or Christopher D. Marshall, *Beyond Retribution: A New Testament Vision for Justice, Crime, and Punishment* (Grand Rapids: Eerdmans, 2001). While Zehr focuses on Old Testament material, Marshall's very thorough exegetical study offers important insights into New Testament perspectives on criminal justice. For a short informational review on restorative justice see Jim Consedine, *Restorative Justice*, 147–56; Daniel W. Van Ness, *Crime and Its Victims*, 101–39; or Lee Griffith, *The Fall of the Prison*, 87–126.

On *critical penology and the politics of imprisonment* see the bibliographic notes at the end of chapter 1 under the section called "The Politics of Imprisonment." See further Michael Welch, *Ironies of Imprisonment* (Thousand Oaks, CA: Sage, 2005). He presents interpretations from historians and critical criminologists of how prisons emerged. His account shows, among other things, how an increased use of imprisonment and a deterioration of prison conditions parallel economic conditions that increase unemployment and so create a surplus of manpower that the workforce cannot absorb. These so-called surplus workers face the prospect of long-term unemployment. Compared to the economically integrated population, such people are more inclined to enter illegal activities.

By absorbing this potentially criminal surplus, the prison serves as a constant tool of social control.

To *link practical theology with issues of justice* and to criticize pastoral care's narrow focus on the individual has been a constant concern of liberation theology. Our own quest for a sociopolitically aware approach to those in prison has been inspired by holistic concern for individual and social transformation as found in liberation theology. It has been supported by earlier attempts to integrate a liberation theological concern for social justice into the care for the individual. Howard Clinebell, *Basic Types of Pastoral Care and Counseling: Resources for the Ministry of Healing and Growth* (Nashville: Abingdon, 1984) suggests it on a more theoretical level; see particularly chapter 2. Stephen Pattison, *Pastoral Care and Liberation Theology* (Cambridge Studies in Ideology and Religion, Cambridge: Cambridge University Press, 1994) practically applies liberation theology in his theory of pastoral care and in his account of pastoral care for mentally ill people and in the context of psychiatric hospitals in the United Kingdom. His publication offers valuable insights into a common failure of chaplains and pastoral care in general to be sociopolitically aware and committed. His findings equally apply to those involved in pastoral care with prisoners.

9

Towards a Theology of Prison Ministry

A long journey through prison and prison ministry lies behind us. On our way we met inmates and heard about how they feel in the context of their daily lives; we asked how prison became what it is today and what role religion plays in it; we listened to stories of inmates, their spiritual breakthroughs, and their inspirations for change; we got to know those who visit prison and what ambiguities they encounter; we discussed how and through what roles visitors support inmates; and finally, we saw that prison visitors themselves experience change and assume a socially bridging role that prepares the ground for a healing approach to those in prison.

This last chapter summarizes the theological motives and faith principles implicitly at work in the attitudes and relationships of prison ministry, and that result from fellowship with those in prison. Together they build *elements of a theology of and for those at the fringes of society*, and are intended to be applicable more widely in any practical theology of social fringe groups. This chapter shows how encounter and fellowship with those in prison leads to a rediscovery of neglected elements of our biblical and church tradition and to new understandings of familiar elements. Before these motives are discussed, some remarks about theological methodology are necessary.

METHODOLOGY: HOW DOES THEOLOGICAL REFLECTION RELATE TO PRISON MINISTRY?

Theology is not faith. Neither is pastoral care. They are both driven by faith, and they generate new faith. Faith does not exist abstractly, independent of a concrete reality, but is shaped by a context and responds to it. What comes *first*, in prison as elsewhere, are basic experiences and perceptions of reality: sadness or joy, frustration or hope, deprivation or strength. Spiritual elements may be attached to these perceptions: spiritual interpretations of imprisonment, feelings of being controlled by evil powers, or the belief of being helplessly subject to blind fate. They are part of people's cultural code and qualify the perception of reality, sometimes causing relief, sometimes bringing additional pressure and suffering. They can emerge from the Christian tradition (as in many Western societies) or from other religious traditions (in contexts where Christianity has had a less culture-shaping role). Yet these spiritual elements are not what we describe here as faith; nor are they theology.

What comes *second* is what we call *faith*. Inspired, in the case of prisoners, by the interaction with other inmates, with Christian staff, with the chaplain, or with visitors who share their faith and present other concepts of reality, inmates develop a specific spiritual interpretation of life. Books, letters, individual reflection, and memories of past spiritual experiences can similarly be part of such a process. Encouraged by these interactions, and sometimes triggered by feelings of a dead end, people embark upon a spiritual journey that can lead to growing understanding, peace of mind, equanimity, and a sense of being sustained, loved, and cared for in the midst of turmoil. This attitude—trust in a life-giving and life-sustaining God—and understanding life and all aspects thereof in relation to God's creating and sustaining presence, is what we call faith. Stories of spiritual transformation (see chapter 4, above) tell how such faith grows and how it leads to changes in attitudes and relationships. The caring awareness and openness toward others, the assumption of a serving role, an attitude that is not overly concerned with one's own benefits—all these are typical fruits of such growth. People who have been touched by such a faith experience, and who have come to know God as the ultimate ground of all our being and as unconditional love naturally venture out into relationships of care. The ministry of visitation by people from outside and the care for fellow inmates by those inside both derive from an attitude of connectedness with God and attachment to him.

Only at this *third* point does *theology* come into play: it tries to interpret, reflect and communicate the faith experiences and spiritual processes of the second level, which in turn refer and react to the primary level of what we called basic experiences. Theology has an auxiliary, clarifying and therapeutic function: to help keep alive the continuity of understanding. It helps clarify which faith *expressions* are appropriate for specific situations; and it corrects where faith refers to first-level perceptions and experiences in ways not congruent with Christian and biblical tradition.

> As an example from our observations above, preaching God's wrath may, in specific situations, be appropriate and thus theologically correct. In the context of prison, however, it exacerbates an existing gap between inmate and visitor and is thus most commonly not appropriate. It is helpful to remember the words of Karl Barth in this regard: proclamation "will continually call the divided [believer and unbeliever] together by proclaiming to believers their merited rejection and to unbelievers their unmerited election, and to both the One in whom they are elected and not rejected."[1]

Theological reflection thus continuously inspires shifts in faith and ministry, and prepares the ground for new spiritual experiences. The *communication* of spiritual experience cannot avoid reference to language and expressions derived from the preceding faith experiences that together build the so-called theological tradition. This does not deny spiritual immediacy: peak experiences with a direct revelatory character. The stories of the Bible recount a number of events when people were directly grasped by the revelatory power of God and experienced immediacy in their relationship to God that transcended the common state of mind. Such immediacy still happens today. However, moments of immediacy are rare spiritual peak experiences. Immediacy is not constantly available but is usually remembered and made present through language and tradition.

The distinction of experience, faith, and theological reflection is an artificial distinction of what, in reality, belongs together. The levels of (a) perception and experience of *reality*, (b) trusting apprehension of God's presence in *faith*, and (c) reflective understanding and communication in *theology* are interwoven. Their relationship is circular: they qualify and affect each other. Faith affects our perception of reality as much as our lived-in world and our context shape faith. Equally, faith experiences do not exist

---

1. Barth, *Church Dogmatics*, 2/2, 326.

in neutral form, independent of theology, but are communicated through theologically formed expressions, the fruits of earlier faith experiences — people, books, songs, rituals, and most especially the Bible; they all are theologically reflected expressions of faith language. Theology too is not an independent arbitrator or an independently judging mental authority that hovers over the life of faith and ministry but is itself affected by faith life. Faith and theology stand in dialectic, mutually inspiring and correcting relationship.

Thus, the inmates' basic perception of reality—the hopelessness, the feeling of being stripped of dignity, the whole misery of life in prison—and their faith experiences on the one hand, and the visitors' experience of fellowship with those in prison on the other hand, form the starting point for theological reflection. Theology ascends from below, from the reality of suffering, and builds the endpoint of men and women's experiences and interactions with God. What theology tries to do is to understand and communicate this process.

The following diagram summarizes how experienced reality, faith life, and theological reflection relate to each other.

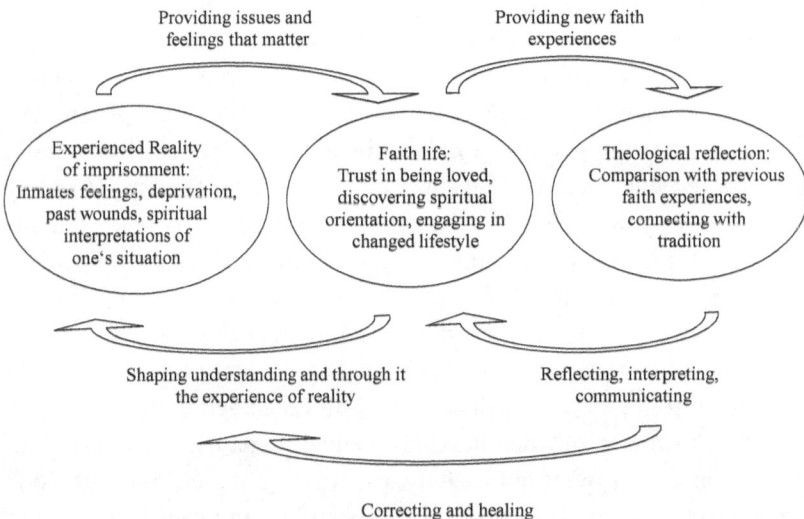

This understanding of theology and its relation to faith and reality is influenced by, among others, Dietrich Ritschl, *The Logic of Theology*. Ritschl reminds us that the subject matter of theology is not

God but talk about God. Theology aims at *examining* the language of believers, at *creatively extending* it through thought and action, at clarifying it, and at maintaining its comprehensibility. Overall, it serves communication in the church.[2] Theology starts with an analysis of the present situation, question, or issue.[3] In an *inductive* process, believers rediscover the relevance and value of the biblical stories and the Christian tradition in shedding new light on their present situation. This inductive process can already be observed in biblical writings where past tradition is rediscovered and understood anew in the light of new experiences of crisis (for example, during the Babylonian exile) or radical shifts in faith life (for example, in the encounter with the resurrected Christ). The present study is close to a liberation-theological approach to pastoral care.[4] It agrees that theology must be 'inductive, pluralistic, experiential, partial and related to (its) environment in order to be relevant.'[5] A theology that claims to be free from its context, neutral and pure in applying the Word of God to a given context, and unaffected in that application by the experience of reality, is nothing but ideology trying to conceal its social affiliation. Theology is an inductive process of reflection that "ascends from the ground up."[6] Our approach argues that a pastoral care that is truly sensitive to the needs of those in prison, that learns to listen and be compassionate, that encounters those in prison with utmost respect, and that remains constantly vigilant to attitudes of condescension and prejudice—such a pastoral care naturally undergoes a shift in perspective and learns to see the world from the perspective of those behind bars. It trusts that even though visitors will always encounter limits in their ability to fully grasp the pain of imprisonment, a sensitive pastoral care and continuous fellowship with inmates have a far-reaching effect, transforming the perspective of visitors and leading to a transformed sociopolitical outlook. This study presents the ministry of visitation with the belief that the thorough learning of the attitudes and skills of pastoral care has an impact on theology, ministry, and social action at large.

2. Ritschl, *The Logic of Theology*, 92

3. Ibid., 102

4. Another example of this is Stephen Pattison's *Pastoral Care and Liberation Theology*. See the bibliographic notes.

5. Assmann, "The Power of Christ in History," 134, quoted in Pattison, *Pastoral Care and Liberation Theology*, 46.

6. Valle, "Towards a Theological Outlook Starting from Concrete Events," quoted in Pattison, *Pastoral Care and Liberation Theology*, 46

The following sections introduce several theological topics that summarize, support, and guide the ministry in prison.

ENCOUNTERING CHRIST IN PRISON

The most direct scriptural basis for prison ministry is found in Matt 25:31–46:

> (34) Then the King will say to those at his right hand, "Come, you that are blessed by my Father; inherit the kingdom prepared for you from the foundation of the world; (35) for I was hungry and you gave me food, I was thirsty and you gave me something to drink, I was a stranger and you welcomed me, (36) I was naked and you gave me clothing, I was sick and you took care of me, I was in prison and you visited me." (37) Then the righteous will answer him, "(. . .) (39) and when was it that we saw you sick or in prison and visited you?" (40) And the King will answer them, "Truly I tell you, just as you did it to one of the least of these who are members of my family, you did it to me."

This word has inspired countless Christians, through all times of history, to engage in diaconal ministry and visit those in prison. However, there is more here than Christ's explicit commandment to care for the hungry, the thirsty, the stranger, the naked, the sick, and the prisoner. The key lies in Jesus's argument: *What you do for them, you do for me. By encountering the people in need, you will meet me.* It is Jesus himself who is there at the roadside, hungry and in despair. It is Jesus who is a stranger without protection and local roots. It is Jesus who is clothed in rags and facing coldness, it is Jesus who is lying sick, and it is Jesus himself in prison, yearning for release together with the other inmates. This word thus upsets any purely humanitarian approach to prison ministry, where do-gooders reach out to the suffering ones on the receiving end. Christ does not need to be brought to prison through visitors, through evangelistic events, or through Christian outreach. He is already there. This is the crucial consequence of Matthew 25. Prisoners thus become—as has already been observed in chapter 5—a lens through which to see God. *In them, we see Christ; in Christ, we see God.*

Matthew 25 does not stand alone; it merely offers the most radical form of God's identification with the suffering. Jesus's whole life—his birth in poverty, his early childhood as a refugee, and his later fellowship with

Towards a Theology of Prison Ministry

those at the margins of society—points in the same direction. His death on the cross, as one stripped of all dignity, is the zenith, the ultimate consequence, of an existence that identifies with worldly failure. In Matt 25 Jesus expresses most explicitly how in the face of the hungry, the thirsty, or the one in prison, we encounter Christ. God reveals himself in prison, among the poor, the sick and the refugees. It is this logic that guides some Christian traditions to understand prisons as places of God's revelation.

Why is it so? Why do we encounter Christ in them? At this point we may come to the end of what can theologically be rationalized. This radical shift in how God reveals himself is part of the upside-down logic of Christian faith and one of its axiomatic principles that cannot further be rationalized. There is, however, an inner logic to God's choosing such a specific form of revelation. Chapter 6 has given a partial answer. At the crisis points of our life, where we are shattered and little is left of what made us, life becomes fragile and transparent for the mysterious yet life-giving and sustaining presence of God: in our limitation, in the fact that we eventually face death in the truth that life is not at our disposal, in our desperate yet failing struggles to attain a tiny bit of immortality—it is through such experiences, where we stand in sheer nakedness, that we rediscover our complete dependence on a grace that gives us life, love, and strength. There we rediscover a grace that does not belong to us, that can never turn into our merit, and that is most intensely felt where nothing is left that helps us avoid recognition of this ultimate dependence. Dietrich Bonhoeffer, who himself suffered many years in prison before being executed for his involvement in an attempt to kill Hitler, described this experience in his letters from prison:

> Life in a prison cell may well be compared to Advent; one waits, hopes, and does this, that, or the other—things that are really of no consequence—the door is shut, and can be opened only *from the outside*.[7]

What Bonhoeffer describes as waiting, as total dependence on the person opening the door from outside, is our total dependence on the grace of God to create, sustain, and redeem us. Experiencing this dependence most strongly is the privilege, albeit an involuntary one, of people in situations of suffering. Visiting them is a journey into our own basic and existential dependence. It is a journey that reminds us that a life based on

---

7. Bonhoeffer, *Letters and Papers from Prison* (Letter on Nov. 21, 1943).

faith in Christ should acknowledge this dependence, respond gratefully to what it receives without merit, and abstain from boasting about one's own apparent strengths and achievements.

There is yet another reason why Christ identifies so strongly with the perspective of suffering. A key text that may help us is Paul's rather mystical meditation in 2 Cor 4:3-6.

> (3) And even if our gospel is veiled, it is veiled to those who are perishing. (4) In their case the god of this world has blinded the minds of the unbelievers, to keep them from seeing the light of the gospel of the glory of Christ, who is the image of God. (5) For we do not proclaim ourselves; we proclaim Jesus Christ as Lord and ourselves as your slaves for Jesus' sake. (6) For it is the God who said, "Let light shine out of darkness," who has shone in our hearts to give the light of the knowledge of the glory of God in the face of Jesus Christ.

In this letter, Paul responds to enthusiastic Christians in Corinth who questioned his spiritual authority (2 Cor 10:10). Their own spiritual experience made them enjoy the reality of salvation and Christian freedom to an extent that the world became irrelevant. Paul was critical of such an enthusiastic understanding of salvation that lost the necessary concern for the groaning and still unredeemed creation. He stressed that the glory of Christ is the glory of the cross, an *upside-down glory* that is shown in its contrary, in the depth of Christ's suffering. If we look at the suffering face of Christ with the mindset of the world, we cannot see glory — but only failure, the end of great hopes, and meaningless pain. Faith means discovering the glory of God not in the glorified and risen Christ but in the *suffering* Christ.

The pastoral relevance of this text is the importance to take suffering serious. In a world groaning with pain, it is indeed one of our great challenges to preserve the balance between the reality of widespread despair and the reality of Christ's resurrection that makes death lose its threatening sting. Faith does not abolish the reality of suffering, nor does the reality of suffering diminish the power of salvation. The inmates are still in prison, subject to dehumanizing rules, waiting for their release. But the prison has lost its spiritual power over them. Many inmates have lost nearly everything—family, friends, status, and money, and the pain of their loss is still with them. Yet, they receive new life through faith; they gain a new perspective and discover that salvation starts in the very now. On their faces they carry a light that transcends their present suffering. The encounter with their transformation is the continuous revelation of God in the poor, the sick, the hungry, and those in prison.

This rediscovery of the poor and marginalized as a place of God's revelation has driven liberation theology and set it in contrast to a long tradition of Christian theology that thinks from a perspective of alliance with worldly power. When theology truly takes its starting point from the poor, it will not be able to enthusiastically ignore the continuous pain of unredeemed creation, and it will firmly declare the presence and this-worldliness of salvation.

A word of clarification is necessary at this point: Are prisoners really the poor, a category that in liberation theology has become so important as a place of God's revelation? Indeed, some inmates are not poor at all. They have successfully hidden their illegally acquired fortunes from judicial attempts of recovery. And even if the majority of the inmates are poor or, if not previously so, have become poor through a costly legal process—do they, as active perpetrators, really fit the category of the innocently exploited poor? Our answer is, they do fit the category of the poor. What makes them fit it is the similarity of their daily experience—being subject to a context that strips them of their dignity and turns them into mere objects and recipients of punishment. Given that they have lost autonomy and decision-making power over most areas of life, their existential situation is structurally identical with the situation of the poor. Even if prisoners' past is different, their present is the same, shaped by deprivation, powerlessness, and brokenness.

In brief, the pastoral consequences for prison ministry are the following:

- Start prison ministry with an attitude of deep respect for those in prison and with the knowledge that they are lenses through which to see God.

- Discover Christ in the face of the suffering: this restores inmates' dignity and affirms their subject status, which has been stripped by the depersonalizing routine of imprisonment.

- Take suffering seriously and avoid glossing it over with spiritual enthusiasm.

- Approach the ministry of visitation as a learning process and as an opportunity to grow spiritually.

Beyond the Walls of Separation

A SHIFT IN PERCEPTION

Matthew 25 reveals a shift in recognizing God through the suffering Christ and through the hungry, the thirsty, the stranger, the naked, the sick, and the prisoner. This shift is paralleled by a reciprocal shift in how God recognizes us and relates to us. Christians believe that in Christ, God brought salvation to humankind and reconciled a disturbed relationship between God and us. However, salvation comes to us not as a new quality in our life but as a *new relationship* to God. God does not save us by magically changing us and giving us the power to resist our pride and our selfishness. Rather, he saves us by changing the way that he *looks* upon us. This is, in very short form, the crucial insight of the Reformation. The key misunderstanding of the young Luther was that he wrongly thought of God's grace as a quality of life, a habit of human being. This belief stood in contrast to his experience of still being subject to the power of sin, despite his devotional fervor and the rigidity of his monastic discipline. Nothing could silence the tormenting doubts about his sinful life until he came to a fundamental breakthrough. Theological language describes it as shift from a *habitual* to a *relational* understanding of God's grace. It happened when Luther, studying Rom 1:16–17, understood that in the process of justification by faith it is not we who change. What changes is rather how God looks at us. Faith is exactly this: to trust that God looks upon us from the perspective of love, not from the perspective of justice, or (closer to the experience of the penal world) God takes a perspective of forgiveness, not one of retribution.

God's new perspective toward us triggers crucial change. By looking at us as if we *were* without sin (despite our still being sinners), God effectively changes our reality and sets us free from our past. He looks at us as if we were righteous, and indeed this allows us to experience change. How is this possible? Perspective shapes reality. Perspective, the channel of seeing, is never neutral. Metaphorically, how we see reality depends on the glasses we wear. Sunglasses make the world darker; unclean glasses obscure our view. Christ is not only the channel, the way, the door, or (less biblically) the window through which we see the otherwise invisible God but also the channel through which God sees us in a new light. This is exactly what Rom 1:16–17 emphasizes: not how we see God through the crucified Christ but how God sees us human beings through Christ. It is as if God changed his glasses, as if his glasses had the suffering Christ painted on them, and God now looks at us through these glasses. God's perspective on us changes; this, in turn, changes reality, for reality is shaped by how it is perceived. The perception of reality is what constitutes it. It depends first on our prejudices and our prereflective attitudes, like in a self-fulfilling prophecy: If you perceive the world around you as hostile and full of enemies, you will be proven right. And if you see society around you as full of precious and interesting people, you will find proof of this as well. Communication theory has thoroughly illustrated the validity of this self-fulfilling prophecy, most famously in Paul Watzlawick's story of the hammer:

> A man wants to hang a painting. He has the nail, but no hammer. The neighbour has one and our man decides to borrow it. But then and there a doubt occurs to him: "What if the neighbour won't let me have it? Yesterday he barely nodded when I greeted him. Perhaps he was in a hurry. But perhaps he pretended to be in a hurry because he does not like me. And why would he not like me? I have always been nice to him; he obviously imagines something. If someone wanted to borrow one of my tools, *I* would of course give it to him. So why doesn't he want to lend me his hammer? How can one refuse such a simple request? People like him really poison one's life. He probably even imagines that I depend on him just because he has a hammer. I'll give him a piece of my mind!" And so our man storms over to the neighbor's apartment and rings the bell. The neighbour opens the door, but before he can even say, "Good morning," our man shouts, "And you can keep your damned hammer, you oaf!"[8]

God's change in the way of seeing us effects change because he sees us not as what we already are but as what we could be—not as a finished product of our past but as open to a future and with the potential for change. Jesus does not teach in abstract ways about sin and forgiveness but by practically forgiving sinners and addressing them *as if they were* without sin. This *as if* is at the root of Paul's doctrine of justification: we are still sinners, but God looks at us as if we were not. This perspective creates room for change, and inmates in prison experience exactly this shift in perspective when approached, not as what they are, defined by their past, but as what they can be, seen by their potential. If we regard them as criminals and "bad guys," we cement them into their sinner status. If we regard them as good (even though they might be bad), they may experience that they are not what they have always been told they are.

God's invitation to us starts with a shift of his perception of us—*a conversion* on the side of God. The ministry of visitation parallels this

---

8. Watzlawick, *The Situation Is Hopeless*, 39–40.

conversion when Christians assume a positive bias toward those in prison. God's shift in seeing us invites us equally to see people not in the shadow of their past crime(s) but in the light of their new life; we refrain from seeing people simply as the products of a background of brokenness and a history of rebellion, and we recognize in each one the creating and re-creating presence of God. Aware of the harm that most prisoners have inflicted on others, prison ministry starts with a conversion and assumption of a positive bias towards those in prison. Conversion starts with our looking at inmates in a new light rather than with our encouraging them to convert.

For ministry in prison, this means the following:

- Remember how perspective shapes reality. How you see inmates is how you affect them.

- Learn to define a person not by what he or she is but by what he or she could be.

LOVE: TRANSFORMING AND TRANSCENDING

We portrayed the shift in perspective as a shift from judicial logic to the logic of love, from retribution to forgiveness. Love is indeed the origin and content of this shift. It is love that cracks so many shells of self-protection and invulnerability. It is this surprising experience of love, expressed in mercy and forgiveness (against all odds, against all merits, and against all previous experiences) that lies at the root of many stories of transformation that emerge from prison. Love breaks through the pain of those in prison—because it has already broken through the pain of God and turned it into new life.

Love, as biblical teaching introduces it, has tremendous relevance for ministry in the penal context. First, *love affects the one who loves*. It makes him or her feel pain. God expresses love most strongly in Christ's pain that turns into revelation, just as human pain can turn into moments of revelation. God loves humankind to the point of (painfully) giving his one and only son (John 3:16). God's love for us humans is aching, as the story of the Prodigal Son shows so intensely (Luke 15:11–32). The father waits in pain for his son's return, not knowing whether it will ever happen.[9] Painful love also shaped Paul's relationship to the congregations he had founded (1

---

9. A parallel parable from the Chinese context that links pain and love with a political theology is Song, *The Tears of Lady Meng*.

Thess 2:7–8). We can partially grasp how love is linked to pain in the experiences of parents with their children: the pain that comes when experiencing the dependence of newborn babies, when recognizing their fragility through their years of growth, when suffering uncertainty about what the future holds for them, when worrying about where they are going, when disagreeing with their decisions yet acknowledging their independence, or when bringing them up and experiencing manifold wounds: often rejected and still forgiving. The roller coaster of feelings that parents ride in the education of their children reflects this mix of pain and love. Love makes a person vulnerable. This vulnerability, the togetherness of love and pain, and the readiness to share in the pain of those we encounter, build an important basis for the encounter between inmates and visitors.

> The Chinese language maintains an awareness of the closeness of love and pain in one of its words for love, *téng ài*: *téng*, is usually associated with pain (e.g., *téng tòng* translates to "pain"); *téng ài* ("to love dearly") commonly describes the love of a mother for a baby.

Second, love *transforms the person who is loved*. Jesus's teaching to love our enemies implies first that there are enemies and that evil exists. Jesus does not naively deny the reality of evil.[10] Yet it also implies that the relationship to the enemy can change. Love can turn an enemy into a friend (for example, through care and acceptance). Such love does not exclude punishment or mean permissiveness, but it gives punishment a twist towards reconciliation and healing. Forgiveness is the most powerful expression of such transforming love. Forgiveness is an attitude most alien to the penal context. Unwillingness to forgive is expressed not only in long sentences but also in society's continuous rejection of ex-offenders after they supposedly have paid the price for their crime(s). The lack of forgiveness is what continues to create harm and what lays the ground for a vicious cycle of hatred. In contrast, an attitude of forgiveness breaks the cycle and introduces an orientation toward the future. Forgiveness suspends the perennial question of whether the individual or the society is to blame for crime. Instead of dwelling on the past, it looks ahead to restoration of broken relationships, transformation of offenders, and reconciliation between offenders and the community (see chapter 8).

---

10. This paragraph's thoughts about love and forgiveness in the penal context are inspired by McHugh, *Christian Faith and Criminal Justice*, 146–63.

Third, *love introduces a dynamic movement* into our life and ministry. This movement of love, which transcends the power of *is* towards a visionary representation (literally a "making present") of what could be, is the golden thread of Jesus's ministry. It is love's visionary power that generates a bias for the lost against the rule of effectiveness, as in the parables of the Lost Sheep and the Lost Coin (Luke 15:1–10). It is a vision of love that leads Jesus in his ministry to pass beyond geographic, ethnic, and religious boundaries, as in the story of the Syrophoenician woman (Mark 7:24–30). It is a virtue of love that leaves behind detrimental prejudice, as in the parable of the Good Samaritan (Luke 10:25–37). A dynamic of love lies behind Jesus's criticism of legalistic interpretations of the Torah and his interpretation of God's commandment that dissolves the boundaries of law towards love. It is a movement of love that makes Jesus reject the logic of condemnation for the logic of forgiveness, as in the story of the woman caught in adultery (John 8:2–11). This same movement continues in the ministry of the resurrected Christ when, after his resurrection, he first appears to his disciples by passing through the door they had locked in anxiety (John 20:19). Ever since then, Christian love has continued to break through human divisions and segregation. Today's prison ministry extends this movement as it continues to pass through closed doors and beyond walls of separation—the visible walls of stone, the invisible walls of social exclusion, and the emotional walls of shame and self-imposed isolation.

A practical theology of prison ministry will remember the following principles:

- Accept that you yourself become vulnerable when reaching out in love.
- Trust that forgiveness is not a sign of weakness but of strength.
- Discover where walls of separation hinder the flow of God's love.

CREATED IN GOD'S IMAGE

The Christian belief that all men and women are created in the image of God (Gen 1:27) is a central argument for the care and support of those in prison. No matter what a person has done, no matter what social category this person belongs to (and in the context of prison, no matter what category of prisoner—recidivist or first-time offender, young or old, local or immigrant, and even no matter whether victim or offender), each and every one still reflects the image of God and deserves to be treated accordingly.

This belief has several implications for the ministry in prison. It first builds the basis for a *positive bias* toward those in prison, supporting our previous reflections. Regarding inmates as created in God's image is a powerful reminder of what they really are and affirms the intrinsic value of each person. Each inmate appears not just as a case, not just as a goal or object of reform programs (Christian or otherwise), but each is a subject with very unique value, each one is equipped with a unique story and prospect, each one deserves to be treated with particular care.

Second, creation in the image of God emphasizes the *essential equality* of all human beings. Every person equally stands in God's grace (Matt 5:45). Nobody, not even the worst sinner, is beyond the reach of God, for even a person at his or her worst reflects the image of God. Nobody is beyond hope. Christian ministry in prison does not know of any hopeless cases. The history of the church is full of stories of God making use of the worst people to extend his kingdom. The belief in the equality of all humans reminds visitors of the needs of all inmates, not only of the devout ones, and to continuously care for those inmates on whom the penal and rehabilitative systems have given up.

Third, the belief that each person is created in the image of God gives *direction* to Christian ministry: it supports, comforts, and stands in contrast to suicidal or other self-destructive tendencies. The Christian visitor will point to every human being's potential to be transformed and to grow in God's likeness. Instead of being perpetually reduced to their shortcomings, people receive the calling to recover their status as creatures in God's image and to restore this relationship. They find repentance when they go through a rediscovery of their human dignity—a rediscovery similar to that undergone by the Prodigal Son in the Bible, who at the low point of his life, remembers his relatedness to his father and indirectly to God as giver of life. (See the story of Dirty in chapter 4).

Fourth, that humans are created in God's image gives support to *criticism of all dehumanizing elements* in punishment. It sharpens Christians' minds regarding those penal elements that only strip inmates of their human dignity. The belief in man and woman being created in the image of God leads to a rejection of any penal philosophy that treats the individual as a means to an end, as the theory of general deterrence does.[11] The

---

11. See the criticism of general deterrence in McHugh, *Christian Faith and Criminal*

doctrine of humanity's creation in the image of God is critical of a political system that tries to maintain social cohesion and order by sacrificing some individuals for the common good, as much political propaganda does. And it is mindful of penal elements that unnecessarily aggravate the suffering of imprisonment and that undermine the dignity of those in prison.

A practical theology of prison ministry, based on the faith that men and women are created in God's image, affirms the following principles:

- Remember that each person in prison equally shares in the joys and wounds, in the hopes and disappointments, in the excitements and frustrations, of all humankind.
- Broaden the scope of prison ministry to include awareness of where the penal system threatens inmates' dignity.

UNDER THE POWER OF SIN

Criminals are not only caught in sin—as popular (Christian) opinion has it—but are also caught in a specific understanding of sin that aggravates their isolation and undermines reconciliation. Sin, as Christians commonly understand it, is based on the assumption of a free will that allows individuals to choose between right and wrong. Crime is the consequence of a wrong choice; it is a fruit of sin, an expression of human pride, and the result of an attitude where the *I* stands at the center. Crime violates not only human order but as an expression of selfishness and the wrong orientation of human life also (and possibly more important) God. Crime is thus, in its deepest sense, rebellion against God.

Such interpretation of crime is not wrong, but when it neglects other aspects of the biblical understanding of sin, it leads to the common misinterpretation of identifying crime with sin and the criminal law with God's justice. This interpretation thus surrounds criminal law and penal apparatus with an aura of necessity and divineness. Punishment is inevitable, not just for social, human, educational, or (in short) worldly reasons, but even more so for theological reasons; for crime is more than an offense against the human community; it is humanity rising against God. This theological legitimization and sacralization of punishment is part of the Western theological and penal traditions and has had the effect of removing criminal

---

Justice, 112ff; similarly also Catholic Bishops' Conference of England and Wales, *A Place of Redemption*, 38–39.

Towards a Theology of Prison Ministry

law from the community. Similar effects were seen in both the shift in the understanding of criminal law and the medieval shift that happened when crime turned from a violation against a person or a community into a violation against the king and the royal order.[12] If punishment responds to a rebellion against God, not just a violation of human law, then it is only natural that any suffering is legitimate.

Against this powerful tradition that identifies crime with sin, the biblical and theological tradition harbors elements of a more holistic and liberating understanding of sin. A first element is the distinction of *sinner* and *sinned against*. The Bible repeatedly emphasizes each person's dual role of being indebted and indebting others, of receiving pain and inflicting pain on others. This dual role appears prominently when Jesus teaches us to pray, "Forgive us our debts, as we also have forgiven our debtors." Chapter 8 already broadened our understanding of inmates to see in them not only perpetrators but also persons who often enough have themselves experienced physical or emotional abuse. Such awareness should not be a reason to take lightly the pain of victims or the responsibility of the offender. However, seeing criminals as persons prevents the common black-and-white mentality of good here and evil there, and the harmful dichotomy of inside and outside. Seeing prisoners instead as both oppressors and oppressed offers a more balanced and just image of those in prison that refrains from reducing them to the crimes they have committed.

The belief in the *universality of sin*—that there is no person beyond the power of sin—further supports such an egalitarian view of sin. Awareness of sin's pervasiveness, repeatedly articulated in the Psalms (Ps 130:3; 143:2), finds most powerful expression in Paul's writings (Rom 7:21ff). Of course, the Christian exclamation "We are all sinners" cannot suppress the popular notion that some are more equal than others, in the realm of sin not less than in supposedly egalitarian political systems. Yet this important part of Christian belief acts as constant reminder that those outside are indeed no better than those inside. It connects Christians, independent of their legal status, as equal before God, even if human law judges them differently.

The lasting and pervasive power of sin over all of us, including Christians—what Luther described as our continuous existence as sinners even when standing under God's forgiving grace (in his famous Latin expression *simul iustus et peccator*)—sharpens our understanding of the human condition and prevents us from falling into the trap of blind optimism. No matter

---

12. See our discussion of restorative justice in chapter 8.

how well designed the improvement techniques or the counseling skills, no matter how serious the commitment of faith or how devout the inmate, failure continues to be part of Christian life. Transformation happens and it is wonderful to see when it does, but sin remains a power in human life. Many inmates fail to thoroughly experience transformation after their faith commitment, and it is important to remember that Jesus's love was not conditional on subsequent transformation.

Jesus's radical interpretation of sin in the Sermon on the Mount exposes human thinking and desire as the root cause of sin. Sin is not confined to the individual acts of sin, nor does it come from outside the human body; rather, it has its roots inside the human heart (Matt 15:18ff). Such understanding of sin brings about insight into the power of evil thought and fosters awareness of our collective participation in sin.

This *transpersonal* dimension of sin has in recent years and under the influence of theology of liberation received increased attention. Sin was too long confined to a narrow individualized understanding that saw it at work only in personal transgressions.[13] In contrast to this individual dimension of sin, the belief in a *structural dimension of sin* affirms that sin happens equally through unjust laws, social structures of exclusion, or oppressive cultural systems. Paul referred to it in the framework of his time when describing his struggle as one against the rulers, the authorities, and the powers of this dark world (cf. Eph 6:12). The biblical writers are obviously aware of the power of sin beyond the individual act, in the mental world of thought as in the powers that transcend the personal realm. Being born into a context that fosters negative thought, growing up without learning the values of life (including the value of self-love), instead learning self-destructive attitudes—all these are equally beyond personal choice, as are the social structures that perpetuate exclusion and hatred. Where laws and economic practices reward corporate greed while at the same time excluding large parts of the population from the profits, hate grows. Where penal policies fail to equip offenders with the skills necessary in the outside world and where an unforgiving society continues to brand ex-convicts as dangerous or suspect, inmates are condemned to ongoing confinement in negative social definitions. The concept of individual responsibility, although important and applicable in the individual encounter that looks beyond

---

13. See Soelle, *Choosing Life*, 82. Pattison, *Pastoral Care and Liberation Theology*, 209ff, offers a thorough criticism of how an individualist understanding of sin shapes most pastoral theology.

the present, turns into an ideology that hides the collective dimension of evil structures.

Sin is usually understood and responded to in moral categories. Sin is the failure to live up to a moral command. Paul's famous description of sin in Rom 7:21ff points to yet another dimension of sin that adds a final element to our understanding of sin in the context of the penal world:

> (21) So I find it to be a law that when I want to do what is good, evil lies close at hand. (22) For I delight in the law of God in my inmost self, (23) but I see in my members another law at war with the law of my mind, making me captive to the law of sin that dwells in my members. (24) Wretched man that I am! Who will rescue me from this body of death?

In chapter 4 we mentioned how inmates experience their situation at the low point of their lives with reference to this text. Some of them painfully realize the gap between what they are and what they could be: their inability *not* to sin. This is what we could call an *existential dimension of sin*.[14] We do not deny that sin has a moral dimension and includes a failure to obey moral commands, but the core issue is a deeper alienation from God, the failure and brokenness we experience, not being up to what we want and are called to be. It is expressed in an inability to love and to receive love, in a lack of self-appreciation and self-love, in a lack of trust and hope. This existential dimension of sin is ultimately the most basic form of what sin means.

Correspondingly, our response to sin should be framed less in moral terms and more in pastoral terms. Dealing with the reality of sin in such a pastoral way avoids the dominant judgmental undertone of much Christian discourse about sin. It allows responses to the power of sin that follow Jesus's example, as in his encounter with Levi, a tax collector participating in and benefiting from an oppressive system (Luke 5:27–32), who was at the same time subject to its alienating power. Levi's awareness of a deep alienation in his own life prepared him to receive Jesus's forgiving invitation and to radically change his behavior.

A practical theology of prison ministry will remember the following principles:

- Avoid identifying sin with a person and an act. Regard sin instead as a power that shrouds an individual and his or her wider life context.

---

14. See on this dimension of sin Tillich, *Systematic Theology*, 2:46ff.

- Get used to thinking of crime not in moral but in existential categories: regard it as an expression of the lack of love in a person's life.
- Respond to the power of sin with pastoral care instead of moral reasoning.

VISITING AND HOSTING

The concluding remarks in Heb 13:1–3 bring us to a further aspect of prison ministry.

> (1) Let mutual love continue. (2) Do not neglect to show hospitality to strangers, for by doing that some have entertained angels without knowing it. (3) Remember those who are in prison as though you were in prison with them; those who are being tortured, as though you yourselves were being tortured.

The text introduces, after a kind of general comment, two basic elements in Christian life: hospitality and the care for prisoners. Listing them jointly does not happen randomly but because of a topical link. The care for prisoners happens, obviously, foremost through visiting—and all the material and emotional support that go with it. We thus have the exhortation to exert hospitality to the stranger followed by the call to visit those in prison. Indeed, visitation and hospitality belong to each other like bolt and nut. Neither goes without the other.[15]

A *dialectic of visitation and hospitality* offers a key to reading the whole story of the Bible—from the moment when Abraham leaves his home to become a vulnerable stranger, dependent on a reception from the residents of an alien land to the period where the Israelites become enslaved guests in Egypt and experience the low point of this dialectic; from the prophetic reminders of Israel's nomadic roots after it had established itself as a nation and the frequent admonition in the law of Moses to care for the alien to Israel's renewed experience of being enslaved aliens during the Babylonian captivity. The biblical tradition keeps all along an awareness of a deeper dimension of hospitality, bringing at times surprising encounters with transcendence. Abraham encounters God's angels in the three visitors (Gen 18), and a poor widow hosts a messenger of God by receiving Elijah (1 Kgs 17). Against the background of such experiences of guest and

---
15. See on the dialectic of host and stranger Ogletree, *Dimensions of Moral Understanding*, 4ff.

Towards a Theology of Prison Ministry

host (being alien in a foreign land and encountering transcendence in the stranger), hospitality turns into a central element of Old Testament ethics.[16] The New Testament extends this line with the story of the disciples who encounter the resurrected Christ in the stranger they host in Emmaus (Luke 24:13–35). The ultimate ground for the dialectic of visitation and hospitality is revealed in the New Testament when in Christ alien transcendence becomes flesh to live among us (John 1:14).

To offer hospitality to the stranger is to welcome something unknown and vulnerable into our life-world,[17] to create space for something foreign, to offer room, to accommodate, to care for and protect the alien.[18] Visiting, on the other hand, implies an attitude of humility and deep respect that confers value on the host. Visitors and strangers do not impose themselves but make themselves vulnerable and accept their dependence on the host. Nowhere has the vulnerability of the guest become more visible than in Jesus, who lived as a stranger and guest in our world—and died on the cross. Visiting has a transforming impact, as the story of Jesus's visit to Zacchaeus shows (Luke 19:1–10). Jesus's mere decision to visit the chief tax collector's house triggered conversion because it expressed so strongly value and love.

The ministry in prison stands in this dialectic of hospitality and visiting. The visitors turn into guests (see chapter 7) and as such allow surprising encounters—to the point of mediating transcendence. Visitors humbly accept the rules of an alien context: both the prison with its strict rules, and the prison subculture with its own code. Their mere presence confers the same values as the visit of Jesus to the house of Zacchaeus or of Jesus's fellowship with the outcasts of society. Most important, visitors make themselves vulnerable and through their vulnerability find a way to connect with the wounds of the inmates. The visiting ministry turns into a learning opportunity for the inmates: to give room to vulnerability, to care for the visitors, to accommodate strangers. Where inmates turn into caring hosts and visitors into those receiving care, the common distinction of carer and recipient is turned upside down. This perfectly matches the experience of many visitors, who feel that they have received more than they gave.

Host and guest meet in *celebration*; visitation and hospitality merge in *conviviality*. Celebration truly happens when we are present in the present[19]

16. Janzen, *Old Testament Ethics*, 38ff.
17. Ogletree, *Dimensions of Moral Understanding*, 2.
18. Nouwen, *Wounded Healer*, 89.
19. Nouwen, "Creative Ministry," 82. See also a more extended discussion of

and are able to take a break from our daily occupations. Jesus's convivial banquets, his presence in the very moment without being chased by an agenda, his generous gift of his time, his not caring about missionary efficiency, his knowing the symbolic character of his ministry—all add up to a ministry of presence. Prison ministry as a ministry of presence (see chapter 6) reflects this celebrative conviviality. Only based on convivial life (or in the case of prisons, where full conviviality is not possible, on a continual visiting presence) can we develop a theology of prison ministry. The convivial fellowship points to the church's existence not for others but *with* others. To visit means to spend time with, to establish relationship and personal contact.

For a practical theology of prison ministry this means:

- Enter the alien world of prison with humility and respect for the existing rules of the prison and for the inmates' culture.
- Trust in the transforming power of visiting and convivial fellowship.
- Remember that presence and life together build the basis for properly understanding inmates.

A HORIZON OF HOPE

The ultimate vision of prison ministry is always healing, transformation, reconciliation, and finally liberation. As Jesus proclaimed at the very beginning of his ministry (Luke 4:18–19):

> (18) The Spirit of the Lord is upon me, because he has anointed me to bring good news to the poor. He has sent me to proclaim release to the captives and recovery of sight to the blind, to let the oppressed go free, (19) to proclaim the year of the Lord's favor.

Jesus's prophetic vision, quoting the prophet Isaiah, builds the horizon of Christian ministry in prison and has several implications. First, the prophetic vision builds a horizon that shapes the whole of reality. Jesus's proclamation calls for a Jubilee year, a year of restoration and reconciliation as mandated in the Torah (Leviticus 25). The Jubilee binds the captive and the captor. Jesus not only announces freedom from captivity and good news for the poor but also involves the other side, calling for release of slaves and

---

hospitality as movement of reaching out to our fellow human beings in Nouwen, *Reaching Out*, 43–80.

Towards a Theology of Prison Ministry

forgiveness of debts. Jesus does not allow his message to be understood in a purely spiritual sense, as proclamation only. Rather, it is a revolutionary act that upsets the reality of social relationships. It can be received spiritually first, without any change in reality, but underneath, the social reality *is* already changing, for Jesus points to what the order of society *could* be. The vision preserves an awareness that the reality of prison, although overwhelming, does not need to be regarded as normal,[20] that incarceration is not part of God's logic. Further, Christians involved in matters of prison and criminal justice discover how crime and punishment are matters of the whole community. In prison, broken relationships within our society and between the individual and the community on one hand and broken relationships between humans and God on the other hand intersect. Spiritual aspects (liberation from addictions, from anger and self-hatred, from past wounds that continue to shape a personality) fuse with social aspects: with a society that often enough rejects offenders, keeps them in a cage of iron bars and behind the no less excluding bars of negative images. Jesus's proclamation reminds us that imprisonment happens in all our names, on behalf of all of us.

Second, Jesus's prophetic vision opens a horizon based on the resurrection. Prisons still belong to our reality, as crimes do. Both crime and the punishing reaction against it are part of our broken world. The proclamation of liberation to the prisoners, standing in such stark contrast to reality, comes to us not as a reality but as a horizon of hope that guides us in witnessing Christ through our individual and social actions. The basis of this hope is the dawn of the kingdom in Jesus's healing ministry and in his presence among us (Luke 11:20; 17:20). Our hope is based as much on the prophetic vision of Jesus as on the revelation and representation of hope in Jesus's life and ministry. Our hope is based on Christ, who held captivity captive (Eph 4:8), although he himself was a prisoner even in death. (For a stone barred his tomb's entrance, where guards stood.)

Third, Jesus's prophetic vision opens a horizon based on the cross, which is, in a paradoxical sense, the lowest point in God's relationship with us humans. Such a hope will always be *upside-down* rather than triumphalistic, and it will be different from simple wishful thinking, longing, or daydreaming.[21] It is the affirmation of meaning and promise based on

---

20. The aspect of prison as abnormal is illuminated in Harvey, "Custody and the Ministry to Prisoners," 82–90.

21. Hall, "Working Theology of Prison Ministry," 171.

deep trust in God's caring presence in one's life, despite reality's being so markedly different from meaning and promise. People in prison develop hope from a unique position as they, in contrast to ordinary Christians who victoriously look back on Christ's resurrection, wait from a perspective of suffering for redemption still to come. Their hope begins not with Christ's resurrection but with his crucifixion.[22] They stand between the cross and resurrection; together with the convicted thief hanging next to Jesus on the cross, they hear the words, "Truly I tell you, today you will be with me in Paradise" (Luke 23:43).

Finally, Christians involved in penal matters will mirror the double ground of hope in the cross and resurrection. They will boldly uphold their holistic vision of justice while humbly admitting Christians' own part in past and present penal failures. The church is built on a solid rock of failure; yet Christians take their hope from the same history of God revealing himself in lowliness and failed lives. The experience that failure can turn into a place of God's revelation, that we can break through the feeling of shame accompanying failure,[23] that there is no need to hide, that from failure the transformation of individual lives and of whole societies takes its beginnings. This is a tremendous message of hope.

A practical theology of prison ministry remembers:

- to keep alive the vision of liberation as a holistic vision that includes liberation from the reality of prison as much as liberation from spiritual captivity;
- to discover the reality of hope in symbolic representations: individual transformations and simple steps of care point to the ongoing power of resurrection;
- to allow the liberty that you proclaim to the captives already to take its form in your mindset.

BEYOND THE WALLS

Imprisonment not only happens through walls and bars but is also harmfully perpetuated in thoughts and minds. The biblical tradition counters this perspective of imprisonment with a perspective of identification: first,

---

22. Ibid., 172.

23. Pattison, *Critique of Pastoral Care*, 162, discusses failure in the life of pastors; his observations equally apply to Christians in general.

of Christ with inmates, then of visitors and inmates as equal in their sin, and finally of hosts and guests in joint conviviality.

The awareness not just that the prisoner is the other but that we are in prison *together with* the prisoner finds further affirmation in both Heb 13:3 and Luke 4:18–19. The first text offers this argument for the care of those in prison: "Remember those in prison, for you are prisoners with them yourselves."[24] This identification points to our continuous subjection to sin and to our spiritual imprisonment; it reminds us that even though our sin may be lawful, we are as much spiritually imprisoned by our worries and our attachments.

Both texts point to a memory of our collective past, an aspect especially illuminated by Luke 4, where Jesus proclaims liberation to the captives with reference to the Year of Jubilee. This year of restoration is based on the remembrance of collective slavery in Egypt. We are called to remember that imprisonment and slavery belong to our collective history; we are what we are on the basis of God's grace, shown in his act of liberation. The ethical commandments of the Old Testament are based not on charity but on memory. Participating in liberation, social restoration, and redemptive care happens because we live on the same ground: if not for having received the same grace of liberation, we would not stand where we are today. We remember our own history and realize its relevance for the present. This attitude enables us to stand in a solidarity based on a fundamental recognition of our essential unity with those in captivity. We are called to participate in the ongoing transforming and liberating ministry in response to, in gratitude for, and in extension of him who has liberated us and given us life.

BIBLIOGRAPHICAL NOTES

On *theological method* see foremost Dietrich Ritschl, *The Logic of Theology* (London: SCM, 1986). For our study particularly interesting is Stephen Pattison, *Pastoral Care and Liberation Theology* (Cambridge Studies in Ideology and Religion; Cambridge University Press, 1994). Pattison applies the liberation-theological option for the poor to the context of pastoral care and chaplaincy in mental health care in the United Kingdom. He understands that most of those involved in pastoral ministry belong to a different

---

24. This translation reflects more appropriately the Greek words; see Harvey, "Custody and the Ministry to Prisoners," 87.

social group than do inmates and do not share the inmates' daily experiences of deprivation. Pastoral-care workers fail to properly understand the suffering of the underprivileged and to adequately assume a theology and ministerial practice relevant for the oppressed and marginalized. He therefore suggests that they should, in a conscious step, opt for the oppressed. His social analysis of first-world society uncovers similar social divisions as those in other contexts. Pastoral-care workers should thoroughly analyze their sociopolitical contexts and become "organic intellectuals" (a term he borrows from Trotsky), who use their resources and skills in the service of the oppressed. Pastoral action should first aim at the social context that causes alienation without neglecting the concurrent need of the suffering individual.

On *theology of prison ministry* see the inspiring reflections in Gerald Austin McHugh, *Christian Faith and Criminal Justice: Toward a Christian Response to Crime and Punishment* (New York: Paulist, 1978). Although his book is concerned with Christians and penal justice in the wider sense rather than just prison ministry, he offers rich theological reflections that apply well to prison ministry. Henry G. Covert, *Ministry to the Incarcerated* (Chicago: Loyola University Press, 1995), offers many biblical references and thorough theological reflection on what happens in the ministry to those in prison. He emphasizes the dimension of the cross and God's *kenosis*, the process of God's emptying himself of all divine majesty to become man among us. Short discussions can further be found in A. E. Harvey, "Custody and the Ministry to Prisoners," *Theology* 78 (1975) 82–90; Pierre Raphael, *Inside Rikers Island: A Chaplain's Search for God* (Maryknoll, NY: Orbis, 1990), particularly chapter 10; or Stephen T. Hall, "A Working Theology of Prison Ministry," *Journal of Pastoral Care and Counseling* 58/3 (2004) 169–78. Hall mentions several elements of a theology of prison ministry: hope, the ministry of presence, forgiveness, inclusiveness, the value of each human being as created by God, and the importance of introducing biblical alternatives to the common understanding of power and dominion.

Appendix

QUESTIONS FOR REFLECTION AND GROUP DISCUSSION

MOST OF THE QUESTIONS can be used both for discussion among visitors preparing for visits to prison as also for group discussion inside prison.

Chapter 1

- How do you see prisoners? How do you explain the crime they have committed? Is it a random event? Or is it rooted in the personality of the inmate?
- If you have been in contact with prisoners, has your image of prisoners changed? How?
- Try to imagine: What elements in your own life would you miss the most if being confined to prison?

Chapter 2

- Why did the concept of the penitentiary fail?
- What are the inherent problems of the treatment or rehabilitation model?
- What can be learned from history about the rehabilitation of offenders? What can be done to avoid repeating past failures of rehabilitation?

Appendix

- For people in prison: If you had to design rehabilitation plans, what would you find the most effective elements of rehabilitation?

Chapter 3

- What do you regard as the most obvious differences when comparing the spirituality of fellowships inside prisons and outside?
- What is the difference between a faith-based prison and a church behind bars?
- Have you experienced opposition from prison management when establishing religious programs? What were the reasons for the management's objections?

Chapter 4

- Have there been moments in your life where you rediscovered spiritual dimensions, and where you experienced a heightened spiritual awareness? Can you remember factors and events that influenced such spiritual changes?
- What feelings and thoughts do men who cry provoke in you?
  For men: When was the last time you cried?
  For women: Have you seen your partner, boyfriend, father, or husband cry? If so, what was the situation?
- When has admission of failure and brokenness in your life has had a liberating effect on you?

Chapter 5

- What is the ministry of the prison chaplain in relation to the prison staff?
- How should Christian chaplains respond to spiritual needs of non-Christians?
- What is the responsibility of prison visitors, both chaplains and lay visitors, regarding prison and justice reforms?

Chapter 6

- Think of a person you regard as genuine: What specific elements of his/her communicative and caring behaviour make you feel this way? Try the same exercise with the other key qualities of a visitor.
- Remember a time when you were in need of care: What did you need the most? What kind of care helped you the most? Share positive experiences of care that you have received.

Chapter 7

- What is the role you like to assume the most when visiting those in prison? What are roles that make you feel uneasy, or in which you do not like to be seen?
- Think of teachers or pastors that you liked most: What aspects of their communicative and role behavior affected you positively?
- What types of physical contact do you like? What types of physical contact do you find intrusive?

Chapter 8

- Why are certain drugs illegal? Why are others not?
- What kind of punishment would be beneficial in our societies?

Chapter 9

- What biblical text inspires you to visit those in prison?

Bibliography

Assmann, Hugo. "The Power of Christ in History: Conflicting Christologies and Discernment." In *Frontiers of Theology in Latin America*, edited by Rosino Gibellini, 133–50. Translated by John Drury. Maryknoll, NY: Orbis, 1979.

Barth, Karl. *Church Dogmatics*. 2/2: *The Doctrine of God*. Translated by Geoffrey W. Bromiley and T. F. Torrance. Edinburgh: T. & T. Clark, 1957.

Bazemore, Gordon, and Mara Schiff, editors. *Restorative Community Justice: Repairing Harm and Transforming Communities*. Cincinnati: Anderson, 2001.

Beckford, James A., and Sophie Gilliat. *Religion in Prison: Equal Rites in a Multi-Faith Society*. Cambridge: Cambridge University Press, 1998.

Berman, Harold J. *Faith and Order: The Reconciliation of Law and Religion*. Emory University Studies in Law and Religion 3. Atlanta: Scholars, 1993.

Berne Eric. *Games People Play: The Psychology of Human Relationships*. New York: Grove, 1964.

Blomberg, Thomas G., and Karol Lucken. *American Penology: A History of Control*. 2nd ed. New Brunswick, NJ: Aldine/Transaction, 2010.

Bonhoeffer, Dietrich. *Letters and Papers from Prison*, edited by E. Bethge. 1971. Reprint, New York: Macmillan, 1972.

———. *Life Together*. New York: Harper & Brothers, 1959.

Bosch, David J. *Transforming Mission: Paradigm Shifts in Theology of Mission*. New York: American Society of Missiology Series 16. Maryknoll, NY: Orbis, 1991.

Bosworth, Mary. *Encyclopedia of Prisons and Correctional Facilities*. 2 vols. Thousand Oaks, CA: Sage, 2005.

Boulding, Maria. *A Gateway to Hope*. Petersham, MA: St. Bede's, 1985.

Brandner, Tobias. "Charismatic Faith and Prison Ministry." *Australasian Pentecostal Studies* 14 (2012) 20–40.

———. "Seelsorge und Freundschaft: Pastorale Rollenvielfalt und Rollenambiguität in der Gefangenenseelsorge." In *Nachdenkliche Seelsorge—Seelsorgliches Nachdenken. Festschrift für Christoph Morgenthaler*, edited by Ralph Kunz and Isabelle Noth, 184–200. Arbeiten zur Pastoraltheologie, Liturgik und Hymnologie 62. Göttingen: Vandenhoeck & Ruprecht, 2012.

Burglass, Milton E. *The Thresholds Program: A Community Based Intervention in Correctional Therapeutics*. Cambridge: Correctional Solutions, Inc., 1972.

Bibliography

Burnside, Jonathan et al. *My Brother's Keeper: Faith-Based Units in Prisons.* Cullompton, UK: Wilan, 2005.

Campbell Alastair V. *Paid to Care?: The Limits of Professionalism in Pastoral Care.* The New Library of Pastoral Care. London: SPCK, 1985.

———. *Rediscovering Pastoral Care.* London: Darton, Longman & Todd, 1981.

Carlie, Michael K., and Kevin I. Minor. *Prisons around the World: Studies in International Penology.* Dubuque, IA: Brown, 1992.

Catholic Bishops' Conference of England and Wales. *A Place of Redemption: A Christian Approach to Punishment and Prison.* London: Burns & Oates, 2004.

Church Council on Justice and Corrections (Canada), and Correction Service Canada. *Satisfying Justice: Safe Community Options; A Compendium of Initiatives, Programs and Legislative Measures.* Ottawa, ON: Church Council on Justice and Corrections, 1996.

Clay, Walter Lowe. *The Prison Chaplain* [1861]. Patterson Smith Reprint Series in Criminology, Law Enforcement, and Social Problems 90. Montclair, NJ: Smith, 1969

Clear, Todd R. "Foreword". In *Restorative Justice: Healing the Effects of Crime*, by Jim Consedine, 7-8. Lyttleton, NZ: Ploughshares, 1995.

Clear, Todd R. et al. "The Value of Religion in Prison: An Inmate Perspective." *Journal of Contemporary Criminal Justice* 16/1 (2000) 53-73.

Clinebell, Howard. *Basic Types of Pastoral Care & Counseling: Resources for the Ministry of Healing and Growth.* Rev. and enl. Nashville: Abingdon, 1984.

———. *Growth Counseling: Hope-Centered Methods of Actualizing Human Wholeness.* Nashville: Abingdon, 1979.

Collins, Gary R. *Christian Counseling: A Comprehensive Guide.* Waco, TX: Word, 1980.

Colson, Charles W. *Life Sentence.* Waco, TX: Chosen, 1979.

———. "Toward an Understanding of Imprisonment and Rehabilitation." In *Crime and the Responsible Community*, edited by John Stott and Nick Miller, 152-80. The London Lectures in Contemporary Christianity. Grand Rapids: Eerdmans, 1980.

———, and Daniel W. Van Ness. *Convicted: New Hope for Ending America's Crime Crisis.* Westchester, IL: Crossway, 1989.

Consedine, Jim. *Restorative Justice: Healing the Effects of Crime.* Lyttleton, NZ: Ploughshares, 1995.

Covert, Henry G. *Ministry to the Incarcerated.* Chicago, IL: Loyola University Press, 1995.

Cowart, John L. *The Prison Minister's Handbook: Volunteer Ministry to the Forgotten Christian.* San Jose, CA: Resource Publications Inc., 1996.

Dammer, Harry R. "The Reasons for Religious Involvement in the Correctional Environment." *Journal of Offender Rehabilitation* 35/3-4 (2002) 35-58.

De Leon, George. *The Therapeutic Community: Theory, Model, and Method.* New York: Springer, 2000.

De Shazer, Steve. *Putting Difference to Work.* New York: Norton, 1991.

Dikötter, Frank. "Crime and Punishment in Early Republican China: Beijing's First Model Prison, 1912-1922." *Late Imperial China* 21/2 (2000) 140-62.

———. *Crime, Punishment and the Prison in Modern China.* New York: Columbia University Press, 2002.

———. "The Promise of Repentance: Prison Reform in Modern China." *British Journal of Criminology* 42 (2002) 240-49.

Dostoevsky, Fyodor. *The House of the Dead.* Translated by Constance Garnett. London: Heinemann, 1961.

Duce, Alan R. "Prison Chaplaincy." In *A Dictionary of Pastoral Care*, edited by Alastair V. Campbell, 218–19. New York: Crossroad, 1987.
Ellis, Lee. "Denominational Differences in Self-Reported Delinquency." *Journal of Offender Rehabilitation* 35 (2002) 185–98.
Foucault, Michel. *Discipline and Punish: The Birth of the Prison*. New York: Vintage, 1979.
Fowler, James W. *Faith Development and Pastoral Care*. Theology and Pastoral Care Series. Philadelphia: Fortress, 1987.
———. *Stages of Faith: The Psychology of Human Development and the Quest for Meaning*. San Francisco: Harper & Row, 1981.
Frankl, Viktor E. *Man's Search for Meaning*. New York: Pocket Books, 1963.
———. *Psychotherapy and Existentialism*. New York: Washington Square, 1967.
Friedman, S., and T. C. Esselstyn. "Adjustment of Children of Jail Inmates." *Federal Probation* 29/4 (1965) 55–59.
Fromm, Erich. *Psychoanalysis and Religion*. New Haven: Yale University Press, 1951.
Garland, David. *The Culture of Control*. Chicago: University of Chicago Press, 2001.
———. *Punishment and Modern Society: A Study in Social Theory*. Oxford: Clarendon, 1990.
———. *Mass Imprisonment: Social Causes and Consequences*. London: Sage, 2001.
Gartner, J. et al. *Rehabilitation, Recidivism and Religion: A Systematic Literature Review*. Baltimore: Loyola College in Maryland, 1990.
Gleason, Sandra E. "Hustling: The 'Inside' Economy of the Prison." In *Correctional Institutions*, edited by Robert M. Carteret et al., 174–87. 3rd ed. New York: Harper & Row, 1985.
Goffman, Erving. *Asylums: Essays on the Social Situation of Mental Patients and Other Inmates*. Garden City, NY: Anchor, 1961.
Gottfredson, Michael, and Travis Hirschi. *A General Theory of Crime*. Stanford: Stanford University Press, 1990.
Griffith, Lee. *The Fall of the Prison: Biblical Perspectives on Prison Abolition*. Grand Rapids: Eerdmans, 1993.
Hall, Stephen T. "A Working Theology of Prison Ministry." *Journal of Pastoral Care and Counseling* 58/3 (2004) 169–78.
Haney, Craig. *Reforming Punishment: Psychological Limits to the Pains of Imprisonment*. The Law and Public Policy. Washington, DC: American Psychological Association, 2006.
———, and Philip Zimbardo. "The Socialization into Criminality: On Becoming a Prisoner and a Guard." In *Law, Justice, and the Individual in Society: Psychological and Legal Issues*, edited by June Tapp and Felice Levine, 198–223. New York: Holt, Rinehart, and Winston, 1977.
———, et al. "Interpersonal Dynamics in a Simulated Prison." *International Journal of Criminology and Penology* 69/1 (1973) 69–97.
Harvey, A. E. "Custody and the Ministry to Prisoners." *Theology* 78 (1975) 82–90.
Hiltner, Seward. *Pastoral Counseling*. New York: Abingdon Cokesbury, 1949.
Hirschi, Travis. *Causes of Delinquency*. Berkeley: University of California Press, 1969.
Hofstede, Geert H. *Culture's Consequences: International Differences in Work-Related Values*. Beverly Hills, CA: Sage, 1984.
Hoyles, J. Arthur. *The Church and the Criminal*. London: Epworth, 1965.
———. *Punishment in the Bible*. London: Epworth, 1986.
———. *Religion in Prison*. London: Epworth, 1955.

Bibliography

Janzen, Waldemar. *Old Testament Ethics: A Paradigmatic Approach*. Louisville: Westminster John Knox, 1994.

Johnson, B. R., et al. "Religious Programs, Institutional Adjustment, and Recidivism among Former Inmates in Prison Fellowship Programs." *Justice Quarterly* 14 (1997) 145–66.

Khoo, Henry. *Shoes too Big: Continuing a Legacy of Hope and Transformation*. Singapore: Armour, 2007.

Kunzel, Regina. *Criminal Intimacy: Prison and the Uneven History of Modern American Sexuality*. Chicago: University of Chicago Press, 2008.

Lahm, Karen F. "Inmate Assaults on Prison Staff: A Multilevel Examination of an Overlooked Form of Prison Violence." *Prison Journal* 89/2 (2009) 131–150.

Lester, Andrew, and Howard W. Stone. "Helping Parishioners Envision the Future." In *Strategies for Brief Pastoral Counseling*, edited by Howard W. Stone, 46–60. Minneapolis: Fortress, 2001.

Li, Chiu Ming. *Revival behind Bars*. Unpublished manuscript.

Liebling, Alison et al. "Appreciative Inquiry and Relationships in Prison." *Punishment & Society* 1 (1999) 71–98.

Liu, Tik-sang. "A Nameless but Active Religion: An Anthropologist's View of Local Religion in Hong Kong and Macao." *China Quarterly* 174 (2003) 373–94.

Madsen, Nancy. "The Power of a Father's Blessing: What Former NFL Pro Bill Glass Has Learned after 36 Years of Prison Ministry." Interview. *Christianity Today* 50/1 (2006) 48–50.

Manning, Nick P. *The Therapeutic Community Movement: Charisma and Routinization*. International Library of Group Psychotherapy and Group Process. London: Routledge, 1989.

Marshall, Christopher D. *Beyond Retribution: A New Testament Vision for Justice, Crime, and Punishment*. Studies in Peace and Scripture. Grand Rapids: Eerdmans, 2001.

Mauer, M. "Causes and Consequences of Prison Growth." In *Mass Imprisonment: Social Causes and Consequences*, edited by David Garland. 4–14. London: Sage, 2001.

McConnell, Michael et al., editors. *Christian Perspectives on Legal Thought*. New Haven: Yale University Press, 2001.

McConville, Sean. "The Victorian Prison: England, 1865–1965." In *The Oxford History of the Prison: The Practice of Punishment in Western Society*, edited by Norval Morris and David J. Rothman, 117–50. New York: Oxford University Press, 1995.

McFague, Sallie. *Metaphorical Theology: Models of God in Religious Language*. Philadelphia: Fortress, 1982.

McGowen, Randall. "The Well-Ordered Prison: England, 1780–1865." In *The Oxford History of the Prison: The Practice of Punishment in Western Society*, edited by Norval Morris and David J. Rothman, 71–99. New York: Oxford University Press, 1995

McHugh, Gerald A. *Christian Faith and Criminal Justice: Toward a Christian Response to Crime and Punishment*. A Deus Book. New York: Paulist, 1978.

McKelvey, Blake. *American Prisons: A History of Good Intentions*. Montclair, NJ: Smith, 1977.

Menninger, Karl. *The Crime of Punishment*. Isaac Ray Award Lectures, 1963–66. New York: Viking, 1969.

Miethe, Terance D., and Hong Lu. *Punishment: A Comparative Historical Perspective*. Cambridge: Cambridge University Press, 2005.

Bibliography

Moltmann, Jürgen. *The Church in the Power of the Spirit: A Contribution of Messianic Ecclesiology*. Translated by Margaret Kohl. London: SCM, 1977.

Morris, Norval. "The Contemporary Prison: 1965–Present." In *The Oxford History of the Prison: The Practice of Punishment in Western Society*, edited by Norval Morris and David J. Rothman, 202–31. New York: Oxford University Press, 1995.

———. *The Future of Imprisonment*. Studies in Crime and Justice. Chicago: University of Chicago Press, 1974.

Morris, Norval, and David J. Rothman, editors. *The Oxford History of the Prison: The Practice of Punishment in Western Society*. New York: Oxford University Press, 1995.

Mühlhahn, Klaus. *Criminal Justice in China: A History*. Cambridge: Harvard University Press, 2009.

Nauer, Doris. *Seelsorgekonzepte im Widerstreit: Ein Kompendium*. Praktische Theologie heute 55. Stuttgart: Kohlhammer, 2001

Norman J. G. G. "Trinitarians." In *The New International Dictionary of the Christian Church*, edited by J. D. Douglas, 985. Grand Rapids: Zondervan, 1974.

Nouwen, Henri J. M. "Creative Ministry." In *Ministry and Spirituality*, 9–100. New York: Continuum, 1996.

———. *Reaching Out*. 1975. London: Fount, 1998.

———. *The Return of the Prodigal Son: A Story of Homecoming*. New York: Doubleday, 1992.

———. *The Wounded Healer*. New York: Doubleday 1979.

O'Brien, Patricia. "The Prison on the Continent: Europe, 1865–1965." In *The Oxford History of the Prison: The Practice of Punishment in Western Society*, edited by Norval Morris and David J. Rothman, 178–201. New York: Oxford University Press, 1995.

O'Connor, Thomas P., and Michael Perreyclear. "Prison Religion in Action and Its Influence on Offender Rehabilitation." *Journal of Offender Rehabilitation* 35/3–4 (2002) 11–33.

Ogletree, Thomas W. *Dimensions of Moral Understanding: Hospitality to the Stranger*. Louisville: Westminster John Knox, 2003.

Oliver, Gary J. et al. *Promoting Change through Brief Therapy in Christian Counseling*. AACC Counseling Library. Wheaton, IL: Tyndale House, 1997.

Pace, Dale K. *A Christian's Guide to Effective Jail and Prison Ministries*. Old Tappan, NJ: Revell, 1976.

Pattison, Stephen. *A Critique of Pastoral Care*. London: SCM, 1988.

———. *Pastoral Care and Liberation Theology*. Cambridge Studies in Ideology and Religion. Cambridge: Cambridge University Press, 1994.

Pederson, Duane. *How to Establish a Jail and Prison Ministry*. Nashville: Nelson, 1979.

Peters, Edward M. "Prison before the Prison: The Ancient and Medieval Worlds." In *The Oxford History of the Prison: The Practice of Punishment in Western Society*, edited by Norval Morris and David J. Rothman, 4–21. New York: Oxford University Press, 1995.

Pew Center on the States. *One in 100: Behind Bars in America 2008*. Online: http://www.pewtrusts.org/uploadedFiles/wwwpewtrustsorg/Reports/sentencing_and_corrections/one_in_100.pdf/.

Pierce, Dennis W. *Prison Ministry: Hope behind the Wall*. Binghamton, NY: Haworth Pastoral 2006.

Pierson, G. R., and R. F. Kelley. "HSPQ Norms on a Statewide Prison Population." *Journal of Psychology* 56 (1963) 185–92.

Bibliography

Ramsbotham, David, Sir. *Prisongate: The Shocking State of Britain's Prisons and the Need for Visionary Change*. London: Free Press, 2003.

Raphaël, Pierre. *Inside Rikers Island: A Chaplain's Search for God*. Translated by Linda M. Maloney. Maryknoll, NY: Orbis 1990.

Rideau, W., and B. Sinclair. "Religion in Prison." *Angolite* (Jan 1981) 31–56.

Ritschl, Dietrich. *The Logic of Theology: A Brief Account of the Relationship between Basic Concepts in Theology*. London: SCM, 1986.

Rogers, Carl R. *On Becoming a Person: A Therapist's View of Psychotherapy*. London: Mifflin, 1961.

Rothman, David J. "Perfecting the Prison: United States, 1789–1865." In *The Oxford History of the Prison: The Practice of Punishment in Western Society*, edited by Norval Morris and David J. Rothman, 100–116. New York: Oxford University Press, 1995.

Rotman, Edgardo. "The Failure of Reform: United States, 1865–1965." In *The Oxford History of the Prison: The Practice of Punishment in Western Society*, edited by Norval Morris and David J. Rothman, 151–77. New York: Oxford University Press, 1995.

Sabo, Don et al. *Prison Masculinities*. Philadelphia: Temple University Press, 2001.

———. "Doing Time, Doing Masculinity: Sports and Prison," In *Prison Masculinities*, edited by Don Sabo et al., 61–66. Philadelphia: Temple University Press, 2001.

Scarry, Elaine. *The Body in Pain: The Making and Unmaking of the World*. New York: Oxford University Press, 1985.

Schilder, David M. *Inside the Fence: A Handbook for Those in Prison Ministry*. Staten Island: Alba House, 1999.

Scott, Jamie S. *Christians and Tyrants: The Prison Testimonies of Boethius, Thomas More and Dietrich Bonhoeffer*. Toronto Studies in Religion 19. New York: Lang, 1995.

Seymour, James D., and Richard Anderson. *New Ghosts, Old Ghosts: Prisons and Labor Reform Camps in China*. Armonk, NY: Sharpe, 1998.

Shaw, Richard D. *Chaplains to the Imprisoned: Sharing Life with the Incarcerated*. Haworth Criminal Justice, Forensic Behavioral Sciences & Offender Rehabilitation. New York: Haworth, 1995.

Sinclair, Kevin. *Society's Guardians: A History of Correctional Services in Hong Kong 1841–1999*. Online: http://www.csd.gov.hk/misc/csd_history/main.pdf/.

Slosar, John A. *Prisonization, Friendship, and Leadership*. Lexington, MA: Lexington Books, 1978.

Soelle, Dorothee. *Choosing Life*. Translated by Margaret Kohl. Philadelphia: Fortress, 1981.

Song, Choan-Seng. *The Tears of Lady Meng: A Parable of People's Political Theology*. The Risk Book Series 11. Geneva: World Council of Churches, 1981.

———. *Testimonies of Faith: Letters and Poems from Prison in Taiwan*. Studies from the World Alliance of Reformed Churches 5. Geneva: World Alliance of Reformed Churches, 1984.

Spitale, Lennie. *Prison Ministry: Understanding Prison Culture Inside and Out*. Nashville: Broadman & Holman, 2002.

Stone, Howard W. *Crisis Counseling*. Philadelphia: Fortress, 1976.

———, editor. *Strategies for Brief Pastoral Counseling*. Minneapolis: Fortress, 2001.

Stott, John, and Nick Miller. *Crime and the Responsible Community*. Grand Rapids: Eerdmans, 1980.

Sumter, M. T., and T. Clear. "An Empirical Assessment of Literature Examining the Relationship between Religiosity and Deviance since 1985." Paper presented at The Academy of Criminal Justice Sciences Conference, Albuquerque, NM, 1998.

Sundermeier, Theo. "Konvivenz als Grundstruktur ökumenischer Existenz." In *Ökumenische Existenz Heute 1*, edited by Wolfgang Huber et al., 49–100. Munich: Kaiser, 1986.
Sundt, Jody L., and Francis T. Cullen. "The Role of the Contemporary Prison Chaplain." *Prison Journal* 78/2 (1998) 271–98.
Sundt, Jody L. et al. "The Role of the Prison Chaplain in Rehabilitation." *Journal of Offender Rehabilitation* 35/3–4 (2002) 59–86.
Sykes, Graham M. *The Society of Captives: A Study of a Maximum Security Prison*. Princeton: Princeton University Press, 1958.
Tam, Wai Lun. "Local Religion in Contemporary China." In *Chinese Religions in Contemporary Societies*, edited by James Miller, 57–83. Santa Barbara: ABC Clio, 2006.
Tannenbaum, Frank. *Crime and the Community*. New York: Columbia University Press, 1951.
Thomas, Jim, and Barbara H. Zaitzow. "Conning or Conversion?: The Role of Religion in Prison Coping." *Prison Journal* 86 (2006) 242–59.
Thompson, Beverley, and Paul Cavadino. "The Role of Non-Governmental Agencies and the Resettlement of Prisoners." *Nacro* (Nov 2000) 1–10. Online: http://www.isrcl.org/Papers/Thompson%20Cavadino.pdf/.
Tillich, Paul. *Systematic Theology*. Vol. 2, *Existence and the Christ*. Chicago: University of Chicago Press, 1957.
———. *The Courage to Be*. The Terry Lectures. New Haven: Yale University Press, 1952.
Underwood, Ralph L. *Empathy and Confrontation in Pastoral Care*. Theology and Pastoral Care Series. Philadelphia: Fortress, 1985.
United Nations Crime and Justice Information Network. "Standard Minimum Rules for the Treatment of Prisoners." Approved by the Economic and Social Council, July 31, 1957 (resolution 663 C I (XXIV), on the recommendation of the First Congress. Online: http://www.uncjin.org/Standards/UNRules.pdf/
United Nations General Assembly. Resolution 39/46. "Convention against Torture and Other Cruel, Inhuman or Degrading Treatment or Punishment." December 10, 1984. Online: http://www.un.org/documents/ga/res/39/a39r046.htm/.
———. Resolution 43/173. "Body of Principles for the Protection of All Persons under Any Form of Detention or Imprisonment." December 9, 1988. Online: http://www.un.org/documents/ga/res/43/a43r173.htm/.
———. Resolution 45/111. "Basic Principles for the Treatment of Prisoners." December 14, 1990. Online: http://www.un.org/documents/ga/res/45/a45r111.htm/.
Valle, Luis G. del. "Towards a Theological Outlook Starting from Concrete Events." In *Frontiers of Theology in Latin America*, edited by Rosino Gibellini, 79–99. Translated by John Drury. Maryknoll, NY: Orbis, 1979.
Van Ness, Daniel W. *Crime and Its Victims: What We Can Do*. Impact Books. Downers Grove, IL: InterVarsity, 1986.
Vose, Robin J. E. *Dominicans, Muslims, and Jews in the Medieval Crown of Aragon*. Cambridge Studies in Medieval Life and Thought, 4th series 74. Cambridge: Cambridge University Press, 2009.
Wacquant, Loic. "Deadly Symbiosis: When Ghetto and Prison Meet and Mesh." In *Mass Imprisonment: Social Causes and Consequences*, edited by David Garland, 82–120. London: Sage, 2001.
Walls, Andrew F. "Missionary Societies and the Fortunate Subversion of the Church." In *Perspectives of the World Christian Movement: A Reader*, edited by Ralph D. Winter

Bibliography

and Steven C. Hawthorne, 231–40. 3rd ed. Pasadena, CA: William Carey Library, 1999.

Walsh, A. T. "Trinitarians." In *New Catholic Encyclopedia* 14:293–95. 15 vols. Detroit: Thomson/Gale, 2003.

Watzlawick, Paul. *The Situation Is Hopeless, But Not Serious: (The Pursuit of Unhappiness)*. New York: Norton, 1983.

Weiss, Robert P., and N. South, editors. *Comparing Prison Systems: Towards a Comparative and International Penology*. International Studies in Global Change 8. Australia: Gordon and Breach, 1998.

Welch, Michael. *Ironies of Imprisonment*. Thousand Oaks, CA: Sage, 2005.

Wicks, Robert J. et al., editors. *Clinical Handbook of Pastoral Counseling*. Vols. 1–2. 3 vols. New York: Paulist, 1993.

Williams, Vergil L., and Mary Fish. "Formal and Informal Economic Systems." In *Correctional Institutions*, edited by Robert M. Carteret et al., 161–73. 3rd ed. New York: Harper & Row, 1985.

Winter, Ralph D. "The Two Structures of God's Redemptive Mission." In *Perspectives of the World Christian Movement: A Reader*, edited by Ralph D. Winter and Steven C. Hawthorne, 220–30. 3rd ed. Pasadena, CA: William Carey Library, 1999.

Wright, Erik. *The Politics of Punishment: A Critical Analysis of Prisons in America*. Harper Colophon Books. New York: Harper & Row, 1973.

Young, Mark et al. "The Impact of a Volunteer Prison Ministry Program on the Long-term Recidivism of Federal Inmates." *Journal of Offender Rehabilitation* 22/1–2 (1995) 97–118.

Youngquist, Neal. "Youth and the Criminal Justice System. Context and Practices within Asia." Paper presented at the VIVA Asia Cutting Edge Conference in Bangkok, Thailand, November 19–23, 2007.

Zedner, Lucia. "Wayward Sisters: The Prison for Women." In *The Oxford History of the Prison: The Practice of Punishment in Western Society*, edited by Norval Morris and David J. Rothman, 295–324. New York: Oxford University Press, 1995.

Zehr, Howard. *Changing Lenses: A New Focus for Crime and Justice*. Scottdale, PA: Herald, 1990.

Zerfass, Rolf. *Menschliche Seelsorge: Für eine Spiritualität von Priestern und Laien im Gemeindedienst*. Freiburg: Herder, 1985.

www.ingramcontent.com/pod-product-compliance
Lightning Source LLC
Chambersburg PA
CBHW031811220426
43662CB00007B/603